Dog Breed Professional Secrets

Ethical Breeding Practices

Sylvia Smart

Wenatchee, Washington U.S.A.

Dog Breeders Professional Secrets
Ethical Breeding Practices
Sylvia Smart

Dogwise Publishing
A Division of Direct Book Service, Inc.
403 South Mission Street, Wenatchee, Washington 98801
1-509-663-9115, 1-800-776-2665
www.dogwisepublishing.com / info@dogwisepublishing.com

Graphic Design: Lindsay Peternell
Indexing: Cheryl Smith
Photos: David Dalton

Limits of Liability and Disclaimer of Warranty:
The author and publisher shall not be liable in the event of incidental or consequential damages in connection with, or arising out of, the furnishing, performance, or use of the instructions and suggestions contained in this book.

Library of Congress Cataloging-in-Publication Data
Smart, Sylvia, 1946-
Dog breeders professional secrets : ethical breeding practices / by Sylvia Smart.
p. cm.
Includes index.
ISBN 978-1-929242-59-7
1. Dogs--Breeding. I. Title.
SF427.2.S63 2009
636.7'082--dc22
2008027591

ISBN13: 978-1-929242-59-7

Printed in the U.S.A.

Dedication

Thank you, Olga Jancic. You believed in me.
I will always love you, my friend.

CONTENTS

Introduction...iv

1. Doing the Right Thing..6

2. Elements of an Equitable Contract.......................................13

3. Beyond Book Learning..30

4. Assessing, Deciding Upon, and Obtaining Breeding Stock.......38

5. Your Kennel...60

6. Financial Management for the Professional Breeder................75

7. Marketing and Advertising..86

8. Involving Your Human Family..107

9. Hiring and Handling Outside Help......................................113

10. What Breeders Need to Know About Veterinary Care............120

11. Preparing Puppies for Their Future....................................148

12. Managing a Stud Dog..160

13. To Show or Not to Show..164

14. Selling or Placing an Adult Dog or Bitch............................170

15. Helping Owners Cope with Loss.......................................176

Resources...181

Author Biography..183

Index...184

INTRODUCTION

This book will teach you how to become an exceptional and successful dog breeder. You will learn how to produce healthy, well-bred puppies and establish a respected kennel name synonymous with quality, integrity, and class. You will be provided detailed, comprehensive guidelines on how to build a superior dog breeding kennel operation without sacrificing your integrity, or undermining your moral responsibilities. I will demonstrate how sincerity and a commitment to "doing the right thing" will guarantee your success. Obviously you will also need to learn new skills, acquire a broad knowledge base, and never stop educating yourself.

Joining the ranks of the truly dedicated and superior dog breeders will change your life for the better. Whether you elect to pursue this on a large scale or on a small scale, you will become a connoisseur of fine purebred dogs, and an expert in your chosen breed. You will meet fascinating, wonderful people and their fabulous dogs.

I really don't know of any other profession that generates the same degree of respect and admiration in a highly competitive field, yet doesn't require either enormous natural talent or a college degree just to open the first door. As a successful dog breeder of superior dogs, no one cares which college you graduated from or who your parents know—your dogs speak for you!

By adhering to the highest standards and paying attention to all the details, you will never produce a puppy at your kennel that you cannot place in a superior "forever" home. No puppy of yours will find its way into a shelter or rescue situation. If you can't make that commitment—you shouldn't be breeding dogs. Do it right! You will be amply rewarded for your commitment to excellence.

This book will *not* address in detail all of what you need to know about whelping and raising puppies—things like pre-breeding screening, nutrition, labor and whelping, complications and resuscitation, dewclaw removal, and tube feeding. It is not a whelping reference book, nor is it a biology lesson on the canine reproductive system, or a guide to writing legal documents. Such reference manuals and guides are readily available (see the Resources section for some suggestions). While it's important to enhance your scientific knowledge of genetics, canine reproduction, and veterinary medicine, the purpose of this book is to provide the information breeders need to know that is not normally included in medical references or in other whelping how-to books designed for breeders.

My goal for this book is to provide you the knowledge I have gained through my many years of being a breeder and interacting and networking with many other successful breeders. Hopefully you can learn from my experiences (both good and bad), then refine it, add to it, and utilize this information to build your own successful breeding program.

Chapter 1
DOING THE RIGHT THING

Purebred dogs are incredibly popular, and there is strong demand for healthy, socialized, and intelligent purebred puppies. This is illustrated by the fact that there are many people who are willing to wait months or even years to acquire a high-quality, healthy puppy sold under a written warranty contract. Often, these prospective owners have to put their names on a waiting list and be pre-qualified by professional breeders before they are allowed to purchase a puppy! In fact some dedicated breeders require the buyers to attend a "Puppy Training and Care" seminar before they will hand over their puppies. Despite these obstacles and restrictions, people are lining up for superior puppies—in 2006 close to a million dogs were registered with the American Kennel Club (AKC) in 155 recognized breeds; the United Kennel Club (UKC) registers over 300,000 dogs annually; and there are many more "pet" purebred puppies that are never officially registered and so aren't included in the basic statistics.

People who want an exceptional purebred puppy have made an intelligent and conscious choice to obtain a dog with a known, quantifiable set of traits and characteristics. And, of course, the best way to accomplish this is to purchase a specific, AKC-recognized breed from an ethical and knowledgeable breeder. These customers don't want to rely solely on luck. It is therefore your responsibility as a breeder to ensure that they are getting what they want and need—consistently tractable, easy-to-train dogs with natural intelligence and a friendly, out-going temperament combined with superior physical condition and a sound genetic foundation.

Ethics and Integrity

My basic philosophy is that breeders who develop expertise in the field and who consistently follow the high road in all aspects of their business can make owning and operating a breeding kennel a successful business. The key to "doing it right" is based on knowledge and the ability to apply what you learn with integrity. When you lay the correct foundation, consistently put ethics and morality in the forefront, and make a point to incorporate basic proven business practices into your kennel operation, your dog breeding business success is assured.

Quality and ethics go hand-in-hand. To become a successful professional breeder you must be meticulous about details, and fanatically clean about your facility, your dogs, and yourself. You have to behave ethically with the public, fellow breeders, employees or contracted helpers, as well as with your veterinarian and his or her staff. Some of the questions that this book will force you to examine include:

- What is best for your dogs?
- What is best for your family? Will you put them first, and will you set an ethical example for them?
- Can you treat others with respect and integrity? Are you an empathetic person? Can you help people who are grieving the loss of their beloved dog?
- Do you have "zero-based" tolerance for deception and omissions—not just for lies and deceit—but also for cover-ups and silence in the face of injustice and blatant greed?
- Can you say "No" to unethical offers from unscrupulous people?
- Will you stand behind your puppies 100%? Will you do it throughout their lives?

To live within the framework of any community in a harmonious and peaceful co-existence is to accept the responsibilities and rules of that community. We live in a society where certain behaviors are considered unacceptable and harmful to the group. These include lying, stealing, cheating, gossiping, and physically or verbally assaulting a person or animal. Some of these unacceptable behaviors are even punishable by law. In the very specific world of dog breeding and related activities, the rules are less "clear cut."

As inside any business or sub-community, there are subtle differences between honesty and being silent when one should speak up, observing violations of rules and regulations but failing to report them, failing to disclose all of the pertinent facts in a business transaction, and going along with unscrupulous activities in order to "not rock the boat" or bring unwanted attention to oneself. The lines between honesty and self-preservation/promotion can become blurred if you are not careful and vigilant. Being ethical means doing the right thing even when no one is watching. Only *you* can protect your good name, your self-esteem, and your kennel reputation.

> ## A Breeder Secret
>
> ### Ethical Standards
> You may have heard lots of definitions of ethical standards. Lets keep it simple: Webster's Dictionary defines Ethical Standards as "Conforming with an accepted standard of good behavior, e.g., in a profession or trade."

If you have ever been caught up in any of the politics of the dog world, you will immediately recognize the ethical dilemmas presented below. When the parameters of integrity become flexible and the fine lines between honesty and deceit appear clouded, you need to take a serious look at ethics versus expediency, and ethics versus winning at all costs. To be ethical, you must bravely face the challenges of mastering the dog breeding profession without compromising your principles. Remind yourself, the sterling reputation you will earn is priceless. Do not compromise when it comes to ethical behavior—not ever.

Ethical Dilemmas in Dog Breeding—What Would You Do?

I am sure if you are making the effort to read this book, than you are an ethical person and would never compromise your ethics in your breeding program. But you need to recognize that professional dog breeders constantly face complicated issues and dilemmas that you may have never anticipated. So to help you prepare for life as a breeder, here are some examples of dilemmas real-life dog breeders have faced. They bring up many complicated issues. As you read through them, try to honestly put yourself in these people's situations and consider how you might feel and react. Then ask yourself, "What would I do?" (Look for the ways these dilemmas were resolved at the end of the chapter.)

Ethical Dilemma #1: The Champion Stud Dog

A nationally ranked AKC champion stud dog is tested and found to have become permanently sterile. His owner/breeder, Katherine, is devastated because she had great plans for the dog. She calls a fellow breeder friend to share the bad news. The breeder she called had been helping her test this stud dog and had given Katherine a referral to a canine fertility specialist to see what could be done for the dog. This breeder/friend was very successful and she has always been kind and helpful to Katherine. She had given her medical supplies for her kennel, and taught her a lot about grooming and showing dogs. To Katherine, she had always been a sweet, kind person.

Katherine is crying on the telephone. She has had several financial setbacks in the past few months, and this is almost the last straw. Her breeder friend offers to sell the sterile stud dog for her to one of her foreign clients for $10,000—enough money to bail Katherine out of her monetary problems. But she can't understand why anyone would want to pay $10,000 for a sterile stud dog. She asks her friend that question. The breeder/friend replies, "Well, don't ask, don't tell. Because he is a proven stud dog, they will never think to ask or to test him themselves. He is highly ranked and appears to be at the peak of health. Once they get him to their country, breed him to a bitch and she misses, it will be too late to ascertain how and when he became sterile. Don't worry so much about them—they have plenty of money, it means nothing to them. What do you care? This will solve your problem."

What would you do?

Ethical Dilemma #2: The Substitution

A breeder worked very hard to train and title his gun dog. After three years of training in the field, his dog finally earned an AKC MH (Master Hunter) title. The breeder was ecstatic, not only because he was proud of what he and his dog had accomplished as a team, but because he could now sell the offspring from this dog for about twice as much as he had previously charged. Having seen his wonderful dog work in the field, hunters were beating down his door to buy puppies out of this MH-titled gun dog. The man bred his dog to two of his own bitches over a three-week period. He was so confident about the outcome that he offered his dog for stud service to four other breeders, and he didn't bother to do a sperm count on the dog because he knew the dog was a proven stud—in fact, he owned one of the dog's sons from an earlier breeding that was now in training.

The MH titled dog bred all of the bitches, and the man collected a full stud fee on each one of them. All were under contract with a guaranteed "two live puppy" clause or a repeat breeding. None of the bitches conceived. A sperm count was taken on his stud dog, and he discovered that most of the sperm were either dead or deformed. The sperm count was also very low. The veterinary fertility specialist doubted that the dog's sperm count would improve, and predicted a 95% probability that the dog was permanently sterile due to a silent low-grade infection that had permanently affected his ability to produce vital sperm.

During the breedings, the dog's owner had not routinely checked the dog's temperature or his penis for any discharge—the accepted protocol in responsible stud dog management. The owner could have returned all of the stud fees that he had collected, and explained to the bitch's owners that his dog had become sterile. He could also have told them to check their bitches because his dog had a low-grade infection. But since he owns the MH dog's son—who has all of his clearances for hips, eyes, and cardio and is already proven on one of the breeder's own bitches—he realizes he could use that male for repeat breedings without letting the bitch owners know. After all, he thinks, the dogs look almost identical. They are the same size and the same color. Even he has to look twice before he can tell which one is the father and which one is the son. He has his own bitches checked out, and they are free of infection. In his own mind he justifies the switch. Why not? The younger dog shows great promise in the field. He will probably get his MH title eventually. What harm could it do to switch the stud dogs?

What would you do?

Ethical Dilemma #3: Who's the Real Mom?

Two litters of puppies are born at a kennel operation on the same night. They are both the same color and the same breed. The first bitch, although acceptable within the description of the breed standard, is not a very "typey" bitch.[1] She has no points towards a championship and no obedience or hunting titles, and her pedigree is fairly "blue collar." She was bred to a nationally ranked champion. The second bitch is a finished champion with a Companion Dog (CD) obedience title. Her sire is also a

---

[1]"Typey" refers to a purebred registered dog or bitch that is typical of the traditional interpretation of the breed standard, and moves correctly.

well-known local champion, and her pedigree is impressive. She has been bred to the same top champion stud as the first bitch. Because of her pedigree and accomplishments, her pups are worth twice as much as the first bitch's puppies.

The first bitch has twelve puppies in her litter. It is going to be difficult to raise them all—they will have to be supplemented every four hours. The second bitch whelped only four pups. They are healthy, and she has plenty of milk. The breeder has put different colored I.D. collars on all the puppies and has marked the second bitch's puppies with a red dab of nail polish on the rear right toes of each one of them.

The breeder decides to move some of the puppies from the larger litter to the mother with fewer puppies. She squirts some milk from one of the second bitch's teats onto her palm, picks up a pup from the first litter (the nicest one she could find) and rubs the pup all over with this milk scent. She places it on the second mother, who immediately accepts it as her own. She does the same with three more puppies—moving each one from the first bitch to the second bitch. At first she only wants to reduce the size of the big litter so that she won't be forced to supplement the pups. However, the puppies from the second bitch are all sold within a few days. She has collected deposits on half of the puppies from the first litter. She is still getting calls for puppies from the second litter. She could easily sell the other four foster puppies as though they were out of the second litter, enabling her to double her money on those puppies. Or she could explain to any visitors that although the second mother is nursing eight puppies, the ones with the red toes actually are part of the first litter and are therefore significantly less expensive.

What would you do?

Ethical Dilemma #4: Genetic Issues vs. Superior Pedigrees
Edward was an artificially inseminated, chilled-semen puppy out of a long line of champions. The procedure that resulted in his birth was an extremely expensive one—and he was the only puppy in the litter! The breeder had planned to show the dog and had several breeders interested in using him as a stud dog. At eight months of age, the breeder found a little round red membrane in the inner corner of his eye and knew he was afflicted with cherry eye. Cherry eye is the name of the condition for a prolapsed third eyelid gland, also called Prolapse of the Nictitans Gland, or PTEG. The third eyelid gland produces 40% of the tears that lubricate the eye. It is possibly a genetic defect because it is statistically more prevalent in certain breeds, but there is no clinical proof of that. In fact, some veterinarians believe it is a congenital defect (not hereditary). Regardless, a dog with cherry eye should not be shown or bred.

What would you do?

What Was the Right Thing to Do?

Ethical Dilemma #1
If Katherine accepts the offer from her friend, her financial problems are over. But if she sells the dog to this foreign buyer, will she ever be able to look in the mirror again? She won't, because she is an ethical and honest person. She walks away from this offer and from the friendship. She is saddened and shocked that her breeder friend turned out to be an unethical person. She lost a friend and a valuable resource for her kennel, but she retained her integrity and her self-esteem. She "did the right thing."

Ethical Dilemma #2

The breeder, in this instance, made the switch and used the son instead of the father. He substituted the son for the Master Hunter sire on all four of the repeat stud services under his warranty contracts. I saw some of the resulting pups—and they were not great in the field—they lacked the ability to think on their own and possessed neither the speed nor birdiness (desire to retrieve birds) of their grandfather. The son never earned his MH title—even though the breeder just about killed him with an e-collar trying to transform him from a mediocre hunting dog into a great hunting dog like his father. What was worse is that this breeder became trapped in his own web of deceit. For the sake of money he continued to sell puppies out of the son, but registered them on the father's name—even though the son was not a line-bred dog.[2] The breeding wasn't the same—because the bitch contributes at least 50% to the breeding, and if her pedigree doesn't line back to the same dog as the Sire's pedigree the breeding is considered to be an "outcross"[3]—and it is the combination of genes that "make up the dog." The bitch that produced the son was not the same bitch that produced his Sire—so everything on the bottom of the pedigree was completely different, and it showed in the "get" (offspring of a male dog). The owner's kennel reputation continued to go downhill as his commitment to quality and integrity had disappeared.

Now he lives each day hiding his operations, fearful that his hired helpers will find out, fearful that someone will swab one of the pups, send it to AKC and find out his secret, which will void all of his puppy registrations! That could bankrupt him. He was no longer able to enjoy hunt training, and the younger dog was blamed for not qualifying for his MH title even though he had run him numerous times. He barely achieved his SH (Senior Hunter) title. This man became bitter and disappointed in his dogs. Every litter the son produced was a disappointment to him. Who lost here? The breeder was obviously the biggest loser. What he should have done is return the stud fees, explain the situation to the bitch owners, and asked some guys in his local hunt club if they wanted to purchase a retired stud dog who was MH titled. The dog was only about four years old—he could have sold him for far more than $7,500. But even if he didn't have that option—he should have always kept his integrity intact—no matter what! He was caught in his own trap.

Ethical Dilemma #3

The breeder did the right thing, and maintained the integrity of her pedigrees and her kennel operation. She let the foster mother feed the puppies until they were weaned—and then she returned them to their correct littermates. The first mother's puppies sold for $1,000 each, and the second mother's puppies sold for $2,000 each. The breeder grossed $12,000 on the first litter and $8,000 on the second litter. If she had sold the extra four puppies at the more expensive price, she could have pocketed an additional $4,000.

Had she not "done the right thing," think about all the issues she would have had to worry about—DNA profiles, puppies that don't grow up to look like their parents,

---

[2] A "line-bred" dog is one who has the same superior stud dog in the third or fourth generation on both sides of his pedigree.

[3] An "outcross" is the breeding of unrelated pairs. They have no common ancestry for at least five or six generations back.

other breeders talking about the poor quality from her Champion bitch. Even the stud dog would have been judged harshly on the inconsistency in the second litter. If other breeders or knowledgeable people had come to visit the puppies, they would have suspected that something wasn't "kosher" about that litter—with half show quality and half not even "typey" puppies. It would be like having half your kids looking like the milkman. Because the sire was presumably not line-bred, the resulting puppies, from two different bitches, were not copies of him. But, even if they had been consistent with his conformation to breed standard—if any of them had been bred, the resulting second generation of offspring would not have held up to the quality of the breeding line.

There is nothing unethical about putting some puppies from one mother on a bitch with fewer pups—it only becomes unethical when you elect to register them to a mother that did not produce them, and then sell them at a higher price.

Ethical Dilemma #4

I did the right thing. I sold this beautiful 8-month old puppy after spending $850 to have his "cherry eye" repaired so that he would not suffer from dry eye for the rest of his life. I sold him under a spay/neuter contract for the regular price of a quality pet puppy—and I also told the new owners all about the surgery, and gave them copies of all of his medical records—just in case he ever had any future problem with this eye.

By the way—always have a "cherry eye" repaired by a canine ophthalmologist surgeon—and do not allow them to just remove the PTEG. The surgery requires skill and experience. If you do not do the surgery to repair it—and you elect to have it surgically removed, the dog will suffer from dry eye for the rest of his life unless his owner runs around after him all day with an eyedropper and administers artificial tears to keep the eye moist.

Summary

All of the above anecdotes describe real-life situations that did occur. There are dozens of scenarios that demonstrate the impact of ethics on this profession. Right now and right here—you need to make your choice. You cannot be conveniently ethical, or semi-ethical, or silently ethical. If you know that you have made poor choices in the past—here is your opportunity to change and evolve into someone of higher caliber moral fiber. My hope and my mission in writing this book, is to infuse this profession and sport with a healthy dose of awareness of how easy it can be to slide into complacency and compromise. Let's all work together to raise the bar, and regain our honor and respect in this highly competitive and rewarding world of purebred dogs!

Chapter 2

THE ELEMENTS OF AN EQUITABLE CONTRACT

Contracts are a key element in the world of the professional breeder. You need them to conduct your business and they reflect your philosophy. While the number and types of contracts you will require may vary, most breeders need contracts with puppy buyers, with people with whom they might co-own a dog, stud service agreements, and perhaps with professional handlers.

Though it would be nice to think that all the transactions you conduct in your dog-breeding business could be verbally agreed to and that no problems would arise that could not be resolved through a pleasant conversation, the reality is that your transactions are business transactions. You need to protect your business, yourself, and those with whom you do business, from potential consequences—both good and bad. For these reasons, you need to create and work with contracts when you enter into transactional agreements.

Contracts are, in fact, simply agreements that have been put into writing. In legal terms, a contract is known as an "express agreement." To be a legal document it must have the following elements:

1. Clearly identified parties.

2. A beginning date.

3. An ending date or ending event or occurrence.

4. A description of the transactions or activities it is meant to cover.

5. The inclusion of compensatory terms (payment in the form of money, labor, or merchandise of some type).

Technically speaking, with these items included and signed by both parties, a contract is legally in place. However, there is a distinct difference between the letter-of-the-law and the intent of an agreement. You will certainly want to make sure that you are able to adhere to the legal aspects of the contract, but as an ethical breeder, you will want and need to adhere to their intent as well.

So that you can fulfill both these obligations, you need to think about anything that could happen relative to a certain transaction and consider how you would rectify any such situation. In my opinion, the best way to write a contract is to be sure you cover all contingencies by carefully thinking through what the worst case scenarios may be. Ask yourself what could go wrong with any aspect of the agreement you want to put into writing, then spell those things out in the contract—and spell out how these situations will be resolved.

How to Find Contracts that Work for You

Fortunately you do not need to reinvent the wheel when it comes to contracts, although you will want to tailor them to reflect your philosophies and needs. One of the best places to find examples of contracts you may be able to use is from other breeders, from dog breeder associations, clubs, and websites. Some breed clubs have a notebook in their club library that has copies of all their breeder member contracts and warranties. This is a wonderful resource, and if your club doesn't have this, talk to the board about setting up such a resource for all the members to access; the internet makes this easier than ever.

If you believe that a particular contract or clause in a contract is suited to your operation, contact that kennel owner and ask him or her if you can use it in your contract. It is polite and correct to ask permission before simply lifting it for your purposes. Most breeders will allow you to use it, and they will appreciate your professional request. This is another opportunity to network with other breeders, as it opens a professional dialog. If not given, you can always incorporate the general content by rewording and altering the sequence to make it unique to your contract. However, part of adopting an ethical approach to this business is to avoid having to backpedal by doing something that seems wrong. The straightforward approach is so much better in the long run!

Once you find a contract you believe fits your needs, you may want another pair of eyes to go over it with you. Especially if you are an eternal optimist, you may need a friend who is a bit more skeptical to go over the contract with you to protect your interests. These things take time and necessitate a somewhat analytical mind. While we cannot all be proficient in every area of expertise, if you wisely recruit help from other people who have talents that you lack, you create a win-win situation.

A Breeder Secret

Do You Need a Lawyer?

As noted above, not always. My original contract was based on one drawn up by the business attorney of a doctor friend who bred German Shorthaired Pointers and Labrador Retrievers. I modified it to reflect the needs of my operation. I deleted some disclaimers written in small print "legalese." Most disclaimers do not hold up in a court of law—especially if they are written in technical legal jargon and buried in small print in a long and detailed document. I modified the warranty to reflect the items that I was willing to guarantee, and I rewrote the language in plain English so that it would be easy to read and understand. If you do not feel comfortable modifying a contract or constructing new paragraphs to represent your specific situation, you may want to pursue legal advice from an attorney who is well versed in contract and consumer law.

Be Clear and Be Specific

Your contract must be specific about what it does and does not cover. Too often, puppy contracts only address the items that are covered—for example, who is to pay for the shipping costs on a returned puppy or a replacement puppy. Return policies and reimbursement policies must be clearly established. Depending on your point of view, state when you will or will not reimburse the purchase price and whether or not your warranty is limited to a replacement puppy. Clearly state in what cases you will or will not reimburse medical expenses and what your policy is concerning injuries to the puppy that occurred after he or she was delivered to the buyer. If you must litigate against a buyer—clearly state who is liable for attorney fees and court costs. Clearly spell out the buyer's responsibilities for the health and well-being of a puppy.

Negotiate Your Interests

Once you have templates for the contracts you need to have, recognize that some contracts will need to be further tailored to some degree through negotiation. Here is a key secret when it comes to the art of negotiation—you must know in your own mind which items are deal breakers for you, and which items you will ask for but know that you would be willing to negotiate or give up in exchange for the things that are truly important. For example, if it is unacceptable to you that a puppy buyer would find the puppy a new home if things didn't work out rather than returning the puppy to you (so you could find a new home), that's a deal breaker. But if you are comfortable enough with the buyer that you could trust him or her in that situation, you may indicate that you would insist on having the puppy returned to you, but if they rejected the clause you would still sign the contract.

Major trade union agreements and world peace treaties have been reached based on this strategy. Sometimes we intentionally introduce items into the contract that although they would be of benefit to us, they are not, in the larger scheme of things, of great significance. Having some leeway in a contract gives us something to give up in exchange for something that is truly important.

Be In Control of the Situation

The basic rule in selling and purchasing, in drawing up and negotiating contracts and agreements, is to always control the situation. Do not give up your decision-making prerogatives. This is your business, and you make all of the decisions. Make them ethically and with empathy, but do not be bullied into paying for someone else's bad judgment. Refuse to be the fall guy. If something is your responsibility, then by all means, stand up and take the hit, using the remedies that are spelled out in the contract—and nothing else. If you did nothing wrong, unethical, or unprofessional, then you don't have to pay the bills or apologize.

There is a huge difference between apology and empathy. You can certainly empathize with someone who has been victimized by an unprofessional veterinarian, and you can sympathize with someone who has lost their puppy due to their own negligence. That doesn't mean you need to make it right. In your desire to be the good guy, don't forget the factor of inference of guilt—if you pay for something that is not your responsibility, it may be assumed that you have accepted responsibility and any future expenses resulting from the problem or defect may also be charged to you. Read the following story—this is what happened to me.

I sold a litter of beautiful, healthy puppies. They all left on the same Saturday afternoon. It was the successful culmination of seven weeks of dedicated care and nurturing of these babies. The Saturday they were picked up was a day of mixed feelings, of tears and smiles, as each one departed with their new families. One of these puppies went to a female career army officer. I even remember that she named her puppy Hunter. He was simply a great puppy. He was already trained to come when he was called. He automatically sat whenever he came up to you, and he was retrieving duck wings and pigeons. He grinned just like his daddy—from ear to ear whenever he brought back a duck wing to hand.

A few days after he left, I got a call from the woman. She was sobbing on the telephone. She had left the puppy with her roommate while she went shopping. The roommate decided she didn't want to watch the puppy, so she tied him to the deck railing of their apartment on the second floor and went inside. When the owner came home and asked where the puppy was, the roommate said he was on the deck. Being a curious and bored puppy, he had gone through the slats of the decking, fallen, and was hanging on the end of a leash tied to the deck railing—dead! She wanted me to give her another puppy to replace him.

First of all, I would never knowingly sell a puppy to anyone so irresponsible. Secondly, I was angry that she had been so negligent as to cause the death of the puppy. Third, just imagine the audacity to ask me in this particular case to replace her dead puppy, free of charge! This was a request from an officer in the U.S. Army. If that doesn't lack integrity, I don't know how to define it. I obviously didn't want to ever hear from this person again or to get any referrals from her. I told her that I was really sorry that she had lost her puppy, but that it would be irresponsible of me to entrust another puppy to her negligent care. As far as getting a puppy for free, it was obvious that it was her roommate who should be scrambling to buy her another puppy. I then hung up the telephone and cried my eyes out for the rest of the afternoon, and several more times during the night. Even now, as I write these paragraphs, my eyes are welling up with tears at the thought of how my poor puppy met such a tragic end.

Puppy Sales and Warranty Contract

For almost every breeder, the puppy sales contract and warranty is the document that you will use the most. This contract and bill of sale is also the simplest of all the contracts you will employ. I have included a copy of the one I use. Through the years, the contract has been modified as various aspects posed a question or an issue arose that was not addressed in the original form. You are welcome to use it or to modify it as you see fit.

A Breeder Secret

Forewarned is Forearmed

Just because the sample contracts I include in this book have met my needs, that doesn't mean they are the right documents for you. It is always your responsibility to obtain good legal advice and suitable recommendations for your business from sources that you deem to be professional and knowledgeable regarding your unique concerns and needs.

SAMPLE CONTRACT: Puppy Sale & Warranty

Date: _____

CONTRACT AND BILL OF SALE

Kennel name: _____

Seller: _____

Address: _____

Telephone: _____ E-Mail: _____

Buyer: _____

Address: _____

Telephone: _____ E-Mail: _____

The seller has, on this date [Month, Day, Year], delivered to the Buyer a [specify the breed] puppy, sex [Male or Female], color/markings [physical description]. The puppy was whelped on [Date]. The Litter Registration Number is _____ _____.

Sire Information: (For example, JESSMOR'S BF FAR AND AWAY, CGC, WC, Call name: "Cruise"; Pointed/BOB Winner + 2 JH passes; DNA#V139715; CHIP#045114017; AKC Registration #SN73384302; UKC Registration #145-488; Color: Chocolate. D.O.B. 12/25/1999; OFA #LR-EL14930M24P1, LR-120520F24M-P1; CERF #LR-29355 (35 months); cardio cleared.)

Dam Information: (For example, BLACK FOREST'S NOW VOYAGER, CGC, Call name: "Camille"; AKC Registration #SN45273406; UKC Registration #R124-322; CHIP #707871. D.O.B. 5/20/1997; OFA Registration #LR98034G24F-T; CERF #LR-20186/2000-33; cardio cleared.)

Amount paid: Deposit: [Dollar Amount] and [Dollar Amount] upon taking possession of the puppy, for a total purchase price of [Dollar Amount].

SELLER WARRANTS AND AGREES:

1. Seller [Full Name] is the lawful owner of the dam, and has full legal right to sell its offspring.

2. The puppy is in sound body and good health at the time of the sale. The puppy has had its first inoculation for parvovirus, hepatitis, distemper, adenovirus, and Para influenza. For maximum protection we recommend that this puppy receive another inoculation at 9 weeks and 12 weeks, and a parvovirus inoculation every three weeks until 21 weeks of age. Buyer is instructed to consult with their veterinarian for advice regarding inoculation and available options such as corona virus inoculations, and additional worming (fecal tests). Seller advises against inoculation for leptospira canicola and leptospira icterohaemorrhagia until after the age of 12 weeks, due to the side effects, which sometimes occur in puppies younger than 12 weeks. If the buyer intends to hunt train this puppy or obedience train this puppy, where it will be in the company of other dogs, I advise inoculation against kennel cough. If the puppy will be working in field conditions we advice inoculation against Lyme disease. Again—consult with your veterinarian! Sellers refer all questions regarding inoculations and worming to qualified veterinarians; our recommendations are merely suggestions, which should be discussed with your veterinarian.

3. Buyer is to arrange a checkup of the puppy by a qualified veterinarian within 48 hours of sale. Seller shall be notified immediately in the event that the dog has a defect. If the puppy is ill (not poisoned) or defective, the buyer is entitled to a full refund of the puppy's purchase price upon the immediate return of the puppy to the seller, together with the signed-off registration papers. Seller's warranty is limited to the refund of the puppy's purchase price upon immediate return of

the puppy, and only under the circumstances described above. Seller does not reimburse for veterinarian expenses.

4. [Kennel Name]'s dogs (herein-after "dog" refers to dogs and bitches) are guaranteed to be OFA certifiable at TWO YEARS of age. The dog must be x-rayed by THIRTY (30) months of age, and the x-ray submitted to the OFA for examination and certification. If the OFA finds the dog to have hip dysplasia, the following requirements must be fulfilled in order to obtain a replacement puppy. It is understood that money is NOT refunded, and that this guarantee is for a replacement puppy only.

- OFA shall be the sole judge regarding hip dysplasia.

- We are to receive a copy of the OFA report.

- If the dog has hip dysplasia, the dog will be replaced upon return of the dog's registration paper, which is to be signed over to me. You may keep the dog if you wish or give it to someone else, but it must be neutered or spayed, and we must have written proof of this from the veterinarian who performs the surgery.

- All freight charges for the replacement dog are to be paid by the owner of the dog.

- Replacement pups may be chosen from any breeding that we have available that is similar in price to what you paid for the dog. If you should want a puppy from a more expensive litter, we ask only that you would pay the difference.

- This guarantee applies to the original owner of the dog, and no dog will be guaranteed and replaced unless our kennel name, is used in front (prefix) of the registered name of the dog.

5. [Kennel Name]'s dogs are guaranteed to be CERF certifiable. The dog must be examined by a DACVO certified veterinarian, by 30 months of age. A written report of any heritable eye disease must be submitted to the seller with written proof that the dog has been neutered or spayed, and the dog's AKC registration papers must be signed over to the seller in order to receive a replacement puppy. All guarantees are exactly under the same terms as the guarantee for hip dysplasia. Eye guarantee does not cover injuries to the eye. Buyer's remedies are for hip dysplasia and heritable eye disease only. No other diseases or injuries or illnesses, and are limited to replacement puppy as provided above.

Buyer: _____ Date: _____

Seller: _____ Date: _____

BUYER WARRANTS AND AGREES:

1. This dog shall be maintained and kept under the personal control of the Buyer, and this dog shall be given adequate housing, food, veterinary

care, basic obedience training, and shall in no manner be mistreated or neglected.

2. This puppy is sold as a pet or working dog (not guaranteed to be show conformation) and breeding quality, and he/she shall not be used for breeding unless the buyer and the seller agree, in writing, to that, in a separate breeding rights agreement.

3. The buyer shall notify the seller if the dog earns any title or certification or receives field trial points.

4. If circumstances arise that would prevent the buyer from keeping this dog, the buyer promises not to discard this dog, and to make every effort to place the dog in another suitable home. This dog shall not be turned over to any animal shelter or rescue organization. If the buyer is unable to locate a suitable home for the dog, the dog shall be returned to the seller together with its signed-off registration papers—free of charge.

5. In the case of male puppies (unless neutered) the seller retains the right to use this male for stud service, free of charge. Seller will notify the buyer in advance if such a service is required, and will make all necessary arrangements, including payment for the pre-breeding blood tests. Seller will also conduct the breeding.

This contract is valid from the date of delivery of the puppy and throughout the lifetime of the dog, or until the buyer transfers ownership of the dog to a third party.

Buyer: _____ Date_____

Seller: _____ Date_____

Be Careful About Veterinary Expenses

One of the most important clauses in my sample contract is the one that clearly states that I do not reimburse for veterinary expenses, and I would advise you not to leave out this clause or include a similar one. Despite their best intentions, some veterinarians may overreact to medical situations by performing extraneous tests and procedures. I have also observed that multiple laboratory tests and multiple remedies are dispensed by veterinarians who are unsure, and perhaps lack diagnostic skills or medical intuition.

Here's an example: I once had a puppy leave my kennel in perfect health. When he arrived at his new home, he must have either gotten into something or for some reason he was stressed. *By the next day,* he had severe diarrhea. The new owners called me, and I told them to take him off of his food, give him only water for at least eight hours, and then give him just a few tablespoons of boiled rice with some boiled/drained hamburger mixed in. Instead of following my instructions, they took him to their local veterinary emergency service. I received a bill for $2,000, *which I paid.* It didn't matter that the services provided were inappropriate in my opinion, or that the veterinarian was not held accountable—breeders are often blamed for anything that goes wrong with the puppy.

After this incident, I now always encourage new owners to spend at least an hour at my kennel playing and observing their "healthy" puppy before they take it home. I work to develop a solid rapport with them and to build a relationship that will benefit the puppy. In cases where puppies who are being shipped, I always deliver them with a USDA Health Certificate from a licensed veterinarian—which I obtain on the ship date or the day before.

I wish the owners would have trusted my experience and knowledge; instead, they fell prey to their own panic. As a result of this, I learned the hard way—and now you can benefit from my experience. Never agree to pay or reimburse the puppy owner for any veterinary bills because you have no control over the medical treatment provided. I highlight that clause in my contract, and have buyers initial that paragraph to make sure they read and understand it. If a buyer raises some concern about it, you can review the parts of the contract that state they are receiving a healthy puppy with multiple guarantees, and that any medical issues can be consulted on together. This part of your contract should not be negotiable. You cannot guarantee something that you cannot control or supervise.

On the other hand, proven genetic defects have nothing to do with environment or care. You are responsible for them because you orchestrated the breeding of the pair that produced the puppy. Always be willing to take back a genetically defective puppy and replace it with a healthy puppy. In order to assess each situation appropriately, do not put that in your contract as it may be misconstrued or taken out of context. Veterinarians lack consensus on what is "genetic" and what is "congenital." Leave those decisions as your prerogative.

As for how to handle a puppy that may have a health issue that deems it defective, remember that even after having a puppy for only a few days, the bond with the person or family is already strong. In my opinion, as the one who sold the puppy, it is unfair and unrealistic to insist that the buyer return a puppy because it has a health defect. He or she paid good money for the puppy, taken good care of it, and may now have to cope with symptoms of hip dysplasia or progressive retinal atrophy. Whether the dog has been with them for two weeks or two years, it is now one of their children! What I ask buyers in this predicament to do is have the dog spayed or neutered (if it hasn't been done already), send me proof of that, and then, if they want, I give them another puppy. Honoring an agreement to provide a healthy dog this way demonstrates your compassion and empathy. Buyers appreciate this and will send you referrals because of how you handled a potentially bad situation. On the other hand, threatening to take a beloved pet or to euthanize the puppy to avoid honoring your warranty is cruel and unethical. Of course, if you breed judiciously and cautiously, you will avoid most warranty issues.

Most other genetic and congenital defects become obvious prior to the age of seven or eight weeks, and you should not release such a young puppy to a new owner unless they were made aware of the defect and agreed to accept the puppy without a warranty (perhaps at a discounted price or free of charge). Some of these issues may be low-grade heart murmurs, enzyme deficiencies, defective tear ducts, drooping lower eyelids, overbite or under bite, deafness, blindness, Monorchid (only one testicle in the scrotum), or Cryptorchid (no testicles in the scrotum), and even breed disqualifications such as color mutations in coat, eye, or mouth and nose pigmentation. Even if the buyer is not intending to show the dog—they would be purchasing a substandard example of the breed, and it should be sold at a discounted price. I would also specify that my kennel name should not be used as the prefix on any puppy with a defect.

My puppy sales contract is not a spay/neuter contract. I prefer to screen buyers and educate them regarding the responsibilities of ownership. I do this for several reasons that I feel are right. In general, I am opposed to the spaying and neutering of puppies—spaying and neutering should be done when the dog has reached physical maturity. The practice of spaying and neutering of puppies contributes to the increased incidence of joint problems in older dogs. Just as postmenopausal women suffer from bone loss and osteoporosis, so these neutered/spayed puppies do not develop proper skeletal substance. When puppies are deprived of hormones and the opportunity to develop to physical maturity, they are subsequently denied the development of bone density. Canine growth plates do not close until around 11 months of age. Hairline fractures, and disintegrating joints result in poor quality of life in later years due to the lack of bone density in these dogs. As far as hunting dogs or working dogs, from my observations, I have to conclude that they lose their "drive" and focus after they are neutered. Show Dogs and Field Trial competition dogs are intact. They are the best-trained and most well behaved dogs in the world—so the assumption that it is difficult or impossible to train an intact male dog is simply not true. Again, this is my contract so it includes terms with which I am comfortable. Other breeders do things differently, but I am not sure they are aware of all the ramifications.

It is up to you to do what you believe is right for your puppies, your buyers, and your business.

Co-Ownership and Contracts

From time to time in your breeding business, you may want to co-own a dog with another breeder or a puppy buyer. Becoming involved in a co-ownership of a dog or bitch may seem like a win-win situation for you and the person with whom you will share the ownership. After all, you'll be splitting costs and reaping double the rewards, right? The truth is that co-ownerships are some of the most difficult arrangements to go into. There are many questions you need to ask yourself and your prospective partner and the answers aren't always clear or easily negotiated. However, they are critical if the partnership is to succeed.

For example, in a hypothetical co-ownership agreement on a brood bitch (a bitch designated for breeding), questions need to be answered in the body of the contract. Most of them are questions related to assigned responsibilities, decision-making authority, and financial liability. These include (but are not limited to):

1. Which kennel name will be at the end of the bitch's registered name?
2. Whose kennel prefix will be on the registered names of the puppies?
3. Who is going to be responsible for veterinary expenses?
4. Who is going to pay show entry fees and related expenses?
5. Who is liable if the bitch bites someone or gets into a fight with another dog?
6. Before breeding the bitch, who will pay for the necessary health certifications and clearances?

7. How will a stud dog be selected for the breeding, and who will have the final decision on this?

8. When the bitch is bred, who will handle the breeding?

9. Who will make the decision of how the puppies will be managed? Who will get pick of the litter?

10. Who will advertise the litter? Will advertising require approval by both parties?

11. Who will physically supervise the whelping process?

12. How will the net proceeds from the sale of the puppies be divided?

13. If one of the partners uses their own stud dog for the breeding, how will they be compensated for that service?

14. Big question: Who will make the decision to spay the bitch, and what will the criteria be for making that decision?

In the case of co-ownership on a male dog, there would be additional questions, including:

1. How will stud fees be split?

2. Who will make the final decision on which bitches are suitable to breed to him?

3. If he is to be campaigned after attaining his Champion title, what are the specific goals and the timeframe for campaigning this dog?

There must be a provision spelling out exactly what is required from a bitch owner in order for them to be allowed to use the stud dog's services on their bitch: brucellosis test; copies of all appropriate health clearances for that particular breed; veterinary check up, including a vaginal smear to check for any infections and a veterinarian's clearance indicating the bitch is healthy and in good breeding condition. Stud dog management details must also be provided, either in the body of the agreement or as an addendum to it.

Other questions might include:

1. What happens if one of the parties to this agreement dies or is incapacitated?

2. If either partner wishes to get out of the contract, what is the process and what are the constraints?

3. If one party is financially injured by an early release of the other party, what will the compensation be and/or what penalties will be applied?

> ## A Breeder Secret
>
> **Choose an Arbitrator**
> An acceptable arbitrator should be named in a co-ownership contract. This is very important because it is usually not cost effective to litigate a contract dispute. The tendency would be for the injured party to just walk away from it. Pick the arbitrator carefully. It might be the breed club board if both parties to the agreement are members in good standing. It might be a third party breeder who has agreed to act as an arbitrator, or it might be someone whom both parties respect and who has agreed to be an arbitrator. There are also arbitrator associations that can supply the names of members who accept arbitration cases.

In a co-ownership agreement, your co-owner may have at least equal decision-making rights, and this can limit your options severely. I heard of one instance in which an owner disagreed with the co-owner about who the bitch should be bred to. She failed to convince the other co-owner that she was right about this. Instead of agreeing to disagree, and allowing a breeding that she did not believe was in the best interests of her kennel's reputation, she had the bitch spayed! This was a bitch who had produced top champions and was still young enough to produce more. This was devastating financially and emotionally to the other party. That unilateral act wiped out the options for the original breeder. By agreeing to a co-ownership, the original breeder had literally risked her chances of becoming one of the top breeders in the country. The bitter feud between them damaged both of their reputations as ethical breeders and effectively closed the door to future opportunities outside of their own kennels. It was an unethical thing to do, and legally the injured party had no recourse for damages because it was, in this case, a verbal agreement made between two friends.

Personally, I believe that friendship outweighs any financial considerations—especially when it comes to the question of whether to breed or not to breed a dog. *The question you must ask yourself before you go into a partnership with a friend is, "Am I willing to sacrifice this friend over a dog?"* Write up the contract, but know in your heart that you probably would never enforce a contract with a friend or family member. The contract is then reduced to a simple list of guidelines so that both of you understand your goals for working together. Then cross your fingers and hope that your friend, or sister, or mother, respects you as much as you respect them.

The Ways Co-Ownership Can Go Sour
Even when you have a well-written agreement signed by both parties, it may be almost impossible to enforce the provisions of the contract. Don't assume that just because you have a written, signed agreement that you are safe from exploitation.

I had a situation in which my co-ownership agreement with a breeder called for a return of my dog from her kennels in 24 months. When that time came, she did not want to comply. It took months of letters, threats, and pleading telephone calls to get my dog back. When he was finally returned, I learned I had handed over a perfectly healthy, productive, proven stud dog that had already produced six healthy litters of puppies, and I got back a completely sterile dog with not even one sperm, dead or alive. I took him to a fertility specialist who did a host of expensive tests on him and concluded that he either had suffered a sever infection that was left untreated, or that he had been chemically sterilized. There was no way to rule out either cause, although the totality of the devastation would suggest chemical sterilization. When I had him neutered to reduce his risk of cancer, I asked the veterinarian doing the surgery if he could tell what the cause was, but he couldn't find anything conclusive.

The breeder's justification for not wanting to return my dog was that she had given me the puppy originally. I had not asked her for the puppy. She called me one day out of the blue saying she had a great show-prospect puppy and asking if I wanted him. I said that I was not looking to add another male to my breeding program at the time. She proceeded to tell me that she was giving me the dog free of charge because it would be a terrible shame to sell him as a pet. (Beware of people bearing gifts. They may have ulterior motives.) I even told her that I didn't do co-ownerships, which she said was fine, so I picked up the pup from her. He was truly a gorgeous puppy—one of the best I had ever seen.

A few months after I had been showing him in the puppy class, the breeder called to ask me to put her name on his registration papers so she could show him at the breed specialty in the prestigious Bred by Exhibitor Class. She assured me that was the only reason she needed to have her name temporarily on his registration papers. I fell for this hook, line, and sinker. After I had all of his certifications completed and had proven him as a stud dog, she wanted to put him on the show circuit with her handler. The written agreement—which I insisted upon—was that he would be returned to me in 24 months, and as compensation for showing him, she and her professional dog handler would have stud rights to use him on their own bitches for the remainder of his lifetime. He did go all the way, but I lost everything I had invested in him—money, time, and great expectations, not to mention that he was a true Mommy's Boy, and I missed him terribly. Since I could not prove, in a court of law, what happened to my dog, I had no recourse. So that I could know he would be happy for the rest of his life, I placed him in a wonderful home with a very dear friend.

The scope of breeder agreements and arrangements is only limited by the creativity of the parties involved. That said, I must strongly discourage you from any contracts that call for co-ownership of your foundation stock. Once you lock yourself into co-ownership of any of your breeding stock, you are in a business partnership whether that was your intention or not. Co-ownership agreements usually go sour within a short time. It is the rare circumstance that works out to the benefit of both parties. Human nature being what it is, everyone wants to win—and everyone wants to win unilaterally.

I share these co-ownership disasters so you can avoid something similar happening to you. Your dogs belong with you! Don't loan them out to anyone for any reason. Don't agree to co-own foundation stock with anyone for any reason. If you want to show your dogs with a professional handler, meet the handler at the show and pay the handler for that day. Train your dog well so he or she can work with the handler. Don't ever, for any reason, agree to any lifetime stud rights on any dog you own! This could be a disaster for your breeding program and your dog's reputation, as it puts you in a position of giving up control of one of the major assets in your business. No one is going to take care of your dogs as well as you. We don't loan out our luxury cars, our expensive jewelry, or our children (although some of us might be tempted to loan out our kids when they enter puberty—and even offer to sweeten the pot!), so don't loan out your major kennel asset—your stud dog or brood bitch.

Dog Handling Contracts

Personally, I do not embrace the concept of needing a handler to show a dog you have bred beyond the regular classes. However, you must be realistic. Almost anyone inside the sport will tell you that unless you are a consummate owner/handler who will be recognized in the show ring, your chances of placing in Group without a professional handler at the other end of the lead are slim, if not impossible. The fact is that although shows are supposed to be about the dogs, they are judged at both ends of the lead—especially at the Group level.

If you wish to campaign your dog beyond the Championship title to gain national ranking, you may also be forced to use a handler. It is the handler who will provide you with a contract. Therefore, be careful—read their contract with a magnifying glass, visit the handler's facility, ask to see the vehicle they are using for dog transportation, and ask to see their grooming area.

I visited several well-respected professional handlers and found some of their facilities to be disappointing. It led me to conclude that not only is the actual contract important to protecting your dog, but your vigilance and stewardship is critical in shielding your dogs from unscrupulous and unethical practices.

Some professional handlers and breeders will keep show dogs in a dark room for weeks prior to a show. They soak them to the skin every night before they are crated and leave them wet until the morning. They do this to cause the dogs to develop thick winter coats. The reduction of daylight hours and the increase in humidity will stimulate coat growth and stop shedding. In my opinion this should not be condoned. Judges who put up dogs in incorrect coat for the season are effectively promoting this practice. It should be penalized so that it is not a good option for exhibitors.

Don't make erroneous assumptions based on appearances and common practices of others around you. Check out a handler's facilities personally, and make sure that the well being of the dogs is his or her primary objective. Just because they are always winning does not guarantee that they are properly managing the dogs entrusted to their care. Remember, your dog can't tell you what's happening to him while he's in someone else's care. It is your responsibility to make sure it's the best. You may even be told that visiting your dog during its show campaign will somehow upset it emotionally and it will not show well. In my opinion, this is not true.

In dog handling contracts, you want to be sure that the expenses you will be expected to pay, which are in addition to the handling fees, are spelled out clearly and are limited to a specific maximum dollar amount. It is better to pay a higher handling fee that's inclusive of all ancillary expenses than to end up being nickel-and-dimed by various add-on expenses. I do not like surprises—particularly on invoices for services rendered.

Failure to disclose anticipated expenses is a common practice among some dog handlers. They contract to handle the dog for a particular show or hunt test, and you get a bill that is almost double the original quote. For example, gasoline, hotel, meal expenses, etc., may be added onto the bill. If the handler is traveling with five or six dogs, she or he will total up all the expenses and divide them by the number of dogs they handled at that particular event. If you are a novice, you may or may not be made aware of it until the bill is presented. Then you might be made to feel foolish as they stand before you and tell you that this is standard practice. They might also say that they thought you were more knowledgeable than that! A condescending attitude is common when someone is trying to con you. If the handler only took two dogs to that particular event, the bill is going to be very high. It isn't your fault that the handler couldn't get more dogs to handle. Why should you foot the bill because they haven't promoted their business adequately?

Stud Service Contracts

The owner of the stud dog provides the Stud Service Contract. A normal stud fee is usually equal to the price of one puppy from that breeding. Breeding fees are separate from stud fees and are charged by some breeders. They can be several hundred dollars to compensate for the time involved in managing the breeding. The stud fee itself may be collected up front or may be due and payable upon registration of the litter. The contract should spell out what documentation will be supplied, and what health checks are required. It should also state the guarantee—which is usually a minimum of two live puppies or a repeat breeding at no charge. The contract should clearly identify both the bitch and the stud dog by description, registration, and microchip or DNA profile number.

Agreeing to give up the pick of the litter as a stud fee is not usually a good idea. What if you produce that superior pup that you have been dreaming about, but you have to give it away to someone else because you made an agreement with the owner of the stud dog? Maybe the stud fee is only $1,500 or $2,000 in cash (it is usually the price of one puppy), but you are giving away a pup that could make $10,000 or $20,000 a year for your business over the course of five or six years for a female, and possibly ten years for a male. That could be $60,000 to $160,000 over the breeding career of the dog. If you are doing it right and you decide that the pup isn't as good as you had thought, and you sell it when it is six or eight months old, the pup will still bring a good price because he is housetrained, obedience trained, and socialized by then.

Never agree to give up the first-pick puppy and do not accept a deposit based on such a promise, unless you are sure you will not want a puppy from that litter. There are some breeders who intentionally keep the more promising pups until they are housetrained, have done some obedience, and are actively being socialized. They want to keep the best for themselves—and make sure the first-pick pup is truly superior as he develops. Breeders typically have their own targeted-market for pups they do not keep for themselves—usually working professionals who just don't have time to train a puppy, but who don't mind paying more for an older pup who is completely trained.

Sample Contract: Stud Service

Date: _____

This is an agreement between [Full Name], the stud owner, and [Full Name], the bitch owner.

[Name of Bitch Owner] will bring the bitch, [Bitch's Name], AKC # _____
_____, Microchip # _____, D.O.B. _____, Color

& Markings _____ to [Name of Kennel and Kennel Address] to breed to the stud dog, [Dog's Name], AKC # _____, Microchip# _____, D.O.B. _____, Color & Markings: _____.

The stud owner [Full Name] will take good care of the bitch, providing a safe, dry, and clean environment. The bitch owner [Full Name] authorizes the stud owner to take the bitch to the closest veterinarian in case of an emergency. The bitch owner promises to reimburse the stud dog owner for any veterinary expenses incurred. The bitch owner also authorizes the stud dog owner to perform vaginal smears and artificial inseminations on the bitch as necessary. The bitch will be bred for three consecutive days—once each day. If a natural breeding is not possible, an artificial insemination with fresh semen from the above dog will be performed. The bitch owner has supplied a current copy of a negative brucellosis test performed on the bitch within 10 days of this breeding and certifies that the bitch has not been in the company of any other dogs since the test was performed. The bitch owner has also supplied copies of the bitch's OFA and CERF certifications, and a letter from the bitch's veterinarian stating that this bitch is in good health and there is no reason that she should not be bred.

The stud dog owner has supplied a stud service packet that includes: copies of her dog's AKC Registration, UKC Registration, OFA Hip & Elbows, CERF, Cardio clearances, a four-generation pedigree, a copy of his DNA Certificate, and copies of any other titles he has earned. A current Brucellosis test (within the last 6 months) has also been supplied and the stud dog owner hereby certifies that her dog has not been in the company of, or bred to, any bitch that was not tested and cleared for brucellosis and had a veterinary health check. The stud dog owner has supplied a photo CD that includes multiple photographs of the stud dog along with appropriate statistical information to support the sale of his puppies.

The stud dog owner guarantees her dog's stud service to produce a minimum of two (2) live puppies. If two (2) live puppies are not produced, she waives all stud fees. There is no separate breeding charge under this contract.

The stud fee is [Dollar Amount], to be paid prior to signing the litter registration papers and no later than six (6) weeks after the puppies are whelped. The stud dog owner promises to post the litter on her website and to assist the bitch owner as much as possible in selling the puppies. The bitch owner promises not to discount these puppies below the minimum price of [Dollar Amount] without prior approval by the stud dog owner.

[Stud Dog Owner's Full Name] _____ Date: _____

[Bitch Owner's Full Name] _____ Date: _____

Summary

If you do your homework, you should be able to provide others with and sign off on contracts that will be workable because you and the person (or people) with whom you're entering into the agreement will fully understand each other. The homework involves looking at as many contracts as possible so you can think about what makes sense and what doesn't. It involves thoroughly thinking through your own circumstances based on the points I've covered so that you feel you've addressed all concerns. And it involves being flexible enough to make something work without sacrificing your integrity or ethics.

Chapter 3

BEYOND BOOK LEARNING

This chapter is all about making key contacts with fellow breeders and exhibitors active in your breed. These folks are, after all, your peers, your friends, and your business associates. Knowing who can help you with what—and vice versa—will not only ensure that your business will grow and prosper, but also that you will become an insider in the dog world. Becoming an insider will gain you access to the collective experience of others and hopefully minimize the mistakes you make along the way. It will help you realize that it is impossible to succeed if you go it alone—and much more fun when you are part of the community.

From my own experience, the key is making and keeping the right contacts. You can do this by:

1. Participating in the sport of purebred dogs.

2. Networking with other breeders.

3. Working with a mentor.

4. Joining and participating in a club (or clubs).

5. Playing fair and behaving ethically.

Learning about the Sport

If you haven't already, you should obtain all of the AKC-related publications regarding dog shows, hunt tests, obedience trials, agility competition, and other activities in which purebred dogs participate. Study them and make sure that you understand them. Even if you are personally uninterested in something like agility, lure coursing, hunt tests, or field trials, to become an expert in the world of purebred dogs requires having a broad working knowledge of the sport. Just as you will eventually become as well versed in veterinary medicine as many veterinary technicians are, you will need to become knowledgeable about AKC rules and regulations, judging criteria, and the inner workings of your breed club. One day you can run for a seat on the board of your local dog club, and competently plan and orchestrate an entire club event in a professional manner, if you decide this is something you wish to pursue.

As you know, reading about something is only part of the experience. You can read every book written on breeding and showing dogs, but until you raise a show dog and step into the ring with him or her, you will not know what it's really like. Then once you do, you'll realize that there's still a lot of studying you need to do.

A great way to gain more knowledge of the do's and don'ts of any activity in which you want to compete with your dog is to attend events and watch. Specifically observe the handling techniques of exhibitors of your chosen breed. Every breed of dog is shown differently, in subtle but important ways. A Labrador Retriever is handled differently than a dog from the Terrier Group. A Standard Poodle is moved around the ring differently than an Irish Setter or a Bulldog. A Pug moves differently than a Pekingese or a Min Pin.

Different breeds of dogs are gaited and stacked differently by their handlers. There are dogs that are stacked quite square, and other who are stretched out in the rear. German Shepherds have their own very unique pose and they move around the ring like no other breed. Some dogs are "free-baited" and some dogs could care less about food. Sight hounds react differently to squeaky toys than a Herding dog might. The best place to observe correct handling is at the Junior Showmanship Ring in the Senior Class. In this ring the handlers are being judged—not the dogs, and most of these kids in the Senior Class are "superior" handlers who go on to become professional dog handlers some of whom go on to earn an annual six-figure income. These are the handlers you will see on TV at the Westminster Dog Show or the AKC/Eukanuba National Championship.

Networking with Other Breeders

It's actually fun and easy to network with other breeders and professionals who work in areas related to breeding dogs. Cultivate relationships with breeders whom you know to be exceptional in all ways (professionally and ethically)—you can never have too many of them teaching you and supporting your efforts. Pick breeders who demonstrate integrity, have a positive attitude, are kind to dogs, don't gossip too much, seem to be making it financially, and who listen well. Visit their kennels, and ascertain that they are clean and their puppies are healthy and free from parasites. Study their warranty contracts, as well. If they live close to you, that is frosting on the cake. These are the people you will call when you have a C-section in the middle of the night—and when you and your veterinarian need four more pairs of hands to resuscitate the pups as they are delivered. It takes another breeder (or a registered nurse or emergency technician friend) to understand that a call in the middle of the night means, "Move it, and move it now!"

When I was actively breeding dogs, I could have four or five people at my vet's clinic within 15 or 20 minutes. By the time the vet was scrubbed in and the bitch was under, we were already standing by, bulb syringes in hand, un-waxed dental floss ready, and Dopram™ on the table. I even had a friend who was a surgical scrub nurse come in once and assist the veterinarian in a C-section because the vet could not get a hold of his veterinary surgical assistant. My EMT friend and neighbor monitored the anesthesia and assisted in the closure. For that type of friendship, you must at least send them thank-you notes and gifts like fruit baskets or flowers. For the breeders who come to help, the greatest gifts are your referrals for puppies—and a willingness to respond to their requests for help, no matter what time it is.

There are always periods in the year when you run out of puppies to sell, and none of your bitches are bred yet. And, especially if your quality is high, you may have pre-sold all of your puppies even before they are born. So if you get a call that you cannot accommodate, and you know that an excellent breeder is expecting a litter to arrive within the next week or two, or one who may have used your stud dog recently, initiate "Operation Referral"—write down what the caller wants, interview them as though you were going to sell them one of your puppies, and if they meet your criteria, get their name and contact information and tell them that you are personally going to contact the breeder and give them a recommendation. When you get off the phone, contact the other breeder and make the referral over the telephone. This is too important to leave to e-mail. If the breeder has puppies, ask her to call the buyers. If not, you call the buyers and tell them you were not able to locate a suitable puppy for them. Never leave someone hanging, waiting to hear from you.

Another way to network with breeders and others who share your interests is to connect with them at seminars or special events. I met some of the most fascinating people at hunt tests in Kansas. Those were the most enjoyable weekends I can remember. Go for the week or the weekend, and by Sunday night, when it is time to go home, you will probably have made some life-long friends. When I did it, I felt like a little kid at summer camp—I really didn't want to go home. I was having such a ball hanging out with people who have the same interests that I have, and watching our dogs do what they love best, that I never wanted to leave. The positive energy and the camaraderie were incredible.

Through this experience, I ended up breeding one of my bitches to a champion hunting dog in Oklahoma who was owned by a wonderful woman I met at the hunt test. I sold one of the puppies from that litter to a hunter from Oklahoma. She sent me the referral because she didn't own any bitches, and didn't raise puppies—but she liked my bitch that had aced the hunt test in Kansas. These are the kinds of personal relationships that will pay off for you in so many ways.

Working with a Mentor

I have a dear friend, Sue Harrington, who mentored me at the beginning of my dog breeding career. I am sure she didn't agree with everything I did, but she was always a lady under all circumstances. She didn't spread rumors or innuendo. She never bad mouthed other breeders or commented on less-than-perfect dogs in the show ring. Although I never purchased a dog from her, I did use her stud dog. She bred wonderful Labrador Retrievers. Of all the people I have met in the dog world, it is she who has most impressed me with her graciousness and her superior ethics. This woman consistently did the right thing no matter what was going on in the breed club, regardless of the current politicking or power struggles that came up, as they do in any organization. She owns Pikes Peak Labradors, a small breeding kennel in Colorado Springs.

The first time I saw Sue at a hunt test dressed in full camouflage with boots and a 12-gauge shotgun cracked and slung expertly over her arm, and with her Master Hunter Black Lab in heel position, I nearly fell over. I had always seen her in the show ring dressed in her grey suit with her hair perfectly coifed, in panty hose, and leather shoes. I knew her dogs had hunting titles, but I didn't realize that she was actually a hunter, and that she trained all of her own dogs on pheasants (which she loved to eat) and ducks. She was in her early 60s then, and it was obvious she was having fun with her dogs. Sue always found time to help newcomers and to demonstrate by her actions how ethical behavior is part of this "gentleman's sport." Today, Sue is considered old school—and I feel privileged to be her friend. She made me want to emulate her behavior, character, and her commitment to improving the breed. Although it has been years since I left Colorado, when I face an ethical dilemma I still ask myself what Sue would do in that situation. That is the best compliment that I can pay her, and I hope that someday there will be someone asking themselves the same thing about Sylvia Smart.

Make it Fun

Keep in mind that networking and developing mentors isn't rocket science. It's not something you have to study or go to business school to master. All it takes is a little effort on your part. Be friendly and seek out the best people. Make yourself available to help others, open your mind to making new friends and to learning new things. The world is full of fascinating people who have wonderful stories to tell you and exciting experiences to share with you. Consider that every person you meet could initiate an adventure, a learning experience, or be someone who will affect your life in some significant way.

A Breeder Secret

Who to Avoid

I will caution you not to become a groupie of some egocentric person who surrounds himself or herself with go-fers to build up a self-important image. You can identify people like this quite easily. They are the ones constantly giving orders and asking for things; for example, "Could you go get some bait for me at one of the vendors? I'll need some for the next ring." Or, "Change Max's collar, I think it's too small. Put the slip lead on him." Decent people treat others with respect. They don't assume that because you aren't a top breeder or handler yet that you are there to wait on them hand and foot. Unless you specifically offer to help, they shouldn't be ordering you around. Imparting information and helping newbies get started is something they owe the sport—and not something that you should have to pay for as their indentured servant.

Joining and Participating in Clubs

Here's my philosophy about getting and being involved in dog clubs—join! If you don't join the clubs and the associations—and you don't contribute—why should anyone in the world of dogs want to help you, mentor you, introduce you to the players, or allow you the privilege of using their valuable breeding lines? If you don't bother to get involved, not only will they not embrace your addition to their ranks, they will resent you and possibly sabotage your efforts.

The cost of getting involved in a club (or clubs) is financially insignificant compared to the benefits you will reap. Investing your time in these activities is not only going to enhance you as a breeder (or exhibitor or other type of enthusiast), but it will expand your base of knowledge and your social connections considerably. When it comes time to advertise and to find homes for your puppies, your membership in prestigious breed clubs and other related organizations is a tangible validation of your professionalism.

There are many different kinds of clubs in which you can become involved. There is your chosen breed's national club (for example, The Labrador Retriever Club if you're a Lab enthusiast like me) or the regional breed clubs. Local all-breed clubs have members who typically own many different kinds of breeds. There are clubs that support a particular activity, like agility, obedience, lure coursing, hunting, herding, and so on. There are also dog-related associations like therapy dog groups, purebred rescue, search-and-rescue, and others.

If (when) you join one of the clubs, participate in as many of its activities as your spare time allows. This could include getting involved with your dog in events, as well as going to club meetings, attending club social events, etc. Once you have been the recipient of the voluntary help and support of members in your local club, reciprocate by volunteering to do training, office work, judging, etc., for the club. You will gain self-confidence, self-esteem, and the respect of your fellow club members by offering to help others who are on the same path. After you have been a member for six months or a year and have gotten a feel for the club, run for office.

Those who have been serving a while are usually eager for others to get involved, and in truth, there really isn't that much work to do during the year. It is only when an event is scheduled that there is about a month of planning, scheduling, and coordinating the activities. Things get more frantic as the event nears, but rest assured that the club president or vice president from the previous year will assist and train you. That way, the following year you can be completely in charge.

An officer's term is usually for two years, depending on the Club Charter. It is a prestigious position, qualifies you as an expert, and allows you to make all kinds of networking connections. I became the Vice President of the Muddy Hunters' Gun Dog Club, which was a NAHRA (North American Hunting Retriever Association) sponsored club. Whenever I sold a puppy to a hunter, I would purchase a year's membership for them in the Hunt Club. This quickly doubled the membership, created opportunities to sell more hunting dog puppies, and allowed me the luxury of watching my own puppies train and develop into competent hunting companions. In turn, my buyers had immediate access to all the NAHRA publications as well as the club training sessions. They only had to pay for the birds for training. The day the club ran the Started Retriever tests, I was beaming with pride—all my pups qualified, and I got to help their owners train them.

A Breeder Secret

Hunt Training

Hunt training usually takes place one or two weekends out of the month. This is a club activity, and most people like to train with a group because it is so much easier to have several gunners, one or more bird launchers, and someone to blow the duck call at the right time. Clubs also arrange for the grounds/permits/insurance, birds, and even ammunition. The club usually has some expensive equipment its members can use to train, too, that the average person wouldn't own, such as bird launchers, pigeon traps, range finders, and remote-controlled bird release cages.

Going to shows, tests, or trials and talking with other experienced breeders/handlers will give you the information you need to sell your puppies. Taking your beautiful dogs into hospitals and convalescence homes to sooth the patients will put you in the right place to demonstrate the wonderful temperament of your dogs. Certainly the relatives, doctors, and friends of the patients will be impressed with your dogs—and at the same time, you will be doing something quite wonderful for the patients and for your dogs.

While preparing for a dog show or setting up a hunt test, for example, you will work side-by-side with breeders and enthusiasts from all walks of life. Don't be surprised if the hunt test judge is a District or Federal Court judge during the week. When you return to the lodge after a day in the field running your dogs in a Junior or Master hunt test, you may find yourself eating your BBQ and corn-on-the-cob next to a famous author or the CEO of a large corporation. Your love and commitment to breeding only the "best of the best" will automatically position you next to others who share your commitment.

A Breeder Secret

Ribbons and Rosettes

The ribbons and rosettes your dog receives at your club's events are quite impressive, and if you take photos—especially when you are a winner or qualifier—you can display them on the walls of your puppy nursery and post them on your website. Buyers love to see this in person or on the DVD that you mail to them. For example, to know that their puppy's sire took the award for highest qualifying obedience score (High in Trial) is prestigious.

It is my experience that individuals who excel in their professional lives are often the same individuals who find relaxation and enjoyment in the company of superior dogs. As the vice president of our hunting club, I once found myself in a muddy hole under a bridge early on a freezing morning with another gunner for the hunt tests. It was rainy and foggy. My coffee thermos was empty. The other gunner introduced himself to me and asked about joining our local hunt club. He shared his hot coffee with me. While we waited for the birds that would be slingshot into the air above us, we talked quietly. He eventually did join our club, and the following year he was elected its president. He turned out to be the Commanding Officer of the local Air Force base.

He brought so many wonderful resources to our club, and together we recruited many Air Force and Army officers and enlisted men from the local bases to join our retriever hunt club. He was a wonderful man, and he taught me so much about leadership and integrity. He owned a charming Golden Retriever who was also his best friend. He was a true Renaissance Man. He had a terrific family, enjoyed the arts, and was well read and educated. He was one of the most interesting people I have crossed paths with in my long and active life.

Never compromise your basic recipe for success. The increase in your income will probably change your lifestyle in some way—or you will elect to put that money back into building your business, acquiring better property, or improving on your kennel facility. But what will you do for fun? Not everyone is excited about dog shows. Some people can't see what is so great about going to a dog show. Truthfully, although I loved the excitement of the dog shows, my most enjoyable recreation came from hunt training my dogs and running them in hunt tests. I have attended agility trials also, and I loved the dog-human team enthusiasm for the task at hand. For myself and other dog enthusiasts, these are very good ways to form a partnership with our dog(s).

As much as I enjoy dog shows and understand their purpose, I think the breeders who get involved in dog-related activities rise above those who don't do anything other than show their dogs. (It's also fun for the dogs to have purpose in their lives.) If it isn't dog shows or hunt tests, it might be agility trials, fly ball, obedience trials, Frisbee™ competitions, or therapy work with special-needs kids or at a hospital or senior home. Some people have a breed that is competitive in herding or lure coursing, sledding or skijoring (a form of sledding with a dog).

In thinking about what my dogs and I can do together, I know I could never be that good at anything on my own! I play the piano, sew, write, paint, photograph, cook, produce videos, rescue kids, and play cards—yet none of my accomplishments comes close to the perfection of working the field with a gun dog! If you asked me who I am, I like to say that I am a writer—and I think I am good at it—yet nothing has been as satisfying as when I was working outdoors with my dog. For families, this is especially true—anything you can find that the whole family can participate in is definitely a step in the right direction. It will pull your family together with laughter and good memories.

Playing Fair and Behaving Ethically

Since networking and being involved with other breeders and fanciers is a key to gaining the knowledge you will need, you want to make sure that you keep your relationships with others healthy. You do that by always playing fair and behaving ethically. As is any human endeavor, competitive dog sports can be flawed. They involve high-stakes competition, money, prestige, and celebrity—all motivations for people to make unethical decisions or to behave badly. Its fundamental nature can't be easily fixed, but breeders and exhibitors can maintain their integrity and set an example for others to emulate. If you vocally harp on the inequities and favoritisms that take place, you will detract from the preponderance of good sportsmanship, camaraderie, and genuine friendship found in this sport. That would be too high a price to pay. Instead, vow to help newcomers to the sport, and show them how to do it ethically and honestly.

For those of you who are already breeders immersed in the world of dogs, if you have been a part of the problem, resolve to become part of the solution. You *can* make a difference. Make sure that the dogs you enter in a show are competitive. Learn to become a superior groomer for your breed so that you can present your dogs properly. Dress professionally and take conformation training classes so that if you have a good dog, the judges will recognize this and award the points to the superior dog in the ring (hopefully, yours!). These are all skills you will learn as you stay in the sport—and continue to make the right contacts by being involved in the sport through the channels reviewed in this chapter.

Chapter 4

ASSESSING, DECIDING UPON, AND OBTAINING BREEDING STOCK

This is the fun part of the process—selecting the breed you want to work with and finding your very first foundation bitches. Your future claim to excellence and healthy breeding lines will be based on how well you do your research, including how well you educate yourself about the breed you choose and how carefully you select your foundation stock. This chapter guides you through these fundamental aspects of establishing your kennel business.

Selecting the Breed

Finding the right breed for you is not only a satisfying process, but also an educational journey. When you have completed it, you will know more about a variety of dog breeds than most people would learn in a lifetime.

Some Considerations for Deciding on a Breed

Above all, I recommend you choose a breed based on what you *love*. You are going to be devoting a tremendous amount of time, energy, and potentially money into your breeding business, so I think you need to be truly devoted to the breed of dog you choose to raise. Secondly, it is obvious that there is much more demand for certain breeds than others (see the list of AKC registrations below). While a "rare" breed may be able to command a higher price, a more popular breed is probably the safer route to go from a business standpoint. But there are a number of other considerations to make before you decide upon your breed. These include:

1. What do you want to convey to a buyer? Make a list of what you think a buyer of a particular breed would be like.

2. What type of person do you think would want this type of a dog? Can you relate to this type of buyer?

3. Do you personally like this breed? Is this a breed that you could live with, that your spouse and children could enjoy?

4. Could you handle puppies of this size? Do you have the space required to house at least two litters of these puppies at the same time?

And there are some more factors that you may not have thought about that you should. These include:

Whelping factors. What do professionals say about the typical brood bitch in that breed? Are they easy whelpers or do they require C-sections? Do they have overly large litters i.e., 13 to 16 puppies in a typical litter? This might sound like a good thing, but believe me, it is not. Stay away from breeds that have very large litters, or you will spend all of your time and resources feeding and caring for puppies, and trying to keep them alive despite the fact that their mothers may not have enough milk for that many pups. There are also some very small breeds that historically only have two or three puppies in an average litter. This is okay if you can house three or four brood bitches and your own stud dog, or you have access to a Champion stud dog within a reasonable driving distance, but it can seriously affect your bottom line over time.

By contrast, very large breeds of dogs are sometimes considered by their breeders to be mediocre mothers, have a high incidence of uterine inertia (labor comes to a grinding halt halfway through the delivery), and experience a high incidence of heart failure and joint issues. And it is rare for dogs weighing more than one hundred pounds to live past the age of eight or nine years.

So-called "Dangerous Dogs." Think long and hard about breeding some of the more "macho" breeds. I know there are wonderful, responsible breeders of these types of dogs. But as a seller, I can't help wondering how do you select buyers who aren't out to intimidate people with their dog? How would you be able to ascertain their intentions, especially in light of the moral issues discussed in the first part of this book? There are also liability issues when you select a breed that is generally considered to be more people aggressive or dog aggressive than some other breeds. I won't argue the nature vs. nurture issues here; suffice it to say you should be smart about this. You also don't want to have any dog on your premises that you cannot allow around strangers, your family, or your other dogs. My advice is to leave those special breeds to those unique breeders who know how to breed them correctly, handle them, and find suitable homes for them.

The following is a list that national insurance companies have printed on their application for homeowner's insurance. It was current at the time I included it in the book; check with your insurance company about its specific policies. While I don't necessarily agree with the accuracy of this list as far as potential risk is involved, you will not argue successfully with an insurance company who refuses to issue a policy based on concrete actuarial statistics. For example, here is a question included in the application for homeowner's insurance:

Do you have any of the following dog breeds, or any mixes of these breeds? You may mark more than one if applicable:

- Akita
- American Staffordshire Terrier
- Bull Mastiff
- Chow Chow
- Doberman Pinscher
- Great Dane
- Pit Bull
- Presa Canario
- Rottweiller
- Siberian Husky
- Staffordshire Bull Terrier
- Wolf Hybrid

Customer Considerations. Another important consideration is to choose a breed that is easier to place with higher income households. Doctors and surgeons, high-level corporate executives, and stressed out computer engineers typically want a soft, cuddly lap dog or a big, solid "teddy bear" type dog. They don't want a dog that is bouncing off the walls, yapping incessantly, or requires ten laps around the block each night just to settle down. Most thoughtful, educated buyers have nice homes, expensive RV's and/or boats, nice clothes, and quality furniture. Many of them take their dogs with them on vacation. They despise doggy drool. Maybe that's not the clientele you want for your dogs and your business, but it's certainly something to think about. Being able to provide the right dog for the right owner and home is critical if you are to be or become successful in the breeding business.

Breed Selection Resources
For those of you involved in the world of purebred dogs already, you know the large number and varieties of breeds there are. For those of you who are reading this book to get started, you'll find that choosing a breed is like putting a garden together—there are lots and lots of possibilities.

It is most helpful to have photos and descriptions to look at in getting a first impression of the many kinds of purebred dogs there are to choose from. The American Kennel Club registers over 150 of them, and there is extensive information about the breeds on their website at www.akc.org. I have also included the list of AKC breeds by popularity according to their registration statistics for the year 2007. It is always interesting to see where a breed falls relative to other breeds in the rankings. There is more information about AKC registration statistics at their website, as well.

There are other resources you can use to research and evaluate breeds. There are some wonderful dog breed encyclopedias available, some of which include breeds other than those recognized by the AKC. Ask for them at your library or look for them online. It is handy to have books like these in your dog library at home—and kids love them, too. There are lots of other websites you can browse for breed information and photos, including the sites of breed clubs, those of other registries, and general information sites like www.dogbreedinfo.com.

Based on current AKC statistics, the following list shows all the AKC recognized breeds by number of registrations. This, of course, can be used as a proxy for current relative demand for pure-bred puppies:

1. Retrievers (Labrador)
2. Yorkshire Terriers
3. German Shepherd Dogs
4. Retrievers (Golden)
5. Beagles
6. Boxers
7. Dachshunds
8. Poodles
9. Shih Tzu
10. Bulldogs
11. Miniature Schnauzers
12. Chihuahuas
13. Pomeranians
14. Pugs
15. Rottweilers
16. Boston Terriers
17. Spaniels (Cocker)
18. Pointers (German Shorthaired)
19. Maltese
20. Shetland Sheepdogs
21. Doberman Pinschers
22. Pembroke Welsh Corgis
23. Great Danes
24. Siberian Huskies
25. Cavalier King Charles Spaniels
26. Miniature Pinschers
27. Spaniels (English Springer)
28. Mastiffs
29. Brittanys
30. Weimaraners
31. Basset Hounds
32. Bichons Frises
33. Australian Shepherds
34. French Bulldogs
35. West Highland White Terriers
36. Papillons
37. Havanese
38. Collies
39. St. Bernards
40. Bullmastiffs
41. Bernese Mountain Dogs
42. Vizslas
43. Bloodhounds
44. Newfoundlands
45. Scottish Terriers
46. Chinese Shar-Pei
47. Retrievers (Chesapeake Bay)
48. Cairn Terriers

49. Lhasa Apsos
50. Pekingese
51. Akitas
52. Chinese Crested
53. Rhodesian Ridgebacks
54. Border Collies
55. Airedale Terriers
56. Alaskan Malamutes
57. Great Pyrenees
58. Bull Terriers
59. Italian Greyhounds
60. Brussels Griffons
61. Soft Coated Wheaten Terriers
62. Whippets
63. Chow Chows
64. Australian Cattle Dogs
65. Portuguese Water Dogs
66. Setters (Irish)
67. Shiba Inu
68. American Staffordshire Terriers
69. Spaniels (English Cocker)
70. Pointers (German Wirehaired)
71. Japanese Chin
72. Old English Sheepdogs
73. Samoyeds
74. Silky Terriers
75. Parson Russell Terriers/Jack Russell Terriers
76. Beaucerons
77. Dalmatians
78. Cardigan Welsh Corgis
79. Belgian Malinois
80. Irish Wolfhounds
81. Border Terriers
82. Fox Terriers (Wire)
83. Giant Schnauzers
84. Bouviersdes Flandres
85. Staffordshire Bull Terriers
86. Schipperkes
87. Swedish Vallhunds
88. Toy Fox Terriers
89. Basenjis
90. Greater Swiss Mountain Dogs
91. Setters (Gordon)
92. Tibetan Terriers
93. Setters (English)
94. Afghan Hounds
95. Norwich Terriers
96. Norwegian Elkhounds
97. Welsh Terriers
98. Borzois
99. Keeshonden
100. Retrievers (Flat-Coated)
101. FoxTerriers (Smooth)
102. Standard Schnauzers
103. Belgian Tervuren
104. Tibetan Spaniels
105. Wirehaired Pointing Griffons
106. Pointers
107. Bearded Collies
108. Australian Terriers
109. American Eskimo Dogs
110. Retrievers (Nova Scotia Duck Tolling)
111. Anatolian Shepherd Dogs
112. Norfolk Terriers
113. Manchester Terriers
114. Kerry Blue Terriers
115. Neapolitan Mastiffs
116. Plotts

117. Spinoni Italiani
118. Salukis
119. Belgian Sheepdogs
120. Petits Bassets Griffons Vendeens
121. English Toy Spaniels
122. Spaniels (Clumber)
123. Briards
124. Spaniels (Welsh Springer)
125. Affenpinschers
126. Irish Terriers
127. Miniature Bull Terriers
128. Tibetan Mastiffs
129. Bedlington Terriers
130. Lakeland Terriers
131. Black Russian Terriers
132. Spaniels (Field)
133. Greyhounds
134. Kuvaszok
135. German Pinschers
136. Black and Tan Coonhounds
137. Scottish Deerhounds
138. Spaniels (American Water)
139. Lowchen
140. Ibizan Hounds
141. Pulik
142. Polish Lowland Sheepdogs
143. Retrievers (Curly-Coated)
144. Komondorok
145. Pharaoh Hounds
146. Sealyham Terriers
147. Spaniels (Irish Water)
148. Dandie Dinmont Terriers
149. Glen of Imaal Terriers
150. Harriers
151. Finnish Spitz
152. Skye Terriers
153. Canaan Dogs
154. Spaniels (Sussex)
155. Foxhounds (American)
156. Otterhounds
157. Foxhounds (English)

As I mentioned briefly in the Introduction, there are a number of dog breeds not recognized or currently registered by the AKC. Some of these are shown in the Miscellaneous Classes at AKC shows as their parent clubs prepare the breed for full recognition. The current AKC Miscellaneous Class Breeds are:

Bluetick Coonhound
Boykin Spaniel
Cane Corso
Cesky Terrier
Icelandic Sheepdog
Irish Red and White Setter

Leonberger
Norwegian Buhund
Norwegian Lundehund
Pyrenean Shepherd
Redbone Coonhound

The AKC also created a holding place for rare breeds in what is called its Foundation Stock Service (FSS), an optional record-keeping service for breeds not currently registered with the AKC. The current FSS breeds are:

American English Coonhound	Jindo
Appenzeller Sennenhunde	Kai Ken
Argentine Dogo	Karelian Bear Dog
Azawakh	Kishu Ken
Barbet	Kooikerhondje
Belgian Laekenois	Lagotto Romagnolo
Bergamasco	Lancashire Heeler
Berger Picard	Leonberger
Bluetick Coonhound	Mudi
Boerboel	Norrbottenspets
Bolognese	Norwegian Buhund
Boykin Spaniel	Norwegian Lundehund
Bracco Italiano	Perro de Presa Canario
Cane Corso	Peruvian Inca Orchid
Catahoula Leopard Dog	Portuguese Podengo
Caucasian Ovcharka	Portuguese Pointer
Central Asian Shepherd Dog	Pumi
Cesky Terrier	Pyrenean Shepherd
Chinook	Rafeiro do Alentejo
Cirneco dell'Etna	Rat Terrier
Coton de Tulear	Redbone Coonhound
Czechoslovakian Vlcak	Russell Terrier
Entlebucher Mountain Dog	Schapendoes
Estrela Mountain Dog	Sloughi
Eurasier	Small Munsterlander Pointer
Finnish Lapphund	Spanish Water Dog
German Spitz	Stabyhoun
Grand Basset Griffon Vendéen	Swedish Lapphund
Icelandic Sheepdog	Thai Ridgeback
Irish Red and White Setter	Tosa

Treeing Tennessee Brindle

Treeing Walker Coonhound

Wirehaired Vizsla

Xoloitzcuintli

Obviously there are many, many breeds from which to choose, and before you get overwhelmed, remember that for your business to succeed you need to make business decisions relative to your selection. While I do recommend that you choose a breed you love, if possible you should choose a more popular breed. You should consider the kind of clients you want and what they like. Before I would get involved in a rare breed program, I would research it carefully. Although it may be an exciting and personally rewarding hobby, it may not be a practical one because of the low demand. There could be severe restrictions on your breeding options—and a smaller gene pool from which to draw healthy breeding stock. Marketing expenses would be high to promote your kennel name and establish a superior reputation. These are all considerations for anyone who desires to excel as a dog breeder. If you did run into genetic issues in a rare breed, there would be little recourse to address them. Where would you find suitable gene pool expansion options? The cons could outweigh the pros.

A Breeder Secret

Dog Breed Registries: Think Global

While the American Kennel Club is the largest and best-known registry in the United States, there are others in the U.S., and there are many around the world. They include the United Kennel Club (UKC) at www.ukcdogs.com; the Continental Kennel Club at www.continentalkennel-club.com; the Kennel Club in the U.K. at www.the-kennel-club.uk; the Federation Cynologique International (FCI) at www.fci.be; and more. You can visit their websites to research breeds that they register.

You do not need to limit your business to the United States. European, Scandinavian, Asian, and South American dog lovers can also be a source of excellent homes for your puppies and for potential show homes as well. If you decide to pursue an international reputation as a breeder and make networking connections with breeders around the world, you need to become familiar with international shipping, customs, health certifications, and quarantine regulations. Via the internet you have access to the world.

Look at the Dogs

The only way to really get to know a dog or a breed is to see it and spend time with it. The best way to evaluate a breed that you are seriously considering is to visit existing kennels and spend time with the dogs and their breeders. Where do you find them? To start with, go to dog shows. Plan on spending several weekends going to shows simply to observe the activities of the people involved in the breed you've chosen. Watch the dogs, watch the people. Watch how the general public reacts to the breed. Talk to the exhibitors and breeders.

Show catalogs list the owners of the dogs entered in the show in the back of the catalog, along with their addresses (no telephone numbers are provided). Collect show catalogs and hunt test catalogs. They are a good resource, and they list both of the dog's parents. If you like what you see, you may want to use that dog's or that bitch's sire for stud service some day. You might want to contact the owner and ask them for information on the breeder of their dog.

A Breeder Secret

Don't Be Conned by Puppies
Remember that all puppies are compelling, so don't grab the first one you see. Take your time—do your homework, research, and compile your facts. In business you need to make business decisions. If you are a sucker for puppies, consult with a hard-nosed friend whom you have instructed to rein in your enthusiasm if you start to "cave."

Obtaining Foundation Breeding Stock

In the books I have read, no one spells out the basics of how to obtain your foundation breeding stock. The truth is that reputable show breeders or field trial breeders are not anxious to sell to some backyard breeder wanna-be—which they may very well think you are. Many of them will only sell pet-quality puppies under spay/neuter contracts. Anything better is either kept in their kennels or traded or sold to their fellow breeder friends and family. I would consider it rare to find quality foundation stock from a breeder who is not concerned about maintaining some breeding rights.

In order to obtain exactly what you want from the breeder whose line you have chosen, you will need to both demonstrate to that breeder that you are not a potential backyard breeder and you should expect to pay a premium to get the quality you require. However, just because you are asked to pay a premium for a dog with breeding rights doesn't mean you're working with an especially reputable breeder, either. Higher prices on female puppies than on male puppies are instituted when novice or backyard breeders sell puppies without breeding restrictions. They may also be associated with AKC Limited Registrations, which were intended to signify a dog was not for breeding to protect the dogs from puppy millers and/or to make sure that pet-quality puppies were not bred. Now it has deteriorated into another source of money for some breeders who are using it not to screen buyers, but to make more money off of puppies that will be bred by anyone. This translates into allowing buyers to breed any puppy as long as they are willing to pay the premium.

The AKC technically disallows selling puppies at two different prices—one "with papers" and the other "without papers." You may sell your puppies at whatever price you decide, but you may not increase the price when AKC registration is included on a puppy from a registered litter. This, in effect, is a sale of AKC registration papers. If AKC acquires proof that a seller is selling AKC registration papers in this manner, they will suspend the breeder's AKC privileges, and all registrations from that breeder may be voided.

Breeders can be very selective about who can and cannot breed their pups by marking the registration application as "not for breeding." This is good for your breeding line once you are established. It is bad for a beginner who wants superior breeding stock. You will need to learn how to talk to breeders in an honest and open way that will convince them you are dedicated to the breed quality, and not just getting ready to churn out as many mediocre puppies as possible. Puppy quality is *paramount* in building your professional breeder reputation. Cubic zirconium may look like a diamond to the untrained eye, but jewelers immediately identify it as a cheap knock-off.

A Breeder Secret

File Your Information

From the beginning of your search, catalog and file the information you collect for easy access. You will be continually building your database. Talk to as many breeders as you can. Ask lots of questions. Their feedback will help you to arrive at the right breed selection to fit your plan, geographic location, facility, and lifestyle.

Become Knowledgeable

In order to approach breeders and exhibitors and ask intelligent questions, the first thing you need is knowledge. In order to gain it, I suggest you do the following:

- Purchase the best books you can find on the breed you want to raise.
- Memorize the breed standard.
- Find a breed-specific publication such as the newsletter or quarterly for the breed, and subscribe.
- Check out the websites of the national breed club and the local breed club.
- Memorize the breed standard!
- Start attending AKC dog shows and breed club meetings in your area.
- Memorize the breed standard!!

Here are a number of other ways you can gain the expertise you will need.

Join the local breed club. If there is no breed club for the breed you have chosen in your area, join the closest one to you. I once belonged to the Pekingese Club of Arizona when I lived in Colorado, because at the time I was attempting to purchase a Pekingese puppy dog to show and eventually breed. Something came up to make this plan out of the question, but while I was a member I received their newsletter and information on litters being produced. It would have been relatively simple to purchase a quality female from one of the members. All I had to do was make a few trips to Arizona and help out with a few club events, get to know some of the members, and be honest about my plans to show and breed.

One of the perks of being involved in a breed club is your scope of options. Depending on the breed, there are all sorts of activities in which you can compete besides the conformation ring. These include hunt tests, agility, Rally, tracking, herding trials, lure coursing, earth-dog tests, multiple levels of obedience competitions, Canine Good Citizen, therapy dog groups, fly-ball, Frisbee matches, search and rescue training, pulling, water work, sled dog competitions, and even freestyle dancing! There are other activities as well, but these are the popular ones. Most of them are excellent family activities, as well as ways to meet new and interesting friends, and have a lot of fun. Being involved in dog activities has enriched and brightened my life in ways that I never imagined.

> ## A Breeder Secret
>
> ### Dog World Demographics
>
> For single women thinking they might meet a man in this sport, I can tell you that dog shows are not a target-rich dating market for single men. I would estimate that at a typical dog show you'll find that 20% of the exhibitors are married couples, 50% are women (married or single), 25% are gay men, and 5% are single guys. At events like agility, obedience trials, lure coursing, and other AKC sporting events, the percentage of single straight guys and gals is much higher. At hunt tests there are a high percentage of men. Probably half of those guys are married and involve their families in these activities, and half of them are single men. These are generally nice guys who are capable of taking good care of their dogs and have the patience to do meticulous dog training over a sustained period of time. You will also find professionals in both sexes involved in all the dog-related activities.

Attend AKC-sanctioned B-Matches on weekends during the spring and summer, where dog clubs award B-Match ribbons and breeders bring out their best pups for conformation training. The judges are usually veteran breed club members. At B-Matches, unlike at regular dog shows, the judges will answer questions and give tips on showing. They may also go over dogs and even tell you how they are evaluating the dog if you ask them to.

Almost no dog is perfect, so knowing a dog's imperfections is important not only for learning to de-emphasize them in the show ring, but also for future breeding decisions. B-Matches are put on by local all-breed clubs, or by specific breed clubs. They are great opportunities to meet breeders, learn about the AKC system, and absorb lots of good information.

Invest in a good digital camera, and start taking pictures of dogs you like. Be sure to always ask permission to photograph a dog. If you really want to open a door on a particularly nice dog, offer to make a copy of the photos onto a CD and mail it to the owner. If you have a digital video camera, that is even better. You will be able to study movement and attitude in the dogs you capture on film.

Represent your intentions honestly. If you are honest and do not make up stories trying to misrepresent your intentions, people will understand that you have integrity and that you are not trying to hide anything. Make no mistake about it—reputable breeders talk to each other, warn each other about unscrupulous buyers, and keep each other informed about any new faces showing up at dog events. One time, I received telephone calls from club members to let me know that Mr. So-and-So with a questionable reputation was trying to purchase female Labrador puppies out of champion sires from all the top breeders in the area. He had put down about three deposits before the story had spread to everyone. Needless to say he was not allowed to purchase any quality puppies from any of the reputable breeders in a four-state area. His deposits were returned to him and he was told that no breeding-quality puppies were available. It is prudent to be honest and to avoid fabricating stories about yourself or your intentions.

Search for a mentor. Be humble. Even if you have a Ph.D. in astrophysics, you still don't know much about breeding dogs. Don't try to impress people with your general credentials, education, or anything else. These people are only interested in your dog-related expertise. You need to connect with someone who will be willing to give you inside information about your particular breed choice.

Dress well—even in casual clothing—and *act professional*. Guys, get a haircut, shave, trim your nails, and polish your shoes or clean your tennis shoes. Gals, leave the dangling earrings and the gaudy bracelets at home, and wear something that doesn't flaunt your great legs or superior cleavage. Why generate envy in the women or invite sexual advances from the men at a time when you are attempting to promote professional connections and create new friendships?

At the Dog Show

Timing. The best time to talk to exhibitors is after they come out of the show ring. Look at the show catalog and find out what time their breed is scheduled to show. If they have won their class, congratulations are in order. If they are grooming and there is still an hour or two before their breed is showing, it may also be a good time to make an introduction and to wish them luck. No one will want to speak to you just before they have to show their dog. Talk to those exhibitors who have the nicest dogs in the ring. Don't necessarily cultivate relationships with the exhibitors or breeders of only those dogs that won a ribbon. Judging opinions are not always consistent with the breed standard.

Watch a dog's gait and stacking ability. You should be able to tell if a dog is moving easily, and if it has a balanced look to it. Unless you are considering an extreme breed like a Bulldog, Pekingese, or Pug, you need to watch the dogs gaiting around the show ring. Think of a beautiful horse and how effortlessly it moves—almost floating on air. Movement is everything about structure, and dog shows are not beauty contests in the traditional sense. A dog that moves easily and freely is going to be a good candidate for breeding. Prancing and high stepping is not a desirable trait in most breeds. Rolls of body fat on the dog's back, sliding from side to side as the dog moves, are the sign of a breeder who is not keeping their dogs in condition.

Think about your automobile when the wheel alignment is correct. The tires wear evenly, and the handling is superior. A puppy that is poorly put together spends his entire life compensating for poor structure. His behind is coming up on his front, his legs bow out or inward, his feet knuckle over, and he is down on his pasterns. His joints wear out prematurely, and this puppy cannot work more than a few hours in the field or in a competitive sport like obedience without tiring. If the front feet are extending beyond a dog's nose as it moves forward, that is a good indication of correct front assembly.

When the dog is standing in its kinetic posture (its natural stance as opposed to being stacked by the handler), do the front feet turn in? If they do, that is a sign of a faulty front shoulder—a "loaded shoulder." Watch the dog from the front as it comes toward you. Do you see the rear feet throwing outward and away from the dog's body? This is a sign of poor rear structure. Chances are that the owner/breeder will be breeding the dogs that you see in the ring. What you are looking for is a way to obtain one of their best puppies as part of your foundation stock while at the same time establishing yourself within the breed club and the breeding community as a serious person.

"Stacking" refers to the handler arranging the feet and the posture of a show dog in the ring. Hand stacking is completely orchestrated by the handler vs. a kinetic stack that is the natural stance of the dog when it is standing. Although "stacking" is expected and requested by most judges—a natural kinetic stance is a better evaluation tool. When a judge asks the exhibitors to "free-bait" their dogs (show them a toy or a treat as you stand in front of the judge), and then he asks them to go around with their dogs on a loose lead—that judge is analyzing structure and movement instead of "fluff" and "presentation." The dogs that such a judge puts up for Winners are probably going to be the best candidates in that ring for breeding potential. Breeders looking for outside stud dogs or to purchase a brood bitch to add to their kennel will be selecting those candidates, based on structure and movement when health and temperament criteria are confirmed. This is another well-kept secret among successful breeders: "fluff" is nice to look at, but it is the structural foundation of your breeding stock that will make you stand out as a breeder. The "fluff factor" may be a factor in some breeds, but all breeds need to have appropriate soundness and substance.

Strike up conversations with the spectators outside the show ring. Most of them are probably breeders, exhibitors, family members of exhibitors, or all three. If you are not already an outgoing person, learn to be friendly. Be curious, and you will naturally be a nice person to talk to. In this business, to be successful, you cannot be an introvert. Learning to explore the fabulous diversity of your fellow dog breeders and exhibitors enables you to cultivate the virtual rainbow of the Dog World. Dog enthusiasts are typically friendly, optimistic, and interesting people. They are easy to engage in conversation—just like their dogs. Buyers like to purchase their puppies from interesting, friendly, and knowledgeable breeders.

A Breeder Secret

Get Prerequisites Out of the Way

Becoming familiar with your breed, existing breeders, and breeding lines within it, going to club events, to dog shows, and remembering everyone's names—all will help you get ready to implement your breeding program. Prepare your facility, your equipment, and formulate a marketing and financial plan for you kennel operations. Visit as many breeding kennels as you can. Within four to six months, you should be in a position to purchase a minimum of two high-quality puppy bitches with breeding rights. You should have had enough time to read all the available books on your chosen breed. At this stage in your project you should be feeling more confident and anxious to implement your plan.

Do not discuss money up front. The dog breeding community is still trying to maintain the genteel façade created by Queen Victoria in England. Although the aristocracy obviously bred dogs for profit, and sold their superior puppies all over the world for large sums of money—it is still not polite to discuss it. In Europe, it is even less acceptable than it is here. No one will actually say that they are selling puppies for profit. For some reason there is some huge stigma attached to selling a puppy, and dog breeders feel uncomfortable admitting that they are definitely "in the black." Realize that top breeders are getting paid what they deserve for all the extremely hard work and care that they put into breeding at this level. But you need to go quietly to the bank and deposit your money without fanfare or boasting. No one but you and the IRS need to know your financial situation.

Choosing Healthy Stock

This is, of course, essential, and the best sources for detailed health information on the breed or breeds in which you are interested are experienced breeders of the particular breed(s). They're the ones who are dealing with their dogs' health issues on a daily basis. This is another reason why I strongly encourage newcomers to join both all-breed clubs and breed-specific clubs. Even veterinarians are not completely familiar with all of the health and breeding issues of each breed.

The following worksheet should help you identify health issues and thus assist in narrowing your search for your foundation breeding stock. Take it with you to dog shows and/or various dog events like hunt tests, obedience trials, etc. Make notations as you view the breeds under your consideration.

Breed Evaluation Worksheet

Breed	Breeder's Contact Information	Health Screening	Upcoming litters and availability

Never purchase a puppy without getting a copy (not just the number) of the sire's DNA profile. This is the only way you can ascertain positively who the sire actually is. If you have any suspicions that the puppy is not out of the sire listed on his registration slip, you may request a DNA check from the AKC. They will send you a swab kit for the puppy, which you will then mail back to them. They will then compare the DNA from the puppy to that of the sire and notify you if it is a match or not. There is a fee for this service.

DNA profiles also protect you as a breeder. I once had an out-of-state buyer purchase a black male Labrador puppy from me. I always had my puppies vet-checked, and I personally checked them thoroughly before they left my kennels. About two days after they picked up their puppy, they called to say that he had a severe overbite and they wanted to return him in exchange for a different puppy. My warranty contract called for them to have a health check performed within 48 hours of picking up the puppy. They said that their veterinarian had brought the overbite to their attention. I knew that this was completely impossible, because none of my puppies had overbites. An overbite is something that is very obvious and cannot be missed.

I knew right away that these buyers were pulling a switch on me. I sweetly replied that, of course, if the puppy had an overbite I would certainly exchange it for a puppy without one—but I must require that they have their veterinarian swab the puppy for a DNA check and certify in writing to me and to the AKC that it was taken from the puppy with the overbite. I told them I was going to order a DNA kit from the AKC, and I asked them to give me their veterinarian's name, address, and telephone number so that I could contact him directly to make arrangements for the DNA Test kit to be sent to him.

They were very quiet on the telephone, and then said that they had to discuss this with their veterinarian and would get back to me. That was the last I heard from them. What they were trying to do was exchange a bad puppy they had either bred themselves, or a pup they got elsewhere, for one of my puppies. This way they would have the pup they purchased from me, and another one from me to replace the defective puppy they got from someone else or had bred for themselves. When you are talking high-priced puppies, getting one for free is lucrative to a crook.

A Breeder Secret

DNA Testing to Safeguard Your Reputation
DNA testing is relatively inexpensive and serves as a useful sales tool for ethical breeders. Although many breeders do not DNA profile their bitches, it might be a good idea. This is especially relevant if you ship your puppies. This practice would give you an advantage over breeders who only profile their males. If the buyer isn't going to visit your kennel, they might like to know that there is a way for them to confirm the identity of the mother. It would demonstrate that you have nothing to fear, and that your pedigrees are 100% reliable.

Back to the Breed Standard

Purchase breeding stock that conforms closely to the breed standard. You may not care for that look, but discerning buyers do. If you choose a particular breed, it must be one that appeals to you in its correct AKC breed standard form. The AKC breed standard (which you should have memorized for the breed of your choosing) is the bible for breeders.

For example, if you like Deer Chihuahuas (the taller, rangier ones), that is fine, you can have one for a personal pet. But, if you are going to breed Chihuahuas and sell them, you had better produce high quality puppies that conform to the standard and could successfully compete in the show ring. If you breed Deer Chihuahuas, it may also be a turn off for those buyers who want the real thing, even if you have both types. The same rule applies to tall, lanky, field type Labrador Retrievers or skimpy-coated, field type Golden Retrievers or English Setters. You must be honest with your buyers about what type of puppy you are selling, especially if you are shipping the puppy and the buyer isn't going to visit your kennels.

There are certain breeds where a size differential exists between the AKC breed standard height and weight range, and the popular pet size. Also, some working breeds may have a bigger or taller minimum breed standard than most pet buyers would be looking for, or they have a greater range of acceptable height or weight within the standard. In these scenarios you have to compromise somewhat, and provide the dog that is most desirable in general.

A Breeder Secret

Evaluating What You Have

For those readers who are already dog breeders and are reading this book to improve their kennel operation or breeding business, you have some hard decisions ahead of you if you are serious about upgrading your breeding stock. You will have to find the resolve to look long and hard at the existing dogs in your breeding program. This is the time for brutal honesty and harsh self-criticism. Each and every dog in your kennel will have to be re-evaluated, and a decision made as to the quality and the genetic contribution the dog or bitch can make to your success. This is not a time to swallow the platitudes of friends and relatives who blindly support you. As far as they know, all of your dogs are show quality, gorgeous potential champions. If you study the structure and movement of each dog against the breed standard, you will avoid kennel blindness, which is the inability to look objectively at your dogs, your facility, and your kennel management practices. Be strong and good luck!

I bred both types of Labradors because hunters demanded the bigger dogs, but pet buyers wanted the blocky/show type. However, I made it clear to my buyers that they are two distinctly different varieties, bred for different purposes. There has been a dialog going on within this breed about splitting it, but breeders who show them are generally opposed to the split. They say that a Labrador Retriever should be able to do it all. The fact is that there have not been any dual champions (FC/CH) in Labrador Retrievers since the 1960's. As the show Labs became shorter and stockier to reflect the British breed standard, the American Field Trial Labs were bred much taller and more elongated and muscular to accommodate the true hunting environment of North America, where the cover is taller and thicker and requires a much stronger, taller, and more robust dog. Because of this, a conformation Labrador cannot do it all, no matter how desirable that might be.

Good breeding decisions are about providing the dog that most owners will be attracted to within the broad interpretation of the breed standard. Of course, if you are showing your dogs in conformation competition, you must go by the strictest minutia of the breed standard. I would always start with the breed standard, and think carefully about any departures from that. Kennel owners, who are breeding to the standard, may justifiably resent you if you intentionally stray far from it. You do not want to alienate other professional breeders. These are the people you want to network with in the future, and share quality stud dogs and superior breeding lines. The dog owners you are pursuing are more likely to appreciate the classic examples of their favorite breed.

Remember, if you breed in such a way as to jeopardize the breed's integrity and consistency, you will become *persona non grata* in the dog world. You must have a well-thought-out plan and you have to be honest. Above all, you will have to pay your dues.

You will also need to learn what characteristics are the hardest and the easiest to breed into or out of a breeding line. For example, a good frontal skeletal assembly is one of the most difficult genetic characteristics to set in a breeding line. You can fix poor tail set, or dippy top lines, but poor skeletal structure in the front would take years of breeding to eradicate from a line—so don't even go there!

Each breed has certain traits that you should avoid at all costs. This is information you learn from the actual hands-on breeders, and from reading everything you can lay your hands on regarding your breed. Breeders will usually be more than happy to tell you—if you just ask politely.

Review the Papers Before the Sale

When you do find a breeder who is willing to sell you breeding stock, make sure that the breeder doesn't put their name on the registration papers as co-owner. Some breeders do that without telling you. When you go to register the puppy it is a shocker to see their name on the back of the registration application. This causes a huge problem because they have your money and you have a dog that you don't really own! Don't listen to excuses about this being standard procedure, or the "way these things are done." Truthfully, that is a despicable practice, and if they try to do that—just run the other way, because they completely lack integrity and honesty.

Co-ownerships should always be done by written contract and prior agreement. The entry on the registration application is merely a confirmation of the co-ownership written contract. This would be like buying a car, paying the money, but never getting the pink slip or registration in your name. There are laws against that. Now that you have been warned about this, you won't have to deal with it. It is better to bring up the subject before you hand over your payment. Before you pay for the puppy, sit down with the breeder and go over all of the paperwork carefully. Take the time to read the contract, bill of sale, warranty, the pedigrees, and health certifications of the parents. Check the back of each page to make sure there are no addendums or additions. If this breeder is ethical and honest, they will encourage you to do this, answer all of your questions in detail, and even share good information about the breeding lines as you go over the pedigrees together.

When I sell a puppy bitch to a breeder, I ask them to please contact me when they are ready to breed—so that I can assist them in finding an appropriate stud dog. In my contract, I always retain breeding rights on any male puppy I ever sell. The wording specifies that any male puppy that is not neutered can be used for stud service on any bitch that I own. Since I am selling hunting dogs, and most of them are never neutered, this was an excellent resource for me. I also explain to them that if I do elect to use their male dog for stud service—it would be to their advantage. The dog would have experienced a professionally "managed" first encounter to condition him for stud service, and he would then be a "proven" stud dog. If they want to use him for stud service in the future, I ask them to call me, so that I can help them make good choices.

About Foundation Bitches

As a beginner, the most economical start is to purchase a puppy bitch. If you can afford it, get two from two different breeding lines. That way you will not have all your eggs in one basket (no pun intended). If one of them turns out to be infertile, or doesn't produce the quality of puppies you want, at least you have the second one to fall back on. Two years of waiting to breed them will not be a total loss. During those two years you may elect to add more puppy bitches, or even a puppy dog to your program. As you become active in your local breed club, you may find someone who has a brood bitch available for sale or lease. If she is good quality and they just want to get one or two puppies from her for their showing program, you might make a mutually beneficial arrangement with them. Make sure that on a lease agreement the beginning lease date is before the bitch is bred—this will ensure that the resulting litter is yours and doesn't belong to the bitch's owner.

If you purchase more than two bitches, don't make the mistake of them all being the same age. If this were to happen, eventually you would end up with a kennel filled with retired bitches. It is a miserable experience to have your wonderful dogs pass away one after the other within the same year, or having to find homes for all of them at the same time when you retire them. Spread bitch purchases over a few years. Plan to keep a daughter from a bitch you are retiring to carry on your line. Once you have reached your planned limit of bitches, make a hard and fast rule—if you want to add a bitch to your breeding stock, you have to find a good home for one of your existing bitches. If you don't take this advice you will end up with a kennel full of unproductive girls who will devour your resources and keep you awake at night worrying about how you are going to keep your business going.

Don't breed your bitch for more than six years. The current recommendation by fertility specialists is to breed twice back-to-back and then skip a season. This is because of hormonal fluctuations that contribute to the incidence of pyometra (infection of the uterus). Of course the frequency has to be correct for each individual bitch. Some have small litters and there is no reason to fear that back-to-back breeding could endanger their health. Other bitches that have extremely large litters or difficulties whelping might require a longer down time between litters.

On average, you can expect that your bitches will be bred for four or five years at the most. Figure two years to mature and be certified, three litters every two years, or roughly six litters. Consider that the average bitch will whelp five puppies per litter (some breeds routinely have seven or eight), and multiply the current prices for quality puppies by the average of 30 puppies over her productive years to forecast your gross return. I always go with the lower estimate to compensate for C-sections, lost puppies, or missed heat cycles.

If you breed your girl after age five or six, it will be harder on her physically. She deserves to be retired, and practically speaking, it will be easier to find a great home for a five- or six-year-old spayed bitch than for a seven- or eight-year-old bitch. As a younger dog, it will also be easier for her to bond with her new owner. A mature, fully obedience-trained adult dog is the perfect companion for a senior citizen, a physically challenged individual, or for hospital therapy work.

If you purchase puppy bitches, you have 18 months to 2 years (depending on the breed) before you can complete their pre-breeding screening tests and be ready to breed them. Most breeds should not be bred too early because they are still maturing mentally and wouldn't make good mothers. The average bitch will cycle once every six months, and cycling begins between eight to ten months of age (some toy breeds are even later). The formula for the range of when a bitch can be expected to whelp her first puppies would be something like this:

[(8 months + 6 months + 6 months = 20 months) + 2 months gestation] = 22 months at whelping date

or

[(10 months + 6 months + 6 months = 22 months) + 2 months gestation] = 24 months at whelping date

or

[(8 months + 6 months + 6 months + 6 months = 26 months) + 2 months gestation = 28 months at whelping date

The accepted practice is to wait to breed until all health clearances come through. The OFA clearances on hips and elbows are the longest ones you will have to wait for. OFA does not issue a final report until 24 months of age. However, many excellent breeders do preliminary OFA radiographs at one year of age. If the X-rays look good, they send them to OFA for a preliminary opinion. If they come back rated Excellent or Good, they feel free to breed the bitch anytime after 18 months of age. There is a bit of a balancing game to be played here. Every breeder you discuss this with will have a different opinion.

A Breeder Secret

In Case of an Accidental Breeding

If an accidental breeding does occur there are several options available to the breeder. If the breeding is one that you could handle despite not having planned it—then proceed to care for the bitch appropriately and care for the resulting puppies. If the bitch is very young—extra nutritional support is mandatory and intensive monitoring for anemia and other complications is warranted. If, however, the breeding is simply not acceptable and there is no way that you wish it to proceed—an ECP injection can be administered. That is Estradiol cypionate. The risk of complications from this drug should be weighed against the risk of the pregnancy proceeding. You have approximately two weeks from copulation to make this decision—although I believe that it is better to proceed quickly once your decision is made. After the eggs implant in the walls of the uterine horns this option is no longer viable. The risks are Pyometra (uterine infection), bone marrow suppression, lethargy due to anemia, and even septicemia. The risks should be discussed with your veterinarian.

Be aware that breed clubs also adhere to a strict code of ethics when it comes to breeding and selling dogs. Some of their rules have not been updated to reflect current medical recommendations, and if you sign the club documents you will be morally required to adhere to their rules. As you build your credibility within the club, you may be able to open a dialog regarding rules that you believe are obsolete. Invite fertility specialists and knowledgeable veterinarians to speak to your breed club. Have them provide supporting data to convince club members that revisions to their rules may be warranted. This will help them realize there are circumstances when certain rules might be detrimental to the health of the dogs, and that accommodations for requesting exemptions when they are appropriately supported by scientific documentation are needed.

A Breeder Secret

Negotiating with Fellow Club Members
I have found that if you take an educational approach instead of an argumentative one the outcome is usually better. Even if you are not successful in having the rules amended, you will not have created animosity within the club membership. Be patient and try again later. It is very important to preserve and support cohesiveness and respect within your breed club. Become the peacemaker and the mediator instead of the person who is stirring up trouble or spreading negativity among the members. When you promote peace and tolerance, your life will gain serenity and a clear sense of purpose. Other club members will recognize your sincerity and will most likely listen to your proposals with an open mind.

When I think back on my experiences, I am reminded of Candlewood Kennels in Wisconsin—a small, dignified, and superior breeding kennel. Some of the top Field Trial Champion lines are out of the Candlewood dogs. Mary Howley has produced 10 National Field Champions since 1990. (There is only one NFC each year.) I wanted to infuse my hunting dog line with the natural hunting traits of the Candlewood dogs, who are born and bred to work in the field. They were not artificially created with electric collars and cattle prods or whips and toe pinchers.

To do so, I purchased a bitch, Camille, over the telephone from an ad in *Field Trial News*. This is a reputable publication that Field Trial enthusiasts read from cover to cover. While there are risks buying a dog sight unseen, the breeding lines and the breeders who advertise in this periodical are reputable. If you aren't sure, it only takes a few phone calls to ascertain a breeder's credentials. In this case, I bought her based strictly on her pedigree. She was a granddaughter of "Lottie" (NFC Candlewoods Tanks A Lot) out of NFC Super Tanker. Lottie was a three-time National Field Champion (NFC)—the most famous Field Trial bitch in North America, and the only bitch to ever achieve that distinction. Mike Lardy trained Lottie. He is one of the top gun dog trainers in the world. Both of Camille's parents were also FC's (Field Trial Champions).

I believed that this was a great opportunity for me to avail myself of that illustrious breeding line. Camille came from a rancher/breeder located in Kansas who was a field trial enthusiast. The breeder was not concerned about breeding rights. He had done the breeding to get a field trial candidate male for himself, and he sold the rest of the litter (nine pups) on the same day the *Field Trial News* was delivered.

Fortunately for me I called in time to get the last available female from the litter. The lesson here is to be decisive and expedient when you find something superior right under your nose. If you know what direction you are going with your breeding plans and are knowledgeable about which breeding lines can help you achieve your goals, you will not need to hesitate and procrastinate until it is too late to seize the opportunities that present themselves. Your bitch's line will set the quality and soundness of future generations of dogs carrying your kennel prefix. A good bitch line combined with a good line-bred stud dog can propel you speedily to the top of the breeder ranks.

Camille arrived, and I was extremely excited. When I opened the crate, I reached in and pulled out a skinny, lanky, black bitch puppy with a long rattail, long nose, and tiny little beady eyes. I said out loud, "Oh my Gosh, I have bought Olive Oil." (For those of you who are too young to relate to this, Olive Oil was Popeye's wife in the cartoon strip—tall, boney, with beady little black eyes close together, and long skinny legs.) The only way I could get Camille to stop crying was to play country western music on the truck radio, at which time she would immediately curl up and go to sleep.

Odd as she was, Camille turned out to be one of the best brood bitches I ever bred to my big, beautiful yellow dog, Custer (Flying With General Custer). All the pups looked just like Custer because he was line-bred on a top NFC line that went all the way back to NFC Super Chief, and he was gorgeous. All the pups had that Candle-wood intelligence and uncanny ability in the field to know exactly where the birds were and how to flush them. They were all black because Camille didn't carry the yellow gene. Most hunters prefer the black hunting Labs anyway, so this infusion into my breeding lines worked very well for me. But my gosh, Olive Oil? Who woulda thunk?

Line Breeding for the Foundation

It's important to understand the principals of line breeding. This is breeding back on the sire's line every three or four generations so that both sides of the pedigree go back (are "lined") to an exceptional sire—i.e., an NFC or a famous show champion. That means that the same exceptional sire appears on both the top and the bottom of the pedigree. Line-bred stud dogs are usually pre-potent, which means that their offspring resemble them regardless of the bitch they are bred to.

You will hear breeders refer to this as doubling up on positive recessive genes. The only way to do this successfully is to be knowledgeable about all aspects of that line—including any negative recessive genes that may be hiding there. When you hear some show breeders saying that it is ignorant to attribute more than half of the genetic make-up of the puppies to the sire and that the bitch line is just as important, that rings true if the sire is not a line-bred stud dog. Do the math on a theoretical breeding pair:

Stud dog's two parents (his sire is an X line, his dam is also an X line) = XX

Bitch's two parents (her sire is a Y line, and her dam is a Z line) = YZ

Sire = (XX) and Dam = (YZ).

Which breeding line contributes the most influence on the outcome? The X line, of course (two X's, one Y, and one Z). In this case we refer to the sire as line bred, and we refer to the dam as an outcross of two unrelated breeding lines. Obviously there is more X than any other genetic package in this combination.

If you used a bitch that was XX+YZ, you would have even more probable contribution from the X genetic package. This is probably why long-time breeders usually look at the line-bred stud dogs from outside their own lines to infuse their breeding lines with consistency and to improve problems they are encountering in their bitch lines.

How do you test this without becoming a genetic genius? Breed the dogs and find out if you get what you need. If you don't get what you want, do not repeat that breeding again, sell all the pups on spay/neuter contracts which state they will not be bred, and they will be spayed or neutered after one year of age and not before, at which time you will supply their registration papers. Keep looking for the right stud dog. The best sign of a successful breeding is the consistent quality of the litter. If you have one great puppy and a bunch of mediocre puppies or worse, you have failed.

In the case of Camille, when I bred her to my line-bred stud dog, I had to ascertain that there was absolutely nothing in my stud dog's line that was connected to her great grandsire on the top of her pedigree. I knew from being knowledgeable about Field Trial Champions that one of her ancestors—an exceptional field trial dog—may have carried the gene for cardiomyopathy (a heart condition) that was passed down through his daughters. Some breeders who had puppies out of this dog's breeding line and subsequently bred them back to that dog's bitch line had produced pups with cardiomyopathy. This is not a scientifically supported assumption, but as a breeder you will have to weigh the circumstantial evidence and draw conclusions that will help you avoid potential disasters. By being aware of the history of the line, and subsequently breeding her only to stud dogs unrelated to that ancestor, I produced healthy puppies without any incidence of cardiomyopathy—and I was careful to warn all the buyers of her pups to never breed them back to that line.

Remember that if the traits you are breeding for are absent in your line, the only way to get them is to go outside your kennels. Just make sure that what you bring in has what you need and is not dragging in some other trait that you don't want in your line. I didn't want Camille's rattail—the Otter tail of a Labrador Retriever is a hallmark of the breed. Fortunately for me, she didn't produce it with the stud dogs I used. One was my big yellow male, Custer, and the other boy was a short, stocky, extremely blocky chocolate male, Cruise, out of show lines, who could hunt. Cruise is one of the sweetest dogs I have ever owned. Camille did carry the chocolate gene, so she produced wonderful chocolate and black hunting pups with him. Consistency was an issue because this breeding pair was a complete outcross, and Cruise was not a line-bred stud dog.

Finding a Stud Dog

The process of finding and obtaining your foundation bitches is also a good time to be looking at available outside stud dogs. For your first breeding I would advise using a proven, established champion stud dog. If there is a breed specialty show scheduled any time soon, try to attend and take a close look at the Stud Dog class. There you have the major sires in the breed together with their offspring from two or three different bitches—a great opportunity to see the consistency and the quality of their offspring. I found that nice bitches, out of superior line-bred sires, often produce lovely sons. Look at the whole breeding line and not just at the individual stud dog.

If you start looking early, you will have the time to gather some good information, take photographs, and even see the get from the dogs you are considering as compatible with your bitches. Collect pedigrees. If you see a dog that you like, ask if he has any litters on the ground. If so, make an effort to go see them.

Chapter 5
YOUR KENNEL

When evaluating your facility, think about how you are going to use it. Consider where you will be breeding, raising, and ultimately selling your puppies. Setting up a kennel requires careful thought and planning so you can get it right. Whatever you do, you will have to live with it for a while, so take your time in the planning stages. I enjoyed the process of planning my kennels. It allowed me to create a healthy and attractive environment for my dogs.

Choosing a Kennel Name

Choosing the name of your dog breeding business is an important and creative process. It will be your kennel prefix—the name that precedes all of the registered names of all the puppies that come out of your kennel. The name of your kennel may become very well known in the dog world. It may grace the front pages of newspapers and dog-related publications. Your kennel prefix will appear on pedigrees, show catalogs, and on your website. If you sell puppies to other successful breeders, your prefix will appear in the pedigrees of all the dogs produced from that line. If your business is passed down to the next generation, this name will carry on into the future long after you have retired. The name could represent your legacy and carry your reputation as a professional dog breeder. Choosing your kennel name and establishing a great business is your chance to do what few people are fortunate enough to do—leave your mark after you are gone.

Linda Vaughn is a respected Labrador Retriever and Norfolk Terrier breeder and an AKC judge who owns Simerdown Kennels in Colorado. I once heard her tell a group of Labrador breeders how she came up with her kennel prefix, Simerdown. It sounds so "British" and sophisticated that I had assumed she found it in a book or got it from an estate she had visited in Europe. I was intrigued by her story. Here is how I remember it. Linda had accumulated five or six Labradors for her breeding program, and they were running around the room excited about something. Labradors, of course, can be gregarious. Her husband was trying to read or watch TV (not sure exactly which). After a few moments of being in the middle of this wild bunch, he exclaimed to Linda, "Can't you get these dogs to simmer down?" She immediately thought that "Simerdown" would be the perfect kennel name for Labradors.

My kennel was Black Forest Flying Labs. It wasn't an original name. I got my first Labrador from my nephew, David Fisher, of Flying Labs in Northern California. I loved the name, and asked him if I could incorporate it into my kennel name as Black Forest Flying Labs. I lived in Black Forest, Colorado, at the time. He said it was fine with him, so Black Forest Flying Labs was born. It turned out to be a good name, except for the confusion of some people who would call me to fly laboratory equipment or rush human transplant organs to various locations. Then I would have to explain to them that "Flying Labs" wasn't a reference to flying laboratories.

I had some other issues with my kennel name, too. Another Labrador breeder started a kennel in Black Forest a few years after mine and used a similar name. I felt that he didn't have nearly the quality of breeding stock that I had and that he was misrepresenting his dogs. Because I had not registered my kennel name with the AKC, there was nothing I could do about this. The other problem with my kennel name was that it was too long. On the AKC registration application there are only 36 letters. The prefix (in front of the dog's name) designates the breeder's kennel. The dog's name is next, and then the suffix (designates the owner's kennel) at the end of the name. If I had used Black Forest Flying Labs on the front of each name, there would be no room for anything else. So for registration purposes, I had to shorten the prefix to BF.

If I had to do it all over, I would have picked a different name. A shorter, classier, more modern name would have been a better choice. You have one shot at this, because registration names are difficult to change. If you don't stick with the same name for your kennel, your advertising dollars will be wasted. You cannot achieve name recognition if you keep changing your name.

Advice in Hindsight

Try to pick a kennel name that starts with a letter close to A so that on alphabetical lists yours will be near the top. The name should be easy to remember—not some combination of letters from your name and your spouse's or child's name that don't mean anything to anyone but you. Classy names are memorable names. Think, too, about how this name relates to your breed of dogs. Some people want to use their own name as the kennel name, like Pamela's Poodles or Mastiffs by Michael. That is understandable, but ego driven. Consider that if you decide to sell your kennel operation or your breeding lines in the future, you would be handing over your personal name to the care of a stranger. For all you know, they could resell the kennel to some sleazy person or even go bankrupt. Also, if you should ever want to add another dog breed or transition to another breed, you don't want to be stuck with your current breed name in the name of your kennels. Do it if you must, but only after having thought about it carefully.

I know some exceptional breeders who named their kennels after an exotic vacation spot. Just as in choosing dog names, pick something that uniquely appeals to you and to your sense of style. If you plan to register your kennel name with the AKC, check out availability and the AKC rules regarding kennel names.

Please don't name your kennel after the wind, the moon, or the stars. You see so many of these kinds of names in the catalogs: Windjammer, Windsock, Wind Whisperer, and Windsong; Moonshine, Moonbeam, and Moonlight; Starlight, Starbright, Starfire, Starstruck, Starstudded, Lone Star, Star Night, Red Star, Blue Star, Yellow Star, etc. In my opinion, these names are worn out and you should be more creative than that.

Try It On for Size

Print the kennel name on your computer in various fonts and font sizes. Consider what your logo would look like with the name. My logo was the silhouette of a black Lab puppy with wings. Doing this will give you added perspective on how it will look in print media. It's funny, but this is what young girls who have a crush on a boy will do—spend hours writing their name with his last name to see how it looks and feels. Remember the movie, *The Wedding Singer*? If she had married the jerk in the movie her name would have been Julia Goulia! Ouch! Be sure to say the name out loud, and have someone else say it out loud to you.

Personally I think cutesy, frou-frou names are not taken seriously. When a person bought a Labrador from me and wanted to name her Tinkerbelle, I gagged. I have a friend who named her cattery Blue Moon. My first thought when I saw this was to say to myself: "I would never use that name, not in a blue moon." But she loves this name and is comfortable with it. To be honest, I think it is a memorable name because of that connotation. It is akin to turning lemons into lemonade. Of course, her dog kennel is named after an insect—which doesn't seem that much more appealing to me, but everyone else seems to love it anyway. What do I know? Maybe kennel names just aren't my area of expertise. However, I am great at naming dogs and cats!

In summary, pick your kennel name carefully, try to imagine it on the front page of a newspaper, or listed in a "Who's Who" of American Dog Breeders. Does it look good? Will it be remembered? Imagine the name on a large sign in front of your facility. Would buyers love to see it on the pedigree of their puppy? Check to see if anyone else has the name or a URL (website address) that is similar.

Zoning Issues and Land Use Regulations

Zoning restrictions are something to investigate and understand so that you can be knowledgeable about them before you establish your kennel. You should also know how the laws in your area are (or aren't) enforced, and what the fines are if at some point you find you are not in compliance. Each state is different, and communities within states can vary widely. Consider where you are and what kind of neighbors you have when evaluating your area's restrictions. Investigate whether different rules apply to you as a legitimate and properly registered business versus being just a resident with dogs.

Before purchasing a property, make sure you know the zoning rules. Carefully review the plot map for the piece of property you are considering. It will show the exact boundaries. Inspect the records for any liens or other encumbrances on the property. These items are important, so don't delegate this research to anyone else. Also, ask around the area about any future development plans under consideration. You might also speak to zoning committee members for the board of supervisors for your county or city (if the property is located in an incorporated area). I almost purchased a property that seemed perfect until I discovered that a turkey farm in the area was expanding and had already purchased the adjoining land to the piece I was looking at. Needless to say, I took my money and ran the other way. If you are not from the area you are considering, visit the local newspaper offices. Ask about zoning disputes, developers, and pending litigation against the county, city, or against developers. Not only will you get some helpful information, but if you do move there, you already have your first local connection with the editor or with an investigative reporter.

What many breeders experience, especially in rural areas (where many breeders choose to live) that are experiencing growth, is that new zoning regulations are often adopted that do not reflect what is going on in the community and are difficult, if not impossible, to enforce. I once lived in an unincorporated part of El Paso County in Colorado. There were about 3,000 homes in this wooded area. None of the lots were less than two and one-half acres, and most of them were five to ten acres. Many households in the area had multiple dogs. Some residents had eight or ten dogs on their property. Many also had horses, and some had cows for roping. The zoning ordinances for this area were very explicit: four dogs was the maximum allowed on one property. At that time, I had 10 dogs in my kennel.

I assumed that if the County officials decided to enforce the zoning laws, they would have to enforce them across the board, and so I was willing to run that risk. Strict enforcement would have meant an all-out range war for this area. I knew that there was also a precedent established regarding zoning law enforcement in the county. A year before, a land developer from California had tried to get the zoning commissioners to enforce zoning laws against having cows near his land. He apparently had planned to build luxury estates on this land. Roping enthusiasts need to have cows to rope—at least in Colorado real cowboys want real cows! What is the point of having a barrel racing, roping horse, if you don't have a flesh-and-blood cow to rope? About 50 double-axle pick-up trucks, with horse trailers in tow, shut down the main access road to this area for a whole day and threatened to shoot any zoning enforcement people if they showed their faces. Needless to say, not one zoning enforcement officer dared show up (besides, most of them had their own cows). The developer wisely sold the acreage and left the county. The chance of anyone from the county trying to enforce these misguided zoning laws was slim. Keep in mind that money doesn't always win over community. I truly admired the spunk and American spirit of those Colorado Cowboys.

Fostering a good working relationship with zoning officers and other county officials (like health officials who may inspect your facility) will always work to your advantage. Instead of complaining and moaning about all the regulations and zoning ordinances that seem "designed to put ethical breeders out of business along with the rotten apples," take the time to study the rules and regulations and embrace those that can benefit your breeding operation. In most cases the regulations are based on common sense—like having clean, painted whelping boxes in good repair, accurate dog records, easily identifiable dogs (microchip or tattoo), health records on each dog showing current vaccinations, fresh water in each kennel run, a clean operation without debris or garbage, appropriate protection from the weather (shade and wind protection), and young puppies housed with their mothers in separate accommodations. Where I lived, the dogs were to be maintained in good health and weight; food was to be stored in closed containers with no evidence of vermin or mold contamination; the kennels were to be free of rodents (rodent droppings); and there had to be some system of waste management (collection and disposal or a functioning dedicated septic system installed away from wells, and not contaminating the ground water). In fact, the only item that I did not agree with was the regulation about the minimum selling age of puppies, which I was able to discuss with an officer to our mutual betterment. As a result of working with the officers and complying with the regulations, I received a rating of Excellent—which I used in my advertising and marketing.

A Breeder Secret

Kennel Location

Obviously there are areas where it is not appropriate to locate a breeding/kennel operation. If you know there are land use restrictions that would conflict with what you have planned, choose another location. However if you are already located in an area and then zoning laws change to your detriment—as in a case where the number of dogs permitted are subsequently reduced—you may be granted a variance that allows you to stay in business.

The old adage that you can't fight city hall is true, but you can make compliance more palatable if you are knowledgeable and ready to answer questions in a non-adversarial manner. Public officials do have flexibility, and they can elect to work with you instead of shutting you down. Most of the inspectors that I met were professional people with common sense, and were dedicated to safeguarding animals' well being. I respect them for what they do, and I am not in disagreement with their general charter. If you disagree with local regulations, you and other nearby professional breeders can and should band together with local dog clubs to address these extremes and to lobby legislators to restore balance and fairness to the process. Compare notes and communicate with each other, remember there is strength in numbers, and working together you can improve your chances that the county inspector who is coming around to certify your kennel will do so.

Sometimes local officials go to extremes that exceed their authority beyond the intent of the law, in a bureaucratic and narrow-minded manner. I am aware of cases where local officials have even solicited bribes in return for favorable rulings. If you believe an official is not operating within the dictates or spirit of the law, you and other breeders should all be concerned and proactive about putting them out of a job. Professional breeders should work together with dog clubs to address these extremes and to lobby legislators to restore balance and fairness to the process. Show up as a group at county board meetings. Smile and be non-threatening. Become a friend of the county, and become an involved citizen—while at the same time protecting your rights.

This is another good reason to be involved with the professional dog breeders' organizations. You can also join small business organizations such as the Chamber of Commerce in your area for the same purpose—to keep your local officials honest, and to have a collective voice. Those who have first-hand experience can give you excellent advice and support.

CC&Rs and HOAs

When you purchase property for a kennel, avoid areas that have restrictive covenants, conditions, and restrictions (CC&R's). Don't rely on a real estate broker to give you accurate information on what those might be. Go to the county courthouse yourself and pull the records on the property you are considering. The CC&Rs will be clearly listed. Also check the zoning restrictions. If you find a property that you don't want to lose because of the possibility of other offers, you can always write up an offer with a contingency clause that if the CC&Rs and the zoning requirements conflict with your intended use of the property, your offer is automatically withdrawn. Give yourself at least two business days to check them.

A home owner's association (HOA) is typically in place for homes or businesses in new subdivisions, planned unit developments, or common interest developments. Anyone who owns a home in such a development is automatically a member. I strongly discourage you from purchasing a home in a planned community with one. Originally, HOAs were intended to maintain uniformity and property values within a planned community, but in my opinion they have almost universally exceeded their mandate and are almost never compatible with a kennel operation.

A Breeder Secret

Don't Neglect High-Tech

If you plan to expand your breeding business, look for a place outside of any planned development, and preferably outside of the city limits, in an unincorporated county jurisdiction. Check for high-speed internet accessibility and cell phone reception before purchasing any real estate. You can't run a successful home-based business without internet access, and you will miss important calls without cell phone reception. If you want to supplement your breeding business with pet-sitting services, you almost have to have a cell phone for emergencies and to reach your customers in the case of a problem at their house. A lot of people don't even have landlines anymore, so you can't rely on them to have a telephone in their house.

There are several things that you can do to minimize land use disputes if you have one where you live. Keep your front yard immaculate, sweep the walkways and driveway, replace dead plants and prune vegetation as needed. When it is time for puppies to go to their new homes, spread the buyers' pickup dates over several days—do not have several vehicles show up at the same time or on the same day with crates in hand. Do not allow dogs or cats outside unleashed or unaccompanied. Always clean up after your dogs immediately. Do not allow your dogs to bark incessantly whether you are home or not. Ask someone to check on them when you are away to find out if they are barking. If they are barking and it can be heard from outside the house, you need to institute a no-bark training program to put a complete stop to it. Don't say it is too much effort. The income you earn from breeding is worth the effort to train your dogs perfectly. A fully trained dog is a pleasure to live with. There is never a good reason to allow your dogs to take over your life or bother your neighbors.

Take the Weather into Account

When I first saw the property I purchased in Colorado, I envisioned the beautiful hillside there blanketed in spring daffodils and crocus flowers, and it was an absolutely enchanting vision. When winter came, however, the same hill covered in ice became an impassable barrier that prevented me from making my way to the dog kennels, which were about 50 yards from my house. I installed safety ropes all the way down the hillside, and went from tree to tree, hanging on for dear life. By the end of the winter I was black and blue from my shoulders to my ankles. I had been blown off the ropes so many times that I could now take a fall like a professional stunt person. If I had anticipated the severe winter storms and blizzard conditions, I would never have chosen that location for my kennel building. It taught me to think about how the weather during different times of the year can have a major impact on the business.

Coping with the Cold

In cold climates, have the foresight to install a thermostatically controlled heating system. Go deeper than the frost line to bring water pipes to the kennels from the house. Install heated water buckets in each kennel run (shield the wiring with metal wiring covering to protect from chewing), and use insulated plastic doghouses inside the kennel building. House two dogs together, so that by sleeping curled up together they can stay cozy. Make it a habit to pick up all the dog poop at least three times a day before it freezes to the concrete, forming "poopsicles." If you don't do this, the spring thaw will be unbelievably gross and smelly—not to mention ugly.

If you live in an extreme climate where electrical outages are a common occurrence, you might already have a backup generator for your house, but you should get one for both the kennels and your house. These are always a good investment, and now that you have the kennels, you can write it off as a business expense.

Be advised that the regular dog-septic systems that are installed in the ground do not work during the winter in climates where the temperature drops below freezing. They just aren't deep enough, and they freeze if they aren't installed below the frost line. At freezing temperatures or lower, the enzymes fail to digest the waste materials. You can make your own doggie septic system with a large plastic trashcan and a long, wide PVC pipe, gravel, and rocks. Call a local builder to find out how deep the frost line is in your area. Install your system below the frost line. If you have a leech field, a french drain under the ground, natural gas lines, or underground telephone lines, you better know where they are before you start digging to lay in water lines or install a septic system. There are companies that will come out and locate all underground pipes, wires, etc. and mark them on a diagram and on the ground in orange or pink spray paint. They are well worth the expense.

Supplying water to your kennels is critical—it is one of the most important things that you need to have. Even if your kennel is located in an attached garage, you need to have running water out there. You don't want to be sloshing buckets through your house, or running hoses from your sink to the garage to wash it down. Whenever you do have to use a hose, make sure you drain it completely before putting it away, because hoses are useless once the water inside of them freezes.

Keep the temperature in the kennel above freezing even for hardy breeds. Provide heated water buckets so the dogs always have access to water. Dehydration is an enemy you need to avoid in your dogs. You might be surprised that dehydration is common in extremely cold climates. Eating snow to survive will lower your dog's body temperature and consume extra calories that you will have to make up by feeding twice as much food. Remember the basics: highly nutritional food; protection from cold, dampness, and drafts; clean environment; opportunities for socialization with humans and other dogs; and appropriate medical care as needed.

Check your dogs' feet when they come back from exercise, and restrict their time outdoors in freezing weather—especially important in medium and small dogs, and in dogs who are not double coated. Make sure they have clean, dry bedding at all times. Do not use straw or hay, as it disintegrates and is then inhaled as a powder, causing lung problems. For older dogs, there are non-chewable heated pads that can be put inside their doghouse. These also work for puppies.

Coping with Extreme Heat

There are three types of hot weather in the United States. In Arizona, where I live now, it is too hot during the summer months to keep animals outdoors. Even with a misting system, the heat is unsafe for man or beast. My dogs and cats are kept indoors in an air-conditioned environment. I set the thermostat at 68°F. I cannot fathom having a kennel in this type of climate without an AC system in place. I provide unlimited fresh water and take the dogs out several times a day to potty and stretch. If it cools off in the evening, we go for runs, play in the yard, or they lay on the patio on the cooler cement. Four months out of the year we live indoors. Eight months out of the year the weather is near perfect outdoors. Advantix™ controls fleas and tics year around. Rattlesnakes and scorpions are an occasional problem, but my dogs were snake proofed and there is a pesticide against scorpions. During the monsoons it is not possible to use Snake Away™ as it gets swept away after the frequent downpours.

When I lived in Colorado, the dogs were outside all summer on 2.5 acres of meadowland. I provided large wading pools inside the dog yard, fresh buckets of drinking water, and I took them to the local lake to swim as often as possible. In the mornings I would hose the kennel runs and the dogs. We were at high elevation so there was always a nice cool breeze in the afternoons and the nights were crisp. At 8,000 feet there were no fleas or ticks to deal with. I kept large fans on puppy pens to keep the flies off and to keep them cool. Females in season were segregated inside double fenced kennel runs, of course. There was no need for AC for us or for the dogs. Poisonous snakes were not an issue at this elevation. Occasional rattlesnakes were rare, and my dogs were snake proofed. I did use Snake Away to keep snakes out of the basement.

In Pennsylvania we had to deal with very high humidity. The dogs were better left inside the kennel building during hot summer days with 2 large dehumidifiers running 24/7 with the hoses from them running outside the building. I also kept large fans directed at the runs and big buckets of cool water inside each run. The males were allowed out during the day and would go swimming in the big pond behind our house. Whenever they were too hot, they would head to the pond and swim and wallow in the mud to cool off. I trained them to stay away from the snapping turtles. In the afternoons I took the females swimming or for a long walk in the cooler woods where they loved to eat wild blueberries and would return home with purple faces. I had to use pesticides and vigilance to control fleas, ticks, and an abundance of other pesky bugs. Grooming and checking for ticks were a daily necessity for dogs and for people. Wasps were common and I carried Benadryl™ and Epinephrine™ with me on dog walks, which I was forced to administer on several occasions. I used Snake Away to keep Copperheads and other snakes away from my house and my kennels. When I left Pennsylvania, I was not sorry to leave poisonous snakes and ticks behind.

Facility Evaluation

Planning how you are going to construct or redesign your kennel is the fun part of your project. Take your time and solicit the input of your family or friends. This will infuse them with the same enthusiasm that you already feel, and will pull them into your project. Keep all the following considerations in mind as you begin and work through all stages of getting your facility completed.

Structure

The intended structure's suitability for dog breeding is an important part of ensuring a successful business. You don't necessarily need a custom-built free-standing building—the facility can be a room in your house, a converted garage or sunroom, an out-building, an unused mother-in-law unit, or even a large insulated shed. For very small dogs, it can be a large laundry room. Some toy dog breeders allow their dogs to have the run of the house, but I would discourage a bitch from taking up residence on your bed because that might become her choice for whelping. Never allow your puppies free run of the house and never allow a bitch to run around your house after whelping. This sends two messages. One, that it is OK to urinate inside the house, and the other is that it is OK to run off from your offspring and leave them alone and unprotected.

I had a friend who bred Chihuahuas. She had wall-to-wall carpeting, and she eventually lost the ability to detect the smell of urine (the human brain's ability to eventually ignore obnoxious odors is a scientific fact). When you entered her house, the stench hit you in the face like a brick wall. Adult dogs and puppies urinated anywhere, at will. She sold her puppies for relative low prices. They were cute, very socialized, and their mothers were sweet, but the breeder's presentation clearly took her out of the running to compete with professional breeders. Mediocrity is a character flaw that cannot be overlooked when it comes to the care of animals or children.

Some breeders of small dogs set up an elaborate and comfortable dog kennel in the basement or garage. Pens can be three to four feet tall. Most of these smaller dogs do not eat their beds (many large dogs will consume an entire dog bed, foam and cover, in a few hours of uninterrupted bliss). Whether you breed small or large dogs, a puppy play area is fun to build and so good for the puppies. Make sure it is easy to clean.

Kennel Area

Make sure your building, shed, or garage is structurally sound, weather proof, and easily cleanable (floors and walls are covered in paint, laminate, ceramic tiles, vinyl, or another non-porous material that can be disinfected). During your planning stages, always consider the ease of cleaning. Keeping your kennels clean and dry will be your biggest challenge. Avoid porous materials that will harbor germs and debris. Avoid plastic buckets, plastic dishes, and other plastic cleaning items. Stainless steel, aluminum, cement, ceramic tiles, enamel, epoxy paints, and metal dustpans are the way to go. The only plastic items that I really loved in my kennels were the large commercial mop buckets with the ringer and wheels, and my large shop vacuum with a long hose attachment to reach all the way into the back of the kennel runs. My next favorite item was my commercial floor squeegee. Adequate ventilation is also a key element.

Make a diagram of your intended kennel area. Measure the area carefully and draw the diagram to scale. Clearly mark all supporting walls, partitioning walls, electrical outlets, windows, doors, steps, and storage areas like closets, built-in cupboards, or shelving. Mark any plumbing lines in the area such as sinks, faucets, and hose hook-ups, both inside and outside of the designated area. Use a large cardboard or poster board with a ½ or ¼ inch grid—it is a great tool for planning. You can use some for planning your outdoor exercise area, too. Use a ruler and pencils. Once you have everything laid out, you can evaluate it much better. Either make separate paper kennel areas that you can move around on your diagram, or pencil in where you would put kennel runs, food storage areas, shelving, and anything else you will need.

Utilize every inch of space, including the areas under stairs, above doorways, and under windows. Small dog kennels can be raised up to waist level, and storage can be placed under their kennel areas. Just make sure you use some type of preformed shower stall or similar device so that the kennel area is washable and will not leak into the storage area. It is so much easier to be erasing and changing your paper plan, or moving around paper cutouts made to scale, than to be moving actual metal kennel runs from one side of the room to another. Standing in the middle of a room to figure out where to put your plumbing lines and electrical outlets, or where to install ventilation fans or lighting fixtures is just not feasible.

My kennel building was set up with a master drain in the middle of the 30'x 25' area. The cement was poured so that the floor was graded toward the center drain. The floor was one big smooth slab of seamless thick concrete. If you are having a concrete slab poured, make sure the contractor doesn't brush the cement. It is essential to have a smooth surface area. A brushed concrete finish will be almost impossible to keep clean as everything sticks to it. The drain in the floor of my kennels led out to the woods—about 150 feet from the kennel building away from the well and away from the leech field. Six 6'x10' kennel runs ran down both sides of the building.

New buildings should be built to code and have safety glass in all doors. If you have screens on windows and wish to have the windows open during nice weather, you should probably think about some type of metal barrier such as rod iron bars or a typical screen door metal grid to go over the screens to protect them from the dogs. Some breeds can chew up almost any material, so your planning has to include consideration of these issues.

I have found that dogs that chew and destroy their kennels are bored and inactive. A well-stocked play yard with lots of toys and knucklebones or cow hooves to chew on will help alleviate their boredom. If dogs are going to be running free in a yard off of the kennel area, or they are going to be running free inside the kennel building (something I do not recommend), consider putting some sheet metal angles up the doorframes on both sides of the doors. This keeps the dogs from chewing up the doorframes.

Kitchen, Infirmary, and Grooming Areas

Depending on the amount of dog food you will be preparing, you may decide to use your existing kitchen, or you may designate a separate food prep area for dog food. Whichever you choose, keep sponges, brushes, and soap dispensers separated from the utensils used to wash the items for human use. Keep the dog items in their own little wire basket.

A Breeder Secret

Fire Alert Stickers
Another item that you may not have thought about are the stickers that people put on the door to tell the fire department how many pets they have. If you want to post those stickers, just write: "Pets are inside this home—number and location are posted on the other side of this door."

I also like to keep all canned dog food and dog-related medications in a separate area of the refrigerator. If you can afford to have one, and you have room for it in your kennels, get a good used refrigerator/freezer for your kennel building or kennel room. It will come in handy for storing medications that need refrigeration as well as cold compresses, opened lactated ringer solution, Oxytocin (stimulates contractions during labor), and Dopram (a cardio stimulant for newborn puppies without a pulse). The freezer section is also good for storing pheasant and duck wings for training hunting dogs, and the unpleasant, but necessary, task of euthanizing deformed puppies or storing stillborns until trash collection day.

It is inexpensive to purchase used kitchen cabinets (which you can paint if necessary), and a sink and garbage disposal unit for your kennel building. A separate dishwasher would make your facility truly professional. Remember that you don't have to have all of these items immediately. But if your master plan is a good one, it will accommodate additional items as you can afford them. Whether you are feeding puppies conventionally or tube-feeding neonates, you will need to keep all utensils and containers scrupulously clean. You will need hot water and detergent, brushes, and a place to air-dry everything that is clean and free of dog hair or airborne contamination.

When you are first starting out, focus on the whelping/nursery area—the nursery should be inside your house, if possible, as it will help to socialize the puppies to humans. You should be able to set up a nursery cam or at least a baby alert system that can sit by your bed at night so that you can monitor the puppies. During the first five to seven days after they are born, you will either be next to the whelping box yourself, or someone else will be assigned to watch the puppies around the clock, which is crucial. After that initial period you will need to set your clock to get up at least every two or three hours to check on the puppies and the mother. You will be monitoring her for mastitis (infection of the mammary glands), and monitoring the puppies for breathing and activated sleep. Puppies move a lot when they sleep; the ones that lie still could have a health problem.

Before you lay out your grooming and infirmary spaces, read the information in Chapter 10 on the pharmaceutical supplies you'll need so you understand what equipment and supplies you need to store, and what type of space you will need in order to work comfortably. A universal rule of thumb from designers is that you need a minimum of 18 inches between things to be able to move around freely. Leave more space if you intend to be moving around with a dog in tow.

Kennel Runs

Average sized dogs—Labs, Goldens, Dalmatians—can be housed in 6' x 12' kennel runs. Make adjustments accordingly for larger or smaller dogs. Depending on their temperament, you can house two dogs to a run.

Each run should include a large Dogloo™ or washable doghouse. Avoid wooden doghouses—they are impossible to keep clean, dogs chew on them, and insects like them. Most dogs like to have a little cave to sleep in where they feel secure and safe. Since we love calm, happy dogs, we try to accommodate that instinct. I prefer the Dogloo type doghouse. It is insulated, sits off the floor, and has an entrance design that keeps drafts off of the dogs. The newer ones have adjustable ventilation openings in the top. Best of all, they are easy to disinfect. The combination of a doghouse and a shelf seems to work well for some breeds. Several years ago the Ralston Purina Corporation put out a quarterly publication for members of their Breeders' Club, which featured some excellent articles on this subject. *Dog World* magazine has also published some well-written articles on Kennel Management and Design. When you are looking at Kennel Management books be sure to look at the copyright date. Some of them are so out-of-date that they are meaningless in today's world of plastics, laminates, and man-made materials. There are also improved methods for heating and air-conditioning, ventilation, filters, and waste management.

Energy and Electric

New energy-efficient building materials and building designs are now available. If you are starting from scratch and not renovating an existing structure, or are modifying one for kennel use, there are some wonderful options today, from affordable solar heating systems to wind-generated electricity, on-demand water heating equipment, and pressurized water delivery systems that cut the amount of water used for grooming in half. These options didn't exist even a decade ago.

Appliances such as clothes dryers and refrigerators/freezers are so energy efficient that it often makes good business sense to throw out the old units and replace them, because in just a few years of usage, they will more than pay for themselves in lower energy costs. Many electric and natural gas utility companies give generous rebates when you purchase energy-efficient water heaters, driers and other appliances. Before making any appliance purchases, check with your utility company first. There is a lot of free information on energy conservation from various conservation groups around the country. Utilize this information when making design decisions.

All exposed wiring should be run through PVC or metal tubing to protect the wires from being chewed and from water damage. When you wash down your kennel runs, you do not want to be spraying water on exposed electrical wiring or electrical outlets, so install the spring–loaded, covered type.

If you are running an electrical fence outside of your kennels, the control box should be inside of your kennel building, close to the door and at least six feet up from the floor so that you can turn it off and on easily, but children and animals cannot reach it.

A Breeder Secret

Color—the Finishing Touch
When deciding on colors to paint the kennel area, select a cheerful, crisp color scheme for painting walls and cabinets, and for your counter tops and wall tiling if applicable. Bright colors with lots of white trim will make your facility look fresh and clean, and pleasing to the eye.

Waste and Water Disposal

Though certainly not the most pleasant part of your business, this is a very important one that needs special consideration. Think about the easiest, simplest, and most economical solutions. You will have to dispose of solid waste that will go either directly into your septic system or into some kind of receptacle that will need to be emptied. You will also need to manage the waste water runoff so it stays off your kennel runs and you can keep your facility clean and sanitary. If it accumulates in some pool outside it will quickly create a health hazard. Even if you use bleach in the water to reduce bacterial growth, it can still create a muddy, oozy, bog. You cannot just dump the waste anywhere. Devoting some time to this subject during your planning stages will save you aggravation later.

Dog waste can be handled in many different ways. Just make sure it is not going to become a major contamination factor. There are companies who will periodically remove it. Small dogs or a small number of dogs shouldn't pose a serious problem, but you have to think now about how you might handle the growth of your business and the resulting additional waste. Waste from puppies can be disposed of in newspapers then put into plastic bags, properly secured, and deposited in your regular waste cans. Read your contract with the waste disposal company and see what the rules are and if they offer alternatives. I do not recommend flushing this down your toilet. Water is an expense in most areas of the country, and cleaning your toilet after dog waste is an unpleasant task.

If you are raising small dogs and are letting them out into your back yard to eliminate, you should set up a small area for their use that's as far from your house as possible. Make it about 6'x 6', install a short fence around it with an opening, and lay pea gravel down as a surface. Take the puppies and teach them to go potty there. This is easy to train because their natural instinct is to go as far from where they live as possible. You should be able to teach a puppy to use such an area in about three or four days of walking him out to it every time he goes out to potty and rewarding him for performing in that area. You can rinse this area down with water and bleach every two weeks.

Pick up the poops once or twice a day and dispose of them. This is so much nicer than walking on dog poop in your lawn! It is a good training method to recommend to your puppy buyers, too.

Trash Bins

If you can accommodate a large trash bin in an unobtrusive area, do it. There is nothing worse than having a bunch of full plastic bags sitting around waiting for the trash service to pick them up. If you have a very small kennel and small dogs, you may not need this added luxury. To maintain cleanliness and order, make sure your trash disposal system is well organized, covered, and free of flies or odor. Use one of the high potency deodorizers to spray it each time it is emptied. I installed hanging flytraps during warm weather to attract and catch flies to keep them off of my dogs and puppies.

Dispose of left over dog food, euthanized newborn puppies, and other items that will decompose and smell bad on the days you have scheduled trash pick up *only*. Until that day, wrap them in plastic and keep them in your freezer. Put a red rubber band around items that need to be thrown out on trash day so you don't have to open yucky things to check them—just grab anything that has a red rubber band around it.

Exterior Cosmetics

The exterior of your kennel (or your house) is the first thing your buyers will see. It is the first impression of you as a *professional* breeder—not a backyard amateur. Whether you are breeding your dogs inside your home or you have a separate kennel building, you want to project professionalism.

Create an environment that represents your breed in its best light. Have a clean, neat, well-groomed front garden with an attractive and classy looking entrance. Plants by the front door should be beautiful. Potted plants are easy to change out for the different seasons so that they look good year-round. To get ideas, look through top decorating magazines, take out the looks you like, and try to tastefully reproduce them. If this isn't something you think you can do well, hire a professional designer. Your buyers should drive up and say, "This looks nice. I can't wait to see the puppies." If you are sending potential buyers a DVD of your kennels, or if you have a website that shows them, the opening footage should be of your walkway and going into your beautiful entrance. It should be a theatrical production, not an amateur home movie.

Fencing

Although fencing is not considered a cosmetic feature, I believe it does have a major contribution to the overall appearance of your property. Make it attractive and compatible with the style of your building—especially any fencing that is visible from the entry side of your facility.

Fencing of perimeters is extremely important in a breeding kennel environment. All bitches in season must be safely enclosed in a double–fenced area. If any get past the first barrier, there has to be a secondary system to keep them secured. Male dogs in search of love are quite resourceful and persistent. Over the years I have heard too many breeders say they had an accidental breeding. Among truly professional dog breeders there are no accidents; they are the result of carelessness and a lack of responsible vigilance.

If you live in an area where there are potential predators of your dogs, like cougars (mountain lions), coyotes, large birds of prey, and so on, you will need strong wooden or metal tops on your kennel runs, as well as tall double fencing around your kennel building with an electric wire or barbed wire along the top. For a cougar, having a dozen dogs locked into kennel runs is like being served dinner. More than once I had to run outside with my shotgun and a strong light to scare away a cougar. If you have small dogs in the house, you cannot just let them out at night to potty, you need to take your big light and your rifle with you. Small dogs are taken in one swift swipe of a cougar's paw. Since predators usually sleep during the day and hunt at dawn and at dusk, you need to be especially careful at night. I never encountered one during the day, and my dogs could run freely on my property without any incident. However, always be alert, and communicate any sightings to your neighbors.

When fencing a field or large play area, you can use field fencing on stakes, but run a low voltage electric wire along the top and the bottom. Make it high enough so that dogs cannot simply clear it in one jump. An 8- to 12-foot tall chain link permanent fence is the optimum fencing for large or medium-sized dogs. It is solid, durable, and looks professional. These can be installed in square or rectangle configurations to accommodate a dozen dogs for exercise (usually breeders will have two of them to keep the males separate), or they are sometimes set up in long narrow lengths of 20 to 30 feet long and 6 or 12 feet wide. I personally don't believe the long narrow ones are very effective, as I have observed all the dogs bunched up at one end.

A Breeder Secret

In Season Indoors
Never put a bitch who is in season outdoors in any enclosure. That would be asking for an unplanned breeding. An amorous male dog can "leap tall buildings in a single bound" to get to his prize. I have also owned a bitch that could be bred right through a chain-link fence, not very comfortable for the male dog, to say the least.

Everyone is familiar with indoor/outdoor kennel runs. These are commonly seen at boarding kennels, animal shelters, and at hunting facilities where trained dogs are leased for the day to hunters on a private game preserve. They can be nicely arranged, but unless you are disciplined about spending time with your dogs, their use could contribute to neglect of the dogs. You get busy, and so gradually you put off getting the dogs out to play. In an indoor/outdoor kennel run, you can leave them without having to take them out for exercise, hand feed them, or interact with them. There is no reinforcement that the dog can attribute to you, and in my opinion this tends to turn them into what is known as a kennel dog—one has grown up living in a dog run, un-trained, un-socialized, isolated from other dogs except for hearing and seeing them through a chain link fence, and not bonded with a human. None of this is in keeping with the business you want to build and the reputation you want to have over time. Don't settle for it in your early planning or you may slip into its convenience.

Chapter 6
FINANCIAL MANAGEMENT FOR THE PROFESSIONAL BREEDER

This chapter is for those who have not run a profitable business in the past. Running a business can be intimidating, but if you follow the rules and do not try to cut corners, it is not that difficult. I do not have the space here to cover all aspects of running a business, but I will cover the most important things that a professional breeder would need to know. For more information, consult the Recommended Reading list at the back of the book.

Setting Up Your Business

You need to be aware that there are several ways you can organize your business. The three most common are:

1. Sole proprietorship or ownership.

2. Partnerships.

3. Corporations (of which there are several alternatives).

Most breeders start out as sole proprietors as this is the simplest to set up and manage. The drawback is that you and your business are considered to be the same legal entity meaning you have personal liability relating to your business, i.e., your personal assets and business assets are lumped together. So if someone should successfully sue you, you could lose your personal assets, not just the business assets. That is something to consider. You will have to evaluate the risk that your business might pose to your personal assets. The more activities you engage in, the more risk of legal problems you run. So, if in addition to your dog breeding business, you are also running a commercial boarding facility or a grooming facility, then sole ownership may not be the best choice for you.

Partnerships are just like sole proprietorships except you and one or more partners pool your resources to run the business. The liability problem is not solved by a partnership, in fact it can be made worse to some extent in that you can be found personally liable for the actions of your partner.

The major advantage of a corporate structure is that you do not have personal liability relating to the operation of the business in most cases. You and your business are viewed as two separate entities. Usually, someone successfully suing your business would not be able to seize your personal assets. But there are some disadvantages including the numerous corporate forms you have to fill out and keep updated, reporting requirements, and additional fees. If you choose to be a "C Corp" you will have to file and pay corporate taxes. If you elect an "S Corp" status, you still have to report your corporate earnings, but can pay those taxes on your personal income tax form at your personal tax rate.

Discuss types of ownership with your accountant and attorney to decide which the best structure for your situation is. Let me remind you that I am not a certified public accountant, a tax consultant, or a tax attorney. Therefore, I urge you to seek out a professional financial expert for advice and to help you get set up properly before you create any financial problems for yourself.

Regardless of what form of business you choose, you will need to get a business license and comply with all of the local and state requirements to run a business.

Banking and Record Keeping

You will need to have at least one business checking account. All income and expenses relating to your business should be run through this account so that you have a clear record of all of your financial activity. Never hide any of your income. When people offer to pay you in cash to get a discount, say no. Never let anyone be in a position to hold something over your head, or to threaten you with exposure to the IRS. Operate your business legitimately.

If you are doing especially well in your business and find you have more money than you can forecast needing in the near-term, open a business savings or investment account. There you should deposit money for unexpected expenses—and you can earn at least a little interest as well. Be careful putting money into a long term investment to earn more interest, since you might be subject to a penalty charge for early withdrawal in case of unexpected needs for that money. Assuming this account offers you ready access to your funds, maintaining such an account will give you peace of mind for such things as veterinary emergencies, sudden opportunities to obtain superior breeding stock, or other unplanned or irregular expenditures. In all of the above situations, you would transfer the appropriate amount back to your checking account, and then disperse the funds from there.

Be Fanatical About Record Keeping

I cannot emphasize enough how important it is to keep good financial records. Get a ledger or a software bookkeeping program—whatever works for you. If you have a software package, you can set up a chart of accounts, which contains specific numbers you assign for each type of income and expense category. For example, you might use numbers starting in the 1000-1100 for all facility related expenses like repairs and construction; 1200-1300 for all outside services such as lawyers and handlers; and 1400 for utilities such as electricity and water. At first it may be difficult to remember the account numbers from the chart of accounts, but after a while, you will automatically enter them correctly and not have to reference a chart. All good accounting software programs will provide you with a chart of accounts that you can use. At any time you can see the exact status of all of your income and expenses.

Using an accounting software program and keeping good records also makes year-end and tax accounting a lot easier—at the end of the year you merely push a button to have all of your expenses printed out by category. You will know exactly what you spent on dog food, dog supplies, veterinary care, cleaning supplies, publications, internet access, training, and so on. And your tax accountant's job will be made a lot easier if you can just print him a well-organized report.

Purchase a mileage/trip book for your car. The cost is a dollar. Record your starting mileage and ending mileage every time you use your car for the business. Enter the destination and purpose of the trip. That means when you go somewhere to visit a kennel, go to a dog show, go to a B-Match, go to take a business class, visit your accountant, or drive to a feed store to pick up dog food, you must remember to record this in your trip book.

Make sure you record any interest you pay on borrowed money as an expense of your business. If you are going to be using a credit card in your business, get one that is dedicated solely to business expenditures. Do not mix your personal credit accounts with the business credit account.

Keep monthly records and year-to-date (YTD) totals. This will help you keep an eye on your budget (see below). Keep all of your receipts in appropriate folders, just in case you need to double-check the accuracy of what you have entered in your accounting software. If in doubt, keep the receipt. I write the type of expense across the top so that I don't have to sort them out later when I can't remember what they were for.

Keep accurate records on every dog you purchase. In your financial books you will enter the date of sale or purchase on each dog or puppy. Make a copy of the Bill of Sale and put the copy in the dog's file. If it is a puppy sold, put a copy in the mother's general file. Put the original Bill of Sale in your financial files. If there is a puppy back clause in your purchase contract on breeding stock, enter that as a debt, estimating what the puppy will be worth. When a dog dies, it is a business loss. Calculate the amount the dog was originally purchased for, all the money put into the dog (training, certifications, and so on), add the value if there was a puppy paid back to the breeder, then calculate what the loss of revenue is to your business. When a dog is retired and sold, the money from that transaction is entered as income.

The Balance Sheet

Your balance sheet provides a quick snap-shot of the financial condition of your business. A balance sheet lists all of your business assets on the left as positive numbers, and all of your business liabilities on the right as negative numbers. At the bottom, you subtract the total liabilities from the total assets. This provides you with your net worth. Easy, isn't it? Here are some of the more common assets and liabilities:

- Bank account balances are assets.
- Accounts receivable (money owed to you) are assets.
- Capital items like kennel runs, doghouses, steam cleaners, vehicles, and computer systems are assets.
- Breeding stock is an asset.
- Accounts payable (money you owe that is due within a year) are liabilities.
- Mortgages, automobile, and equipment loans are liabilities.

Keep your balance sheet up-to-date, as you may need it to obtain a loan at some point to expand your business, purchase real estate, or purchase other business-related equipment. Your banker will want to see it at that time. Believe it or not, some large breeding facilities have ultra-sound, x-ray equipment, and a full service laboratory. These purchases normally require financing.

Keeping a Budget, Having a Plan

Hopefully, you know at least a little about budgeting. The accounting software you buy should have an easy-to-use budgeting feature. This is important to your success, your peace of mind, and your relationships. Budgeting is critically important for breeders because, unlike many businesses, your income will not be steady week to week or even month to month. In this business you make money principally when you sell a litter of puppies—but puppies do not arrive on a monthly schedule. Stud fees are usually generated semi-annually because most bitches cycle twice a year (around Jan/Feb and again around June/July). There are exceptions, but that is the norm. Occasionally you may sell an adult, trained dog, but that is not a regular occurrence. You may find ways to generate income throughout the year by conducting training classes, grooming, boarding or pet sitting, selling retail products, etc., but generally speaking, your income will not be a set amount that's deposited monthly into your account.

Here's a way of thinking about budgeting and forecasting in this business: You may sell two or three litters in the summer and another two or three in the fall. If you have five brood bitches, you may have one year with ten litters and the next year only five or six. Calculate 63 days of gestation, and about two months until the puppies can leave, which equals four months from breeding to final payment. During that period you have on-going expenses like food, supplies, utilities, advertising, veterinary charges, insurance, and so on. You will need to budget your money.

Remember that money in this business doesn't come in regularly each month, it comes in lump sums. This means that you have to plan ahead for everything. You can't just assume that because you have thousands of dollars in the bank at any given time that you won't run out of money before the next litter is sold or before your stud dog will make some money for you—and don't assume that every pregnancy will end in a successful outcome. Never spend money that you haven't made yet.

Forecasting expenses is a great exercise in keeping you real. As you sit down with pen and paper or at your computer, start thinking about how you will be spending your money in the coming year. This can be both sobering and liberating at the same time. How can that be? Well, to do a zero-based budget, you are forced to consider every aspect of your business, estimate the income and expenses for the next year (including inflationary increases), and think about ways to economize or reduce costs. Sobering if the numbers don't look good, liberating if you can see the path to success in your budgeting process.

Health Insurance—For You

Health insurance is a big issue for anyone running a small business like a breeding/kennel operation. If you are not covered by your spouse's health insurance or insurance from another source, you will have to budget for that, too. Buying health insurance as an individual business owner can be ridiculously expensive—to the point where it is almost a luxury item. If you are in decent health, you may elect to purchase catastrophic illness coverage with a large deductible ($5,000 and up) as a means of keeping your premium affordable. But even in that case, it could cost you at least a couple hundred dollars a month in premiums in addition to having to absorb the high deductible in case you get sick. Of course, you can choose a more traditional plan with lower deductibles, but the premiums will be higher.

You may be able to take advantage of group medical plans through associations you might be a member of or through organizations like Costco. If your business grows and you have enough employees you may be able to form a group and get lower rates than you would as a single person but then, of course, there is the issue of what you would pay as an employer for your staff. There are also health care savings account (HSA) insurance programs that you might want to investigate which, assuming you stay healthy, can be a good way to save money for future illness or retirement. In any case, health insurance is important, and you need to find a way to obtain some kind of coverage even if it is only catastrophic health insurance. Contact a trustworthy insurance professional and review your options.

Cutting Costs

When you think about it, a reduction in expenses is basically the same as an increase in profits. It's worth spending some time considering how you might manage this. For example, if you are paying someone to come once a week and work all day cleaning your kennel runs, maybe your son or daughter could work one hour a day, cleaning one kennel each day per a schedule that you set up—and do it for less money. If this is a consideration, but you aren't sure if it will work, do it on a trial basis for a week or two, get the bugs out, and then if it is successful, budget it into your forecast accordingly.

If you are buying your dog food at a feed store, you are paying extra. If you have six or eight large dogs, it might be more cost effective to open an account with one of the dog food manufacturers and have a pallet of 25 bags delivered directly to your kennels. You can also be on the Breeders' Club discount program, which can cut the price of a 40-pound bag of kibble almost in half. You might also want to take advantage of the factory distribution specials. Sometimes they sell you 25 bags minimum to get two free bags. Additionally, some of the manufacturers' rebates are fabulous. I used to get $60.00 in factory credits for every 400 pounds of dog food purchased. I would cut off the weight labels from the bags and mail them to the manufacturer. They would send factory "dollars" that I could use to pay the distributor. Spread over a year, this made for huge savings. If you don't have enough dogs to justify this, maybe you can partner up with another breeder in your area and split the dog food between you. A pick-up truck is all you need to make this work. Even with small dogs, you can join the manufacturer's Breeders' Club and get a substantial discount—and free puppy packets.

Forecasting expenses and formulating a budget might cause you to look for even more ways to cut down on expenses. If you operate your business without a financial plan, you may not take advantage of all the ways you can increase your profits and, in the worst-case scenario, you will not succeed financially as you will sink into debt and make poor decisions based on financial expediency and last-minute solutions to complex problems.

A Breeder Secret

Buying in Bulk
I used to partner up with local dog breeders to order vaccines, special kennel supplies, dog food, and puppy formula. This way, you can buy larger, less expensive quantities, or take advantage of the opportunities to buy several and receive one (or several) free offers. Many catalog supply houses also waive the shipping costs if your order exceeds a set amount.

For most breeders, it is difficult to generate a lot of profit from day one, so watching your costs when starting a business is critical. You will also likely have a lot of initial expenses and it may take some time before you have a big payday relating to selling that first group of top-quality puppies. You should be able to begin to bring in substantial amounts of money consistently over time—substantially more than your expenses—but until that time, you need to carefully follow a budget and not allow yourself to be too quick to withdraw funds from your business account.

Paying Yourself
One thing that many new business owners forget is to pay themselves a salary or monthly draw. This may be difficult in the beginning, but you should have the goal of

paying yourself on some sort of regular basis as soon as you can. One technique is to calculate all of the initial expense you had in starting up the business, then divide that amount into 24 or 36 equal payments (you decide which). This is a way of reimbursing yourself for your start-up costs within a reasonable amount of time—if you can't pay yourself back in three years, then perhaps you need to reevaluate your business operation. I recommend you budget this as a fixed expense (not adjustable) as it will force you to create a budget with enough money left over to compensate yourself.

You need to find a happy medium between optimism and realism. At first, everything will be going out and nothing will be coming in. One good way to supplement your income during the initial phases of your business is by taking care of another breeder's dogs or puppies. An established breeder who is very busy will often place a litter with another breeder to raise the puppies, or even to have the puppies born at the other breeder's facility. This is hard work, but also good experience. The fee is usually substantial, depending on the size of the litter. This is a good way to be earning some money while you are waiting for your own puppies. Be sure to have a written agreement with the breeder that clearly states how much you will be paid, and that there will be no deductions from that amount for any reason. Typically, they pay the veterinary expenses, supplies, and food, and they pick up the puppies on a specified date and time.

Capital Investments

Capital investments are assets you purchase that support your business enterprise. While a professional breeder may need relatively few capital investments compared to other businesses, they can still be substantial. For a breeder, the following are typical capital investments although not every breeder will need each:

- Kennel runs
- Computers
- Breeding stock
- Refrigerators
- Steam cleaners
- Air conditioning units
- Ventilation equipment
- Dog houses
- Dog trailers
- Duck blinds
- Bird launchers
- Gun cabinets

Capital investments usually involve a substantial amount of money, especially for someone new to the business. The ideal is to be earning enough money from your operations so that you can save enough money to pay cash for these investments as they come up. If not, you will need to borrow money. If you are going to get a loan, be realistic in your analysis of the project and be able to prove on paper to both yourself and your lender that it will have a substantial positive impact on your business and will significantly increase your earning power. Many people are afraid of borrowing, but I recommend it as long as you are being realistic. No one ever got anywhere with one foot in the air. Look for low-interest options, and think of this as renting money. Every month when you make that payment, think about how you can pay it off even faster and save the interest.

Expenditures for capital items must be accounted for in your bookkeeping system. You need to know how much you paid for each item, when you purchased the item, whether or not you can depreciate the item, and when or if you sold the item. Consult with your accountant on any major purchase so that you are confident that you have the information you need in the right form.

Consider Investments Carefully

Even if I plan to pay cash, when I want to consider a capital investment in my business, I try to assume the posture of someone coming to me to borrow money from me. I try to look at the project from that standpoint—sort of like getting outside of yourself and finding a way to be objective about something that you want to do. Maybe your real motivation isn't coming from a business perspective. Maybe you want to remodel your kennel food prep area just because it would be so cool to have a real kitchen area in the kennel building and it would make you feel so professional to own a kennel operation with a modern kitchen and dispensary incorporated into it. On the other hand, maybe you could wait a year or two and actually move to a better property where such an investment would be justified.

Perhaps it would be smarter to purchase two more brood bitches and install a small nursery area in what you are considering for a food prep area. If you prepared the dog food in your kitchen for another year or two, purchased two brood bitches and produced three more litters per year from the two bitches, you might have a lot more money for your project in the long run. Since it takes almost two years before you can breed a bitch, the sooner you get more brood bitches, the sooner you will be able to get a return on that investment.

Income Taxes and Deductions

I've saved the part of running a business that most people want to avoid until the end of this chapter. I hate paying taxes—but paying taxes is part of owning a profitable business. The good news is that many breeders pay more taxes than they need to because they are not aware of the literally dozens and dozens of legitimate tax write-offs and deductions that you are allowed to take. Just hope that you make enough money that you will need all of the "write-offs" and tax shelters that are available!

Be meticulous about keeping receipts. I recommend that you put all of your receipts and bank statements in an archive box labeled with the correct year. Take the time to clear out all of your financial filing cabinets for the year, bundling each type of receipt and stapling them together or putting a rubber band around them or a clip to secure them, depending on the bulk of papers. If you are ever questioned or audited by the IRS, having this information well organized will be very important.

Your accountant should help you do your taxes unless you have just a very small operation with minimal income and expenses. Most accountants now have some sort of a tax planner form asking you for all of the information they need. Normally this will include your year end balance sheet and income statement and any comments you have on your financial information. They will also want to see:

1. Personal tax information.
2. Interest paid and interest earned documents from the bank.
3. Interest paid to mortgage companies or banks.
4. Credit card interest statements that pertain to business expenses.
5. Copies of vehicle licensing fees.
6. Copies of property taxes paid.
7. Estimated quarterly tax payments you may have made.

Subject to the review of your accountant, you can generally take the following expenses as deductions against your income:

1. Utility bills (home businesses can deduct a percentage of these expenses).
2. Show or seminar expenses (gasoline, meals, motels, entry fees, etc.).
3. Veterinary bills.
4. Subscription medications.
5. Insurance payments.
6. Outside labor and contracted labor.
7. Vehicle repairs/maintenance (only on a separate vehicle for the kennel business).
8. Restaurant meals with clients (no matter where you go, talk about dogs and puppies)—however normally only 50% of the cost of meals is deductible.
9. Leasing or renting vehicles for business purposes.
10. Dog shipping expenses (don't forget airport parking fees).
11. Office expenses (copies, faxing, packaging, and shipping).
12. Airline tickets (for example, when you fly to a dog show and enter at least one dog).
13. Dog food for dogs you plan to sell.
14. Dog supplies.
15. Office supplies.
16. Professional charges (attorney, accountant).
17. Advertising.
18. Communication equipment (cell phones and fax machines).
19. Internet access fees.
20. Business licensing fees.
21. Dues for professional associations.

22. Magazine subscriptions.

23. Dog show or performance event entry fees.

24. Special dog-handling clothing and shoes.

25. Dog training equipment.

26. Cleaning supplies for the kennel.

27. Dues for professional associations.

28. Registration fees.

29. Materials for facility repairs and maintenance.

In general, breeders are not aggressive enough in claiming these legitimate expenses. If the answer to the question, "Do you use it in the business?" is yes, then it's a business expense. You may need to take care to separate expenses between dogs you keep as pets yourself vs. dogs you are raising to sell to clients.

Accountants and the IRS

I have said it above, but I can't emphasize enough the need to use a qualified accountant (preferably a CPA). Don't rely on a bookkeeper or a tax franchise to give you the correct answers to your questions. Smart people do not prepare their own taxes or make decisions that may have tax ramifications without using the services of a professional certified accountant. They are worth every dime they cost; when you combine your business and personal return, you will be surprised at how economical their services are. Try to find one that has actually worked for the IRS, as they are the ones who really know how to play the game. My accountant gave me excellent advice: "Declare all of your income. Hiding income is a felony offense. Write off every allowable write-off you can think of. If the IRS doesn't accept a deduction it is just a mistake; you pay the tax on it, and go on your way." It is advice I heed daily.

If you have significant earnings, use legal tax shelters to alleviate your tax burden. You can find ways to avoid taxes or ways to defer taxes by working with your accountant. If you can only defer the taxes, it may be until a much later date when your taxable income is negligible. An experienced, knowledgeable accountant will know about tax shelters, spreading income over several years, depreciation, and how to structure your tax return to keep as much of your money in your own pocket as legally possible. He will also know what *not* to deduct because it activates a red flag on your return and generates an automatic audit. Even if the deduction is legitimate, is it worth it? I never feel guilty about withholding my hard-earned income from Uncle Sam.

If you have a CPA doing your taxes and you declare all of your income, you should have nothing to fear from an audit. I was audited once. My accountant got so angry about it that he went back over my taxes with a magnifying glass and reviewed every single aspect of my return—and the previous year's return as well. Even though he had prepared those tax returns, he proceeded to bring back another $1,500 for me! He didn't charge me for going to the audit, either. That is the policy of many CPAs. If you do your taxes with them every year, they do not charge you if they have to go to an audit for you.

Remember this fact—if the IRS audits you and you represent yourself at the audit, they have the right to ask you anything about any portion of your return and to require supportive documentation for anything on that return. If your CPA represents you at the audit, they can only ask him about the line items that were flagged for the audit. In other words, when you get the notification of the audit, they will list on the notification which items are in question. They cannot ask your CPA about anything else on the return because he is not the taxpayer. This is a very good reason not to go to an audit. An even better reason is the fact that the average person gets stomach cramps and nausea when the words IRS AUDIT are even whispered. I was never audited again. When my accountant passed away, I cried harder than his wife and children. I loved that man! If you declare all of your income, you never have to lose sleep because you are worried about the IRS.

Summing Up

In summary, here's what is critical to your kennel's financial management:

1. Keep accurate records.

2. Separate dog breeding income and expenses from your personal income and expenses.

3. Maintain a separate bank account and credit card for business expenses.

4. Record every transaction related to your dog breeding.

5. Track expenses and income—date, source, vendor, description, form of payment, and amount.

6. Keep all receipts and cancelled checks or check stubs—cash and credit.

7. Maintain a record maintenance system to organize all your documentation.

8. Use an accountant!

Chapter 7

MARKETING AND ADVERTISING

Are you intimidated by the prospects of marketing and advertising? You don't have to be, because you are a consumer. You have been a consumer all of your life—think about all the experiences you have to draw on. Every decision you make as a consumer is affected by someone else's marketing and advertising, whether it's how the information to make a purchase gets to you, how an item is packaged, what the price is, or what your final experience is with the product. Think about the things you buy on a regular basis. Do you have brand loyalty? How was that brand built? Are you an impulse shopper, looking for things that are interesting—or on sale? All of these considerations are part of marketing and advertising. There is no reason that you, too, can't do a superior job of marketing.

If you are feeling a lack of confidence, check out some up-to-date marketing books from the library or browse the topic at your favorite bookstore. The *Guerilla Marketing* series of books by Jay Conrad Levinson seems to be the new bible for everyone from small business owners to marketing executives. Learning about marketing is your homework assignment, so spend an afternoon or evening browsing the marketing section of a large bookstore while drinking lattes or espresso. It's fun to take a friend on this assignment. This is now Dog Breeders' U, and you need to immerse yourself in this core course.

Getting Started

Start your marketing and sales campaign early. I recommend getting a desktop publishing software program. Microsoft Office Publisher™ is one that has the basics that most small businesses need, and there are several other workable programs on the market. Since many of your puppy sales are going to come from referrals by veterinarians, groomers, dog trainers, existing customers, other breeders, and your website, people need to be able to learn all about you. One of the simplest and most effective ways is with a tri-fold brochure that you can create with a desktop publishing program.

This brochure can be sent with a photo CD or a DVD of your kennels when someone calls you. You should drop off some brochures at your local veterinary clinic. Consider paying the vet techs a referral fee for buyers who purchase a puppy from you. Vet techs don't make much money; a referral fee of $50 or $75 is warranted for a good referral. It should be paid with a personal thank-you note attached. Veterinarians usually will not accept a referral fee and might be insulted if you offered them one—even though they pay clients a referral fee in the form of a discount on their next visit. Once a vet tech or a veterinary receptionist receives a referral fee and the buyers are ecstatic about their puppy, they will continue to refer customers to you regularly.

I've found that people who can easily afford a high quality puppy are a target market best reached through referrals and the Internet. In order for you to get a sound referral, you need to be outstanding. If other dog world professionals don't know you, start introducing yourself. A quality brochure given to local veterinarians, groomers, and trainers can work well so long as you give them every opportunity to get to know you.

Working Your Website

In this day and age, having a website for your breeding business is a must. Start building your website, whether you are doing it yourself or having it done professionally. Make it classy and target it to your specific market. Do not go with one of the free website set-ups that are covered with all kinds of banner and sidebar advertising and have constant pop-ups that interfere with reading your site. No matter what, you do not want to look cheap.

Ultimately, about 90 percent of your sales will likely be generated from your website. Even if the initial inquiry came from a different source, the buyer will be sent or will go to your website to view the dogs and puppies and to find out more about you as a professional breeder. They will compare your kennels with other kennels. This is your opportunity to exceed their expectations.

Until recently, it was very expensive to have someone design a professional website and maintain it. The first one I had done for me in 1992 cost $650 for the design and $20 a month to maintain! There are many more options today. For do-it-yourselfers, one is www.homestead.com, where you can set up a professional-looking site using their extensive database of templates and their photo gallery. The process is so simple that anyone can build a site in just a few hours. Once you build it, you can make all the updates and changes easily. You do not need to be a computer expert to do it—if you can type and you can click, you can do it! Check out my writing website at www.sylviasmart.com and see what I built in three hours.

Since your website is your door to success, think carefully about your design choices. Lets assume your targeted demographic is people between the ages of 35 and 65 who are educated and financially sound. If that is the case, design your website with that demographic in mind. Find ways to get people to visit your website by promoting it through magazines, breeder referral lists, etc. Most breed clubs have a breeder referral page on their websites, so use it. If they have a page announcing litters that have been born, it is an excellent place to list your litter, or if they have an upcoming litters page, this is even better.

Once you have a site, directing buyers to it is the key to success. Talk to internet specialists about improving your website positioning through search engines; there are numerous ways to do this. Many publications and services provide information regarding website promotion. You can also submit your site on Google and Yahoo by going to their sites and clicking on "submit," then following the directions. Discuss this with your website provider or other web master companies.

If this seems like a lot of work in an area you know little about, remember, self-education is crucial to success in any business. Think of it as an investment in yourself. Even if you are hiring someone else to perform a task, you need to understand exactly what is being done. If someone else is going to host your site and implement your changes, get a guaranteed turn-around time from them in writing with a clause that says if they don't make the deadline you don't pay them for the month. It is so common to sign up and then have to beg them to make changes in a timely manner. It is still most convenient and easy to control your own site and make corrections, changes, and additions yourself.

When you create your kennel name, research available website URLs and hopefully you will get one that is easy to remember, reflects your kennel name, and makes a statement about your kennels. If you already know how to set up your own website, you are ahead of the game and that is wonderful. The flavor and design should be bold, contemporary, sharp, personal, and warm. The website should provide lots of good information about you, what you do, your philosophy, your experience, and most of all it should reflect your love of dogs and your commitment to excellence. Tell buyers why you selected this breed. What makes this breed the best of all choices for them? Write as though you were writing a letter to a friend, telling them about your excitement, and your enthusiasm. If you are just starting out and you don't have show photos of your own, ask the breeder who sold you the puppies if they would allow you to feature their Champion Sire, and also the Dam, as the parents of your puppies, at least until you have your own bragging rights. In the future when you begin to breed your bitches, and you breed them to Champion Sires—most stud dog owners will allow you to have a photo of him on your website with his pedigree, and list of accomplishments. It is free advertising for them, and a chance to promote their stud dog to other breeders—especially if the puppies you produced are superior quality. Make sure you list the owner's name and contact information under the photo, making it clear that he is not your dog, but he is the Sire of your puppies and is available to approved bitches. I would only keep the photo up until all the puppies are sold.

Consider what style of photo goes with the breed you have. Sporting dogs need warm, earthy colors, photographs of dogs in the field, swimming, or sitting at your feet in front of a fireplace, etc. Lap dogs should be photographed on laps, sitting on pillows, sniffing pretty flowers in the garden, or playing with children. Working dogs might be photographed doing what they were bred to do—or just being with their human families. If you attend some B-Matches, take some good photos of the puppies in the show ring—fill your website with these positive images. Here is a breeder who is doing something with their puppies. There they are in the park with the judge going over them. There they are with you, getting their first Puppy ribbons! Take photos of them at puppy kindergarten, learning to sit and to come. If you have kids, get some shots of them licking kids faces and chasing balls. This demonstrates your involvement with the puppy in a family atmosphere. This dispels any suspicions that you might be a puppy miller with acres of wire cages holding poor, pitiful puppies.

Make sure you have lots of great puppy photographs. If you don't have puppy photos yet, ask the breeder you purchased your puppies from if they can let you use some of theirs until you build up a library of excellent puppy photographs. I suggest you take photographs of your foundation puppies as they grow. A digital camera is one of your best investments. They are easy to use, and it is easy to edit your photos—if you have the software you can do wonderful things with a simple photograph. I use Microsoft Digital Image™. Get a basic photography book and learn how to shoot good puppy and dog photos. The main mistake most people make is taking their photographs too far away from the subject, and not getting down on the level of the puppy or dog to take the shot.

A Breeder Secret

Photo Faux-Pas

Never have any dirt or debris or junk in your photographs. Don't photograph a litter of puppies with spilled puppy food on the floor or with excrement of any kind in the background. (You shouldn't have excrement on floors where there are dogs or puppies, anyway.) No *flies* in the photos. You would think that would go without saying, but I can't tell you how many times I have noticed flies or dirty floors in the background of puppy photos. Think about this every time you photograph. Always have the light source behind you or from one side—not in front of you, or lower than you. Practice a lot—with a digital camera it costs nothing to shoot 100 photos and then keep only the best ones.

Web cams can be quite interesting. A breeder friend of mine is married to a computer specialist. He built her a fabulous puppy nursery in their large basement. He also installed a web cam focused on the whelping box. It was connected to her kennel website, so anyone could go on line and watch the whelping box on a live feed at any time of the day or night. This was great for selling puppies—people loved seeing their puppies being born. She would call the prospective owners when her bitches went into labor. Sometimes she would have long conversations with them during the whelping process as they watched.

You do need to be aware of what can happen with Web cams, however. One day my friend arose early and decided it was a good day to put the puppies outside for an hour of fresh air and clean the whelping box. It was a hot day, so she stripped down to her bra and panties. She carefully scrubbed and disinfected the box and all the puppy pens, hung clean water bottles, and replaced the bedding with clean fleece. It took over an hour to complete the task. As she turned to view her work, she saw the little red LCD light glowing on top of the cam positioned on the wall behind her. The entire process had been broadcast on her website! She was mortified.

If you do community work with your dogs, including therapy work or search and rescue or even Junior Showmanship classes, foster care, or rescue work, make sure that information is on your website. Buyers do not just look for pictures on a website—they like to support charitable or volunteer involvement. It makes them feel good and it is the right thing to do. If you are doing these things, you deserve their support. This personal information also allows the buyer a better understanding of who you are and what your philosophy is in general. Everyone wants to be friends with someone who is active, caring, community conscious and trying to make the world a better place. They would prefer to purchase their new family member from someone who's out there doing good rather than someone whose only concern is money. If you haven't already discovered this, being a good person is a whole lot more fun than being greedy and selfish. You will find this will put a smile on your face most of the time!

Be your own best promoter. Post show photos of your dogs on your website, especially if you have shown them. Put lots of thought and effort into showcasing your dogs, your kennel, and yourself. Say how special your dogs are, how they are socialized, what activities you do with them, how smart they are, or how funny they are. Tell the buyers why they would absolutely want a puppy from you. Tell them what makes your kennels or your breeding lines better and more special than any other they could choose. Take the risk out of the purchase by spelling out your guarantees. Your guarantee should not require the return of the dog, just proof of spay or neuter at the appropriate age. That is a big plus for the buyer. These guarantees give you the edge over most other mediocre breeders. You are then highly competitive in finding the very best homes for your puppies. You put your money where your mouth is, and you stand behind your puppies. This approach will also keep you vigilant about what you breed.

If you take all the precautions and perform all the necessary screening tests when selecting your foundation breeding stock—and you are using a judicious approach to breeding outside your own kennels—you should have an extremely low warranty replacement expense. In all the years that I bred and sold puppies, I only had to replace one pup—and she was only marginally hip joint challenged. I believe that is the highest endorsement of superior breeding. Some breeders would have said she was OK to breed, but my motto is "only the best should be bred." She had been sold to someone who thought they wanted to breed her, so I gave them another puppy.

I recommend setting up PayPal™ on your website, which allows your customers to pay you by credit card. Setting up a PayPal account is easy to do. The charge for this is per transaction, and is minimal compared to having to set up your own system to accept credit cards through a bank. PayPal also has savings accounts that pay more interest than conventional banks. It is easy to work with, and a convenience for your buyers as it eliminates the dilemma of deciding when to ship a puppy while a personal check clears at the bank. The truth is an out-of-town check may take up to 10 days to clear.

It used to be common practice to accept money orders or cashiers checks, but lately there have been many cases of these being forged. If you part with a $2,000 puppy and the check is cancelled or doesn't clear the bank, what do you think your chances are of getting your puppy back—or the money for it? Without PayPal or your own credit card system, you have a potential problem when the buyer is not local.

To avoid scams, never accept any payment that is in excess of your price. A common scheme is to overpay you and ask you to refund the difference or send it on to a third party. When you do that, the original check or money order turns out to be forged or bogus, and you have already sent money back to the maker or forwarded it as per their request. Banks don't notify you of the forgery or counterfeit until several weeks later when they deduct the amount from your account. One recent scam is to send you an overpayment with a counterfeit money order or cashier's check and ask you to pay the person who picks up the puppy at your kennel—supposedly to pay for hand-delivery of the puppy. They even generously tell you to keep any difference for yourself as a tip! Of course, when you attempt to contact them when the check or money order bounces, they are no longer available and their telephone number is disconnected. With all that in mind, cash (check it for counterfeit), PayPal, or a personal check drawn on a local bank where you can wait until it clears or cash it at that bank are your best (and only) options.

Print Advertising

Another way to keep your kennel in front of people is through print advertising. Magazine ads are effective. Some monthly publications worth considering are *Dog World, Dog Fancy,* and *Gun Dog* (for Sporting breeds). *DogsUSA* and *PuppiesUSA* are annual publications. Though these are expensive advertising options for display ads, buyers and serious competitors will purchase and keep these magazines for at least a year. Keep in mind that magazine deadlines are several months prior to the publishing date. I liked to place magazine advertising that hits the newsstands before November (this covers Christmas, New Years, and Valentines Day), and again in March or April, which covers the summer vacation period. These are the primary puppy adoption months.

Advertising should be consistent. Look at national marketing campaigns and you'll see they all have a single thread—either a motto, a certain style, or a celebrity who endorses the product over and over again. The style of your ads, the content, and the photographs should ring out class, quality, superiority, and an unusual commitment to your breed choice. Study some of the car ads, and take their lead.

Your ads should be simple and elegant. For a display ad in a magazine, the photo should be absolutely professional—high resolution, and vivid. Obtain the photography specifications from the publication and set up your camera accordingly. The puppy in the photo should be an excellent example of its breed. Eyes should be clear and surrounding colors used in the photo should contrast nicely with the puppy's coat. The print font should be easy to read, yet stand out. Avoid ad copy that sounds too cute or otherwise unprofessional. Your kennel name should be prominent and in a larger font than the text. List your website address, telephone number, state, and that shipping is available. (If you do not ship puppies, do not advertise nationally; it would be a waste of your time and resources.) Unless the breed name is part of your kennel name—which is not a good idea, anyway—make sure you have the breed name on the ad. I have looked at a number of ads where no breed is mentioned, and from the photo, the puppy could be a Mastiff, a Boxer, a Bulldog, or something else. When the photo is of a puppy, it isn't always easy to tell which breed it is. The magazines sometimes put ads in the wrong section because they can't tell which breed it is, either. Most breed sections of dog magazines are listed in alphabetical order by breed. Some listings are divided by group (Sporting, Toy, etc.), and then alphabetically by breed. Before you place an ad, get a copy of the magazine and study it. Make your ad stand out in the crowd.

Advertise in the annual dog magazines. Study the publications and analyze the best ads. I believe that a quarter-page ad is the minimum size if you want to get the biggest bang for your buck. If you really want to advertise in a particular monthly magazine, but the price is just too steep, get a sales rep on the line and ask them what they can do for you to reduce costs so that you can afford to advertise at least twice a year. They do have lots of options and can offer you some special discounts. Keep in mind that within a year or two you should no longer need to advertise at all. If you are doing it right, you will be selling your puppies strictly by referrals and through your website. You may achieve that by the end of the first year. Don't sign any long-term marketing or advertising contracts with anyone. A rare breed may require a lot more advertising and marketing in order to educate buyers about the breed. A very popular breed like Yorkshire Terriers or Labrador Retrievers needs very little promotion because everyone knows what these are and why they are popular. The question, then, is only quality—and selling yourself and your kennel as the best source.

A Breeder Secret

Newspaper Advertising
Use newspaper ads as a last resort. Many less than reputable breeders use classified ads to sell puppies. Classified ads are probably not going to reach your likely key target market, middle to upper income households, in any event.

The Psychology of Sales

A friend who I mentored years ago is a good example of someone who could have been very successful if she had understood the psychology of sales. She had some difficulty selling her puppies, even though they were high quality and she took wonderful care of them. She just didn't understand marketing. One day I was visiting her, enjoying her current litter of Labrador puppies. A buyer came by to look at the pups. When they asked her about the temperament of a particular puppy, she said "he's hyper, he's wired." My response would have been to describe the puppy as outgoing and active, very curious, and full of puppy energy. See the difference? I would point out that the puppy was friendly, ready to play, and wonderfully curious. I also would have shared with them that I believed he would grow out of that exuberant stage after puppy-hood. I would show the buyer how to view this puppy's personality as a definite plus. The truth is that this puppy was the pick of the litter! I love a curious, friendly, energetic pup. These are the ones who, in the end, make the best dogs as adults—particularly if you want to show them. These are the secrets of a successful dog breeder—the secrets that I wrote this book about.

When anyone had reservations about purchasing a hunting Labrador puppy from me, I would take them to the meadow with one of Custer's pups, and tell them to hold the puppy where it couldn't see me. I would move away, throw a pheasant wing upwind from the puppy, and then ask the hunter to release the pup. The puppy would hit the ground with its nose down, then stand straight up with its nose in the air, turn toward the pheasant wing and lock up on point. This would be a five or six-week-old puppy, barely weaned off its mother. The puppy would then trot off toward the pheasant wing, find it, and holding it high in the air, prance back to the buyer, proudly displaying its trophy. To really show off, I would then reach out my hand toward the pheasant wing in the pup's mouth and issue the command, "Give." Since I had been training these puppies from the age of four weeks to give on command, the release was immediate and with a wagging tail, because the puppy knew it would have another chance to retrieve the wing.

A Breeder Secret

A Commitment to Excellence

Make sure that every puppy that leaves your kennel is a living, breathing celebration of your commitment to excellence. In other words, give your puppies the opportunity to sell themselves—even if all the puppies at your kennel are already reserved. After playing with your reserved puppies, the buyers will give you a deposit to reserve a puppy from one of your upcoming litters. Talk with your customers specifically about the temperaments of the puppies that you have for sale. If the puppies aren't born yet, talk about the parents' personalities and achievements. Discuss how you raise puppies so that they always come when they are called. This is a big selling point. These are the secrets of a professional dog breeder.

Telephone Etiquette—and Sales

When the phone rings and you determine someone is calling you about purchasing a puppy, you should have several things in mind to accomplish:

1. You want to come across well over the phone and sound friendly, knowledgeable, and professional.

2. You want to determine whether the person is a good candidate to purchase a puppy.

3. You want to convince the prospective buyer that your dogs are the best.

Before you begin to talk with someone on the telephone, smile! Smiles come through on the telephone. Believe it or not, they do. There is a special tone in the voice of a caller who is physically smiling. Take time with the caller. Do not rush them. You can always heat up your dinner later or cook dinner a few minutes later than usual. You need to give them your undivided attention. Your family needs to understand you are not to be interrupted on business calls unless it is a real emergency. Remember that the caller has called at a convenient time for them, and they may have a list of breeders to call. This is your opportunity to make a good impression on them.

Prepare a cheat sheet to use for incoming puppy inquires. Use one for every call about a puppy purchase, and file it once it's completed. A cheat sheet should include this information:

```
Date: _____

Name and telephone number: _____

E-mail _____cell # _____

Referral? _____

Gender ___ M   ___ F

Family makeup: ___ #adults   ___ #children under 5 yrs   ___ over 5 yrs

Pets: ___ Cats   ___ Dogs   ___ Other _____
Housing: ___ Home owner   ___ Renter in house   ___ Apartment

Work: ___ Outside the home   ___ Hours away   ___ Work at home

Dog owner history: _____
```

Be personable. Ask questions about the buyer's children, their ages, their relationship with the dog they lost if that's their situation, etc. You want to help families find the perfect dog for them. If you truly feel that way, your voice will convey your sincerity. When you open up your heart to people, it is you who ends up being the beneficiary. A wonderful part of our profession is actually being able to place a sweet puppy into a loving home where it will bring years and years of joy and happiness to the members of that family. How many people can be a part of that?

After speaking with them for a while and getting some personal information from them, you should have a feel for the person on the other end of the telephone line. You will now decide if you want to let them have a puppy or not. If the first words out of their mouth are to ask the price of the puppies, I would stop smiling and show no interest in placing a puppy with them. With few exceptions, people who ask the price first are looking for a bargain—and have no appreciation for quality. They are probably wasting your time, and would not purchase a quality puppy anyway. If they ask the price at the end of the conversation, give it to them. If they respond by commenting that the price is high, educate them. Tell them that one hip replacement is over $2,000, and that the average visit to a veterinarian for even the smallest problem is over $250. Your puppies are healthy. If you did your job right, they should remain healthy for many years and experience longevity with good quality of life. Also tell them that your contract commits you to taking the dog back at any time they cannot keep it, for any reason, and making sure it gets a new home or it stays with you for the remainder of its life. That is the commitment of a true Professional Dog Breeder. Stand behind your puppies—they are the best! Don't worry, you won't be getting them back—they're too good. If you do get one back because of a special situation, it shouldn't be hard to find that well-bred dog a new home.

A Breeder Secret

Make Friends with Your Phone
The telephone is your friend. Good telephone skills will make or break your kennel success. So if you aren't good on the phone, practice.

Discuss socialization and nutritional support for the mothers and for the puppies. Be sure to talk about the puppies you have, by name. Tell them how little Joe always cocks his head to one side when you talk to him, and how Marjorie immediately sits and looks at you with her ears up when you say her name, or how Sam always carries his tennis ball around in his mouth and stores it in the food dish while he is eating so he can keep an eye on it. Tell an inpatient buyer how Norma Jean can't leave for a few more weeks because she is a Mommy's girl and likes to sleep between her mother's front paws. Make prospective puppy owners feel like they have played with your puppies and know them personally. Soon you will find yourself in the wonderful situation of never having puppies available because they are all reserved either before they are born or immediately after birth. That is when you invite potential owners over to play with the current litter to see what kind of puppies you are expecting in the next litter.

Listen to people carefully, and give them time to express themselves. When they are finished talking, repeat what they told you. Never make them feel rushed. You are showing them that you were really listening, and that you know this is a big decision for them, and you are pleased that they are doing their homework and taking it seriously. Never be in a hurry to accept a deposit. In fact, I have actually refused a deposit and told the buyers to sleep on it. Purchasing a puppy is a big decision, and you only want your puppies to go to homes where everyone is 100 percent sure they will be loved and become family members. If you hear any hesitation in the person's voice—as in, "I better send you a deposit now or I'll miss out on getting one of your puppies"—your response should be that you will hold the puppy for 24 hours and they should call you when they're sure. Not one person to whom I gave that reassurance ever changed their mind. (Obviously, before the puppies are born, you can always add their name to your waiting list for another 24 hours before you require a deposit. After all, you don't actually have puppies yet.)

If prospective buyers tell you they just lost their dog and are heartbroken, you need to truly sympathize with them, because they are in pain! People who have lost a long-time companion dog are suffering severely. I cried more over losing my Lab of 12 years and my Pekingese of 15 years than I ever cried for my grandmother. It sounds strange, but I didn't really know my grandmother, and my dogs were my best friends all of my life. You can sympathize with a buyer who has lost their canine family member—people feel it. They know instinctively that you are genuinely sad for them and wish to help them. There is nothing phony or silly about helping a fellow human being who is suffering, regardless if they end up with one of your puppies or not.

When you talk to customers, your belief in your puppies will come across without making a huge effort to promote them. Be matter-of-fact about your prices, your conditions of placement, and your ability to satisfy their need for a puppy especially suitable to them. If you believe the customer is right for one of your puppies, just keep imparting interesting and factual information to them until they say they definitely want a puppy from you, or at least want to make an appointment to visit you if they are within driving distance. Talk about skeletal structure and movement, using the analogy of a wheel alignment on a car and how the tires wear out if the alignment is poor. The same is true for a puppy, who will wear out because his front assembly and rear assembly don't work together properly.

In order to place your puppies, you have to believe in them. I know that I have repeated this statement more than once in this book, but it is the key to finding the best homes for your puppies. You have to know that your pups are the healthiest, most wonderful puppies in the entire nation. You have to build the foundation of your kennel in such a way that there is no doubt in your mind that your puppies are the best of the best. I actually came to the point where I would watch the Westminster Kennel Club Show on TV and point out the flaws in the dogs, or watch Crufts and point out the inferior grooming of the European dogs vs. the American entries. Eventually, you will develop a good eye for superior structure and subsequently for correct movement in the dogs, and maybe even for the level of grooming.

Repeat Sales and Referrals

If you do your job right, every sale will generate new buyers. Often the original buyers will return to purchase a second and even a third puppy from you!

I once took a deposit on a puppy that was not born yet from an elderly couple over the telephone. I never met them in person. Their neighbor, who knew me personally, had referred them. The wife had terminal cancer and had been told she had four to six months to live. She had promised her three grandsons that when they moved into their new house she would buy them the yellow Labrador Retriever puppy that they had always wanted. Since she wasn't going to be around for the move-in date of their house, it became my job to provide the perfect puppy for her young grandsons. They sent me payment in full for the puppy, and the husband told me to call him when the puppy was ready to go.

About five months later I carefully selected a wonderful, friendly, brave little puppy named Max who was seven weeks old and ready to go. I called the man to tell him about Max. He cried over the telephone, as his wife had passed on just a few weeks before. He made an appointment to bring his grandsons and their parents to my kennels the following Saturday. He didn't tell them where they were going or why. He had instructed me to keep the puppy in the nursery and to take them in through the house so they wouldn't suspect a thing. When they arrived, he brought them into my home, and they were all looking very quizzical as to why they were heading down the steps to my basement. I sat them all down in my training room, and then I went to get Max. When I brought him out, I put him in Grandpa's arms and announced to all of the family that this was Max, a gift from their Grandma to them because she loved them all so much. Everyone was sobbing, and little Max was doing his best to lick up all the tears from all the faces. His tail was wagging so hard I was afraid it might fly off.

I sold a yellow Lab puppy to a professional couple who were both high school principals in a major ski resort town in Colorado. They named the puppy Lucy (after the show, *I Love Lucy*). The next year they came back to purchase a black Lab puppy, whom they named Ethel, and the third year they returned to purchase a chocolate puppy they named Molly Brown. During those three years, they must have sent at least ten referrals to me. Always put at least a dozen business cards in your puppy packets. Thank the person in writing or by e-mail for their kind referrals. This puts you far above the average dog breeder. People like to be thanked in a special way. It only takes a minute to write a brief note and drop it in the mail. I know we all send e-mails these days, but there is something to be said for opening the mail and seeing a card with a sweet puppy photo on it, and inside a note that says something like, "Thank you for referring [name of person] to me to purchase a puppy. I really appreciate your thoughtfulness. How is Joey doing? Does he still lift up his right paw when he wants attention?" This makes you incredibly special to the owners, and you'll get more referrals from them. You will also put a smile on their faces that day.

If you do not have what a person is looking for, and you cannot change their minds to take what you have—males vs. female, black vs. yellow, or smooth coat vs. rough coat, etc.—and they don't want to wait for your next litter, then be generous with referrals to other breeders. Don't just make the referral, but also contact the breeder(s) you referred the buyer to and let them know that you have sent them a *bona fide* referral! They will be delighted, and there is a good chance that they will reciprocate in the future. If nothing else, they will have a positive opinion about you. Only make referrals to breeders that you know are members of your breed club, active in the breed, appear to be professional in their deportment, and absolutely breed high-quality dogs.

A Breeder Secret

Referral Caution

Never make a blind referral to someone you do not know, whose dogs you have never seen, or on whom you have not received positive input. The referral ultimately reflects back on you, and if you don't know the kennel you're sending the buyers to, you don't know what the puppies will be like.

Always tell the buyer that you are going to make a personal referral for them, and give them the names and spelling of the kennels. Buyers are impressed that you will take the time and make the effort to help them find a healthy puppy. They will send you referrals, or maybe they will decide to wait for your next litter. If, in the end, you don't have what they want, haven't convinced them to wait for your next litter, and you have given them the referrals you think are appropriate for them, there is one last thing you need to do, and that is to close your conversation with a statement like this:

> Whether you purchase your puppy from me or from someone else, always keep my telephone number and feel free to call me with any questions you might have in the future regarding your puppy. If I don't have the answer for you, I will help you find it. My main concern is that all puppies get the best care and training possible. Thank you for calling me, and I'm sorry that I don't have the perfect puppy for you today. Good luck in finding your puppy!

The Puppy Packet

No puppy should leave your kennel without a puppy packet—it's like purchasing a car and not getting an owner's manual. The packet is essentially the owner's manual for the puppy. It is all the information the new owners need, secured inside a three-ring binder.

Your puppy packet should make you stand out in a crowd of good breeders. Your packet should sparkle with professionalism, caring, and money-saving tips mixed with the typical obligatory items found in most puppy packets. This is the packet that your buyer will be taking to their veterinarian for the puppy's check-up. (If you want referrals from veterinarians, having clients bring in puppies with professional packets is sure to make an impression on them.) Include a color photo of the pup with his full name below it on the front of the binder.

A Breeder Secret

CDs for the Puppy Packet
Purchase a CD label-making software program (they are very inexpensive) and make up a new label for each litter. Put your kennel name on the top, a good quality photo of puppies in the background, the date of birth of the litter, and print your kennel phone number around the edge of the CD, in a circular print. The CD label program is user-friendly and fun. Use transparent jewel cases, which show the colorful, professional label on the CD. This is another item that moves you to the top of the list as far as attention to detail.

This is what belongs in your puppy packet (as well as anything else you decide is pertinent):

- Sales contract and warranty.
- A copy of the sire's DNA profile certificate.
- Copies of the sire's and dam's certificates of registration.
- A certified four-generation pedigree for the puppy.

- Copies of all the health certifications of both parents.

- 8 x 10 photographs of both parents—head shots or stacked shots.

- A 5 x 7 photograph of the puppy at five weeks. (I like a close-up of the puppy being held in your hands with his face toward the camera and his two front paws over your fingers.)

- The puppy's health record, which will include dates of all vaccinations already given and what the dates are for future shots.

- List of first aid supplies.

- A photo CD of your kennels, yourself and your family, your dogs, dog shows, various dog events, newborn puppies, and anything that relates to this puppy.

- The puppy's birth collar taped to a colored card with the name and date of birth, and a paw print from the newborn puppy (use edible kids' paint for the paw prints because the mother will be cleaning it off with her tongue).

A Breeder Secret

The Birth Collar

A puppy's birth collar is the original color rickrack that is tied on the newborn puppies to identify them for weight and health tracking purposes at the moment they are born. The rickrack is changed at least twice a week as the puppy grows. The original newborn puppy collar is a very special and unique gift for the new owners. Some of them will actually cry when they open the packet and see how tiny their puppy was at birth. Some owners will take the collar home and have it mounted and framed. It is something unique and unusual—something that money cannot buy. How many people have their puppy's very first newborn collar?

Inside the binder, you should insert a set of colored dividers with index tabs. Label the tabs as follows:

- Contract and Warranty.

- Breed standard.

- Parents.

- Health records.

- Training information.

- First Aid.

- Titles (list of all available AKC and UKC title abbreviations and their definitions).

- Certifications (list of certifications for health or temperament, or working).

- Suppliers (list of catalog or internet suppliers of merchandise and medications).

- Recommended Reading (books and other material about the breed).
- Breed Clubs (local and national breed clubs and contact information).
- Recipes (for anything from treats to shampoo to rug cleaner—anything you have tried).
- The puppy packet should have your business card stapled to the inside flap of the folder or notebook.

The first page in the binder should be a "Thank You for Adopting Me" letter from the puppy to the new owner and should read something like this:

Dear Owner:

Thank you for giving me a "forever" home, for being patient, for being kind, for training me to be a good dog, for understanding that I am a baby dog—and I get tired quickly. So please don't wake me up to play with your kids when I fall asleep in the corner. If I wake up, please take me outside to potty because I can't wait very long. If you see me circling, that means I have to go NOW. If I make a mistake, please don't yell at me, or smack me on my bottom, because I will get scared and not understand what I did wrong. My breeder says that I am very smart—so just give me a few weeks to learn your way of doing things. I will try my hardest to please you. Thank you for always having fresh, clean water out for me, and for feeding me 3 times a day until I am at least 6 months old. Thank you for always moistening my dry food so it will be slippery and I won't choke on it. If I eat too fast, please spread my food out on a cookie sheet to help me slow down. Thank you for making my home a safe place for me, by removing electric cords and poisonous plants from where I can chew on them, by not leaving items around that I can chew up and swallow, and for crating me in my nice safe crate if you can't be with me to help me learn your rules. I promise to grow up quickly and be the perfect dog for you. **I promise to love you unconditionally for as long as I live**.

Signed,

Your Puppy

A Breeder Secret

A Very Special Puppy

Making a big deal out of the acquisition of a puppy is important. Understand that some people do not have children because of infertility, genetic diseases, or because their lifestyle wouldn't accommodate a child. Sometimes there is something in their background that prohibits them from adopting a human child. Getting a puppy is the closest they will ever come to becoming a parent! For those buyers it is very appropriate to give them a puppy gift. Some of them will send out announcements to their friends and family with a photo of the newborn puppy. You can supply that for them! If you track your puppies correctly, you can give them the time of birth, the birth weight, and even the presentation (breach or frontal). If you want to, you can set up a video camera and supply them with a DVD of their puppy's actual birth. What other breeder has ever done that? You can also use your desktop publishing program to create a beautiful birth certificate for each puppy.

Rewarding Your Buyers

One of the best ways to generate referrals is to cultivate existing customers. An excellent way to do this is to make up a special gift certificate, which is good for a certain amount off the cost of the purchase of another puppy. Make out the certificate to the original buyer exclusively. They or a close family member such as siblings, parents, grandparents, and children can use it. Place the certificate in the puppy packet, date it, sign it, and put in an expiration date that expires in 24 months from the date of purchase.

Make notes on your calendar to send birthday cards to the puppies in each litter, every year. This puts your name in the minds of the buyers, and they will appreciate it that you bothered to remember their sweet dog on his or her birthday.

It is easy to flag these dates. When a litter is born, you will make an entry on your calendar for that date. Open a sub-file for Suzy on every litter she produces during her lifetime. Each sub-file will contain all of the information pertaining to that particular litter. Not only their official documentation, but also the dogs' call names and information about each buyer. Later, you can personalize your communications to them. There is no way you can remember all of this information without taking notes.

Depending on what holidays are close to the puppies' birthdays, make up special cards. For example, the week before March 17th, make up St. Patrick's Day Birthday Cards, include a personal note, and mail them to all the puppies from that litter and their owners. Here's an example:

Dear Grandpuppy:

Happy St. Patrick's Day and a Very Happy Birthday!

It seems like just yesterday you were here at our house playing with your brothers and sisters.

Hope You Will Come To Visit Our Doggy Summer Camp. It Will Be A Lot Of Fun. We Have a Pond to Swim In, and Lots of Room to Run and Play with Your Cousins in the Meadow.

Your Doggy Mom and Dad Send Their Love.

Kisses from Grandma Sylvia

There are limitless unique and fun ways you can keep in touch with your puppies and puppy buyers. You can send Christmas cards or postcards, holiday email greetings, or gourmet dog biscuits. These are all items that will keep your kennel name in front of your buyers. When the puppies are about two or three years old, it is time to suggest a new puppy as a companion for their grown dog. Don't be pushy—just ask them if they think the time is right to get a little brother or sister for their dog. If you sell additional puppies to their littermate owners, send an announcement with a photo of the new little brother or sister puppy. This will often generate another reservation. You can be creative and do something like this: "Here is a photo of your sister's new little brother, Gordon. He is actually your half-brother too. Your sister, Twinkle, is so happy to have a playmate! She asked me to send you a photo of Gordon."

When you place your puppies, put your kennel name and contact information on everything you give the new owners. If you are providing puppy-training crates with your puppies, apply preprinted stickers to them (take the time to design a high-class sticker with your kennel logo). Some breeders provide T-shirts, grooming kits, puppy care books, pens, calendars, coffee mugs, and other promotional gifts. Be creative, and do what you can within the restraints of your budget. I found that the least expensive and most productive way to generate repeat business is to call or e-mail your buyers and forward puppy photos of your current litter.

Remember that the personal touches are the most effective. A personal e-mail asking the owner how Charlie is doing (Does he still cock his head to one side when he wants attention?) means a lot more than a pen with your kennel name on it. Few people are going to wear a T-Shirt with your kennel name and logo across the front of it; in fact, any apparel item may not be effective. What might work better is a really nice dog brush with your name and telephone number imprinted on the back of it, or a quality leather leash and collar for a full-grown dog (the puppy will grow) with your kennel name imprinted into the leather, or a gold-tone dog tag with your kennel name and telephone number etched on it.

Ancillary Products and Services

If your facility is large enough, you should consider supplementing your breeding business by selling products or offering services. These can include collars, leashes, and other basic supplies; grooming supplies and services; training; boarding; day care or camp; and so on. Don't do any of these things until your business is established and you are making a nice profit—not until then is it time to consider taking on additional products to increase your profits.

Grooming Services

Consider renting out a space at your facility to a professional groomer. This can be great for your business so long as the service is also of the quality you expect. A groomer's credentials should be top-notch, and you should watch him or her work with dogs—especially your breed. Make sure the groomer can present a professional image. When interviewing for a groomer, assess their overall appearance and personality with this in mind. Talk with him or her at the interview about cleanliness and order. Provide professional smocks and grooming tools if you are hiring the groomer to work for you.

Be cautious when you hire a groomer or lease an area of your facility to a groomer. If you are leasing, you might want to find a way to calculate the electricity and water expenses separately from your kennel utilities. The expense of setting up a grooming facility can be financed through various grooming supply companies. Take advantage of any freebies they are willing to provide as long as their products are good. Remember to find out what the insurance cost is going to be, as your exposure to risk will be higher. A groomer who is an independent contractor should supply you with proof of insurance coverage, and this should be spelled out in the contract between you and the groomer. Discuss this with your insurance agent, as they may want a copy of that endorsement. You don't want to find yourself liable for anything that your insurance company will not cover just because you have a grooming facility at your kennels. And don't forget to check out zoning requirements in your area to make sure an activity like a grooming operation is permissible.

Boarding

At some point, you may decide to go all out and have a boarding facility or provide contracted pet-sitting services. Some of the largest breeding kennels also incorporate a dog boarding facility along with a cat condo wing away from the dogs. Boarding kennels must be kept separate from breeding kennels because of the risk of infectious diseases being introduced into your breeding kennels.

A boarding kennel can be a gold mine if it is close to a major metropolitan center and if it is properly managed. It can also be a ball and chain around your neck. Licensing and insurance issues are magnified. A lot depends on how you are able to staff the facility. The considerations are more than can be addressed in this book. I only mention it because often a successful breeder will expand their business by combining it with this related service.

If you elect to run a pet-sitting business on the side—and you are going to use employees or independent contractors for this service (where they go into homes and take care of people's pets at their home)—each employee needs to be insured and bonded.

Summer Camp

On a small scale, I always offered my puppy buyers the option of dropping off their dogs during summer vacations. I called the break, Grandma's Doggy Summer Camp. With two fenced, lightly wooded acres for the dogs to romp and play in, it was a nice change for them from city life. With Labrador Retrievers, it was fairly common to have them all running together without any fights or threatening behavior, but not all breeds are that easy and this should be a consideration. I would not accept dogs that were not neutered or spayed, and I would only accept Labrador Retrievers because I know their temperament. I charged significantly more for this service than all other boarding facilities in the area and I restricted my boarding business to only dogs that I had originally sold, and their companion dogs. The owners supplied all of their dog's food and signed a waiver/disclaimer form that basically said that I was not responsible for any medical emergencies or other issues. They also signed a medical permission slip and financial responsibility form. You would think that with these requirements and the fees I would not have been very successful, but in fact, price was not as important to my clients as the safety and enjoyment of their dogs. In the end, I made a significant amount of income on this little side business.

Retail Product Sales and Marketing

If you have the right type of set-up at your kennels, you could sell retail articles there. To purchase wholesale items for resale, you will need to have a business license and you will need to be set up to accept credit cards, to collect sales tax, and then remit sales tax collected to your state. This sounds difficult, but it really isn't that hard to set up. The government provides good information on running a retail business. The SBA (Small Business Administration) is a good place to start and the information is free. There are even volunteer organizations that will provide free consultations from retired business owners. All of this information is usually available from your local bank. When you go to get your business license from the local County or City office—they will provide brochures, forms, and contact information for all of these services. The SBA also provides government guarantees for small business loans, and in some urban locations designated as redevelopment areas, there are government grants and subsidies available if you qualify.

Besides having any number of dog-related items for sale, from basics like bowls, collars, leashes, grooming products, crates, beds, odor eliminators, toys, and treats, you could explore boutique items like canine apparel, gift cards, stationery, and whatever else interests you and your buyers.

Puppy Starter Kits

The idea is to make shopping easier—and enjoyable—for your puppy buyers. One thing you could do is assemble a puppy starter kit that would include everything a new owner would need to outfit and care for his or her pup. Simply list the items on a flyer with the total price, and offer it to your buyers when they send you a deposit on a puppy. Some of them will welcome such a thing, and some will want to shop for these supplies on their own. Many will already have equipment from a previous dog. But if you are serving an upscale clientele and if you have really nice things in your kit, many buyers will purchase it. Your mark-up on those items would be 50-100 percent, depending on what you include and where you obtain it. This is a nice option for many breeders, and could generate you some additional income. Here is what you might want to include:

- Puppy training crate (large enough for puppy to stand up and turn around only).

- Washable crate pad.

- 8 pounds of the puppy food you are feeding your puppies.

- A 1-pound bag of the smallest puppy biscuit treats to use for training.

- Stainless steel food and water dishes.

- A high-quality pin brush and steel wide-toothed comb.

- A pair of high-quality canine nail clippers.

- An appropriately sized Kong™ toy, which is an important training tool.

- An appropriately sized Nylabone™ chew toy.

- A quality collar and leash.

- A box of baby wipes with lanolin.

- A spray bottle of Bitter Apple™ chew deterrent.

- A pooper scooper and a roll of biodegradable baggies.

- A puppy packet from a leading dog food manufacturer that typically includes dog food coupons and a crate-training manual.

Newsletters

Newsletters are great tools for staying connected to your puppy buyers—and generating new sales. If you have the time to produce a newsletter, you can publish it online monthly, bi-monthly, or even quarterly. It doesn't have to be too fancy; the idea is that you want to feature items of interest to buyers of your breed.

You can feature current litters and upcoming litters. You can post various activities that encourage your customers to participate i.e., agility, dog parties, dog hikes, and other fun mixers where they will see you in person if you place most of your puppies locally.

The newsletter can also give buyers health updates applicable to the breed, workable training tips, gourmet recipes (which will make them want to print it out and keep it), and a place to brag about their puppy/dog if you ask them to submit information to you on their dogs.

Eventually you can decide if you want to open this to subscriptions as another creative source of income. You would be giving your buyers a gift of a one-year free subscription—and if they want to continue to receive it, they would subscribe annually. If you charge $20 a year, and you end up having 50 or more puppies a year, that equals about $1,000 in additional income. If you double that by adding subscribers who are not your puppy buyers—it can grow from there.

Offer other breeders one-year gift certificates to your newsletter to give to their buyers. If you do not keep it breed specific this concept would be highly expandable. Every year you add new buyers and new subscribers. In 5 years you could have $5,000 from puppy buyers and another $5,000 from other subscribers—bringing your newsletter income to $10,000 per year by the 5th year. That doesn't even take into account price increases, or advertising dollars you may generate from outside sources. The beauty of this is that there are almost no expenses other than your own time. An online newsletter has no printing costs, no postage costs, and no unsold copies—only your time.

Internet Product Sales

You can generate income from your website in several ways. One is to provide links to various dog-related companies who will sign contracts with you for a percentage of the sales generated by your website (sometimes known as affiliate sales). Life's Abundance Dog Food has a distributor program where all sales are computer-generated from your individual website for their product. The food is expensive and not available from regular stores. All the details you need can be found on their website at www.healthy-petnet.com. There is a one-time set-up fee, and there is a monthly fee to maintain the website. You then put a link on your website directly to the Healthy Pet Net website in your name, and when someone orders, they issue checks to you for sales made off of your site. The food is good quality, natural, and the purchased quantity delivered automatically by UPS to your customers on a pre-arranged timetable. You simply promote the food in your literature and on your website.

There are some excellent natural grooming supply manufacturers who will sell their products to you at wholesale prices. Advertise them on your website and in your kennel facility—if you have the room and the time. See the previous section on retail product sales and marketing.

Chapter 8
INVOLVING YOUR HUMAN FAMILY

The joys in this business are definitely best when shared with family and friends. It is certainly a lot more fun to attend an agility trial with your family. You can sit on the grass and have a picnic, instead of just running your dog through his paces and going back home.

Family Involvement

If you are married or in a relationship, you understand that there is no greater blessing for your dog breeding business than a spouse or partner who is hands-on and involved in supporting your endeavor—if only for those nights when you have been awake for 12 hours straight delivering a litter of puppies and you need someone to keep an eye on them for an hour or two while you recuperate. Even better is a true partner who shares the wonder and miracle of birth with you—making coffee, exclaiming over each new life as it enters the world, and rubbing your back between deliveries. Those special people who cheer you on, laugh and cry with you, and don't think it's crazy to spend the weekend at a dog show or an agility trial are worth their weight in solid gold. Treat them with respect and kindness. They believe in you. You must show your appreciation every day and share your money with them!

In the case of a young couple going into breeding, there are special gifts to be gained. First of all, it can be considered a great dry run for eventual human parenting. The skills needed to raise a child over 18 years of his or her life are almost identical to those they will need in the first 18 months of a dog's life. These skills include consistency, the ability to break training down into incremental steps, using a reward system, mutual respect, patience, dedication, the ability to focus, and assistance in problem-solving. It also gives a young couple the opportunity to learn to communicate about issues that are always sensitive—finances, rearing, and of course, ethics.

Not everyone, of course, will have a supportive spouse or partner, at least not initially. A reluctant partner might be convinced if you take them to visit a successful breeder. Going over a detailed financial plan with them also demonstrates that this endeavor is not just a dream—but also something tangible. If you have a comprehensive written business plan that you can show your partner, and you are honest about the work involved they may see the potential for success. Don't mislead them about you doing all the work—because this will not be the case. There will be times when they must participate to some degree. If your plan is sequential and logical—this will go a long way in addressing their concerns. There will also be situations when you cannot participate in social functions or family activities because you have to address the immediate care of your dogs and puppies—they should be made aware of that too. When you cover the positive and the negative aspects of your project honestly it imparts credibility to the overall program. I have to assume that you would never be with anyone who wasn't already a dog lover. Also, promise to share your profits with them! This is what usually puts it "over-the-top." Of course, you can always lend them your copy of this book.

A Breeder Secret

Unsupportive Partners

In my experience, sometimes the single biggest problem novice breeders have is dealing with their spouses or partners. Many spouses/partners admire the guts it takes to go into business for oneself, but they are hesitant to fully support their partner. There are many reasons for this, including not understanding why anyone would want to stretch herself that much, or feeling unsafe or financially insecure.

It's not surprising to me that many successful breeders are single women and mothers. I think it takes a parent-type, nurturing personality to care for puppies. The care of puppies is a very intense and demanding occupation. If a breeder doesn't have the capacity to empathize with the dog's situation during whelping, weaning, and transitioning to a new home, the quality of the puppies' character will be damaged. A puppy is a complete package that includes physical attributes, sound health, mental stability, attachment capability, tractability, an appropriate gentle temperament, and a brave spirit. We have all observed puppies that cower in the corner when you try to pick them up, or hover over their food, growling as though any minute they will bite your hand if you even think about touching their dish. It is not only pitiful to observe these reactions to their world, but such puppies may never find loving, nurturing, forever homes, because their spirits are skewed and distorted.

How the Family Can Help

Involving your immediate family in your dog-breeding business can be an excellent opportunity to become closer, teach youngsters about responsibility, and to legitimately enhance their self esteem—but it doesn't happen magically or by itself.

If you are starting a dog-breeding business and are still working at an outside job, you will need the cooperation of everyone in your home to help you. Just remember that it is your family members who can make or break your dog kennel success. Be clear about what you think each member of the family can—and can't—do, and assign tasks that are complementary to their abilities and interests. For example, poorly handled telephone calls lose potential homes for your puppies—and waste your advertising dollars. Rather than risk this potential disaster, make it a rule that children can't answer your kennel telephone. List a cell number in your advertisements and make sure you have a professional voice message on your phone. You must also return calls within a reasonable time.

Involving Young Children

It is best left to parents to determine what age-appropriate tasks are suitable for each individual child. Children mature at different rates. Coordination, memory, focus, and attitude determine how much responsibility a child can handle. There is no "one job fits all" rule.

Youngsters can learn so much from delivering newborn puppies, participating in supervising natural breeding, and learning how to do artificial inseminations. It is also heart warming to watch kids learn and grow from these kinds of experiences. As they see puppies grow and develop, human children learn what it takes to be a loving parent—the responsibility we accept to train puppies, to keep them safe, and to find the perfect homes for them. When you are ready to give a child his or her own puppy to raise, to care for, to train, to show, and possibly even to breed, it creates a very special bond between the child and the dog. Dogs give unconditional love, and that is something we cannot give our children, as there are always conditions between humans. No matter what we think about ourselves, we can never give the same kind of love that can be received from a special dog.

I started a foster child on this road when he was only eight years old. He was too young to show his dog in Junior Showmanship, so he showed it in the Open classes in competition with adults. He did very well and received many compliments from judges and exhibitors alike. The experience gave him self-confidence and poise. He also learned about dressing appropriately. Once, when he had competed successfully in the show ring against a professional dog handler, she came over to congratulate him after the ribbons were handed out. He looked very nice that day in a beige suit, peach-colored dress shirt, a brown paisley tie, and brown leather shoes. He and his chocolate Lab presented a perfectly matched pair. The handler leaned over and said, "Do you know why you beat me today?"

"No," he replied, grinning in a wide smile.

"Because you dressed better than I did," she exclaimed, then shook his hand and told him what a great job he had done in the ring. I wanted to hug her myself for the time she took to acknowledge his efforts.

Involving Teenagers

Teens can assist, but an adult should have the primary responsibility when it comes to caring for your dogs. You should be prepared to supervise and double-check everything assigned to them until they are proven to be consistently responsible and trustworthy.

In my experience it is a rare teenage child who is capable of consistently taking on serious responsibility. Teenagers are "unfinished," and hormones rule their brain and bodily functions for a number of years. In truth, you cannot trust them to always do things right; often they just do their chores to get them done, with little regard for attention to detail and little thought to the consequences of their actions—or inactions.

The following are some true stories that I'm sharing in order to graphically demonstrate the seriousness of this topic. Just imagine that the following incidents happened at your kennel:

Inexperience. It only takes one distracted, immature teenager to miss the signs of mastitis in your bitch, and by the time you get home and realize there is a problem, the bitch may have developed massive septicemia, spiked a fever at 106°, and died a painful death. The teen in charge was giving this bitch food and water for several days, since she was moved from the nursery to the kennels. It was assumed that her pups were weaned, and her milk was dried up completely. Thinking the teen was keeping a close eye on her, you never checked on the bitch yourself to make sure she was OK. Though the teen was involved, this disaster is your fault! You will never forgive yourself for this. The lesson is you must examine every dog in your kennel at least once a day.

Inattention. A teenager I employed is in a hurry to meet a friend after school. One of their chores before they can go anywhere is to feed the six-week-old puppies in the afternoon. The teenager throws some dry puppy kibble into a puppy saucer and puts it down for the pups. One of the puppies gulps down the dry food and the kibble gets stuck in its throat, causing the puppy to choke to death. The teen was told that all puppy kibble must be moistened first with warm water and mixed to make it slippery so that the puppies won't choke on the food. By the time I discovered this situation it was too late. Every Heimlich maneuver and every attempt to dislodge the kibble packed into its throat failed. This puppy died in my arms—and there was not a thing I could do about it.

How would you like to have made the telephone call to the buyer who had purchased this puppy, visited it, had its photo on their desk at work, and e-mailed photos of this puppy to all of their friends and family? I can tell you that it was personally one of the worst calls I have ever had to make. Recently when someone told me that their toddler got something stuck in its throat and they had to perform the Heimlich maneuver on the child to dislodge the stuck food, I burst into tears as the entire episode replayed itself in my mind! We don't forget something like this.

Irresponsibility. You have to run to the grocery store. Your brood bitch is in the first stage of labor. You have installed her in the whelping box in the nursery, and you anticipate that it will be several hours before she will actually give birth. You assign your teenage daughter to sit with the bitch until you return, just in case a puppy should arrive sooner than you think it will. Your daughter has assisted in previous deliveries of puppies, and she knows the procedures for handling newborn puppies. Her girlfriend is over visiting, and they are both absorbed in a TV show. Before you leave, you remind your daughter to keep her eye on the whelping box. When you return 30 minutes later, the girls are still watching TV, but there are drops of blood all over the floor, indicating that your bitch has been walking around the room in heavy labor. As you approach the whelping box, you see your bitch sitting quietly, looking at a dead puppy still encased in its sac, with the placenta attached. Your bitch didn't remove the sac, and your daughter was unaware of the entire episode. Not only is the death of the puppy unnecessary and completely sad, but you also just lost a $2,500 puppy over a 30-minute run to the grocery store. Your daughter is hysterical over the dead puppy, and she blames it on you. She will remember this incident all of her life.

If you understand their limitations and take full responsibility for following up on them and your dogs, your teenagers can be a great asset in your business. A teenager who is interested and demonstrates the ability to make decisions, follow through on commitments, and do a good job, may be given the ultimate reward of breeding his or her own dog. Perhaps an arrangement could be made wherein a percentage of the profits made on the dog could be set aside for future opportunities like education or vocational schooling. Did you know that there are college scholarships awarded through AKC for Junior Showmanship achievements? Did you know that admission to medical school or veterinary school is also based on the student's extracurricular activities, and the potential contributions those activities would make to a medical career? Many veterinarians have a mentoring program in their practice. If your child has an interest in this pursuit, why not capitalize on it through participation in a very enjoyable family activity?

On a personal note, I have foster and adopted children. Working with me in the kennel, they got to start over from "day one," and learn about a mother's natural love. Should the mother dog accidentally lie on a puppy and kill it, by talking about it together, they can understand that she did it by mistake, and we can forgive her. I believe this is an important lesson for these children. They need these experiences to heal and to go forward with their lives. They need to forgive what was done to them because of alcohol or drugs and understand that it was done through ignorance, and was not their fault. After all, almost all puppies are either adopted or fostered. These kids can identify with that completely. The fact that the puppies they raise are expensive and desirable can also give the children a sense of special worth and importance.

A word of caution is appropriate here. When dealing with hurt children—those who have experienced abuse and/or neglect, you must be vigilant. These children may be your adopted or foster children or they may be ones you hire to help in some way. Remember that some of these hurt children have issues with animals. Although we may not like to face these issues, it is imperative that you supervise these children around your dogs. If you are thinking about doing foster care or adoption while you are breeding dogs, you would do best to make sure the agency knows that you will not accept children with a history of problems with animals. This is not the appropriate forum to discuss these issues, but psychotherapists can provide insight into this matter.

When one of my foster sons was about 12, he was helping me hold onto a bitch that was tied with my stud dog in the act of breeding. We had laid the pair down on a blanket. He was holding my stud dog's head in his lap while I held the bitch and stroked her head, talking to her softly. This particular stud dog usually tied for about 45 minutes. As we sat waiting for them to release, he asked me, "Do people have ties like the dogs do?" Without taking a moment to consider the opportunity I was presented with this question, I said, "No, people do not tie when they have intercourse. It is unique to dogs. I don't know of any other mammal that is tied during mating." I immediately realized that I had completely missed this once-in-a-lifetime opportunity to keep this boy celibate for quite a few more years. All I had to say was, "Of course they do." That is one of the few times that I have regretted my honesty!

The Rewards of Working Together as a Family

When children make an effort and truly contribute to the family business in a measurable and obvious manner, it automatically creates genuine self-esteem in the child, pride by the parents, and it impresses puppy buyers, too. When this happens, another lesson is in order for these kids—compensation for a job well done. You must provide opportunities for them to gain monetary compensation. This is an important lesson in life, which will stand them in good stead in future employment or entrepreneurial endeavors. It is—have a plan, work to implement the plan, and build a strong financial base. These are the building blocks for a life free from boredom, free from financial restraints, and free to explore their unique talents. You will be able to convey these lessons to your children through your example.

Rely on Your Dogs, Too

I have talked about incorporating your family into your kennel operation. I want to close this chapter by giving you this important bit of wisdom that I have gained over my years as a professional dog breeder, foster/adoptive parent, and a biological parent.

Truthfully, you need the therapeutic benefit of your dogs to sustain healthy relationships with your human family. Your dogs can get you through hard times and difficult choices. They have a deep reservoir of love that they will freely share with you and your family. Spend some quiet time with your dogs each day. This is the major pay-off of being a professional dog breeder—you can justify hanging out with a half dozen or more of your best friends everyday, soaking up their admiration and affection for you! How many people do you know who can boast that kind of a job? If anyone asks you why you are sitting on a blanket in the sunshine in the middle of the day with six tired dogs sleeping around you next to a pond, tell them you are "working."

Chapter 9

HIRING AND HANDLING OUTSIDE HELP

Before you go and hire someone—anyone—make sure you really need the help. Has your business grown enough to support this major expenditure? Ask any small business owner, and they will tell you that the largest expense of their business is payroll. Going from a family run business to one with employees is a precarious milestone in the growth of your operation. You need to budget seriously for this—and absolutely know that you can generate enough income to justify it.

Entrepreneurs do not hire employees to avoid doing the work themselves, they hire employees because they know they can increase their business substantially by adding laborers; or they can improve and grow their business faster by adding employees who possess talents that they are lacking, thus freeing themselves to do what they do best for their business. For example, if I am a master dog groomer who can groom a dog so well that it will absolutely win at the dog show, I might hire a weekly bookkeeper to keep my paperwork straight so I can concentrate on doing my thing. If, in the long run, the paperwork being done while I was grooming the dogs translates into having Champion breeding stock to increase the price of my puppies—and thereby paying many times over for the bookkeeper—then that is superior business management. One of the major mantras in the corporate business world and in the real estate industry is "highest and best use." This refers to putting all available resources of time, money, and physical assets to the best possible utilization for the greatest return on investment.

About Independent Contractors

Independent contractor labor refers to workers who do not fall under regular employee rules or description. According to the IRS, if the worker is an independent contractor, you (payer) have the right to control or direct only the result of the work done by him or her, not the means and methods of accomplishing the result. Generally independent contractors work with or for more businesses than just yours and usually perform distinct tasks on a regular basis (cleaning and bookkeeping are two typical examples). An independent contractor essentially is running his own business, and is responsible for keeping track of and reporting his own income and taxes. So when you use independent contractors instead of employees, you do not withhold income taxes, social security, health insurance, or other employee taxes. There is no need to pay overtime or holiday pay. Using an independent contractor can therefore result in a very substantial reduction in cost, paperwork, and hassle for you. You can research the legal definition of independent contractors at www.irs.gov/businesses/small.

Small businesses often run afoul of the IRS by using independent contractors when in fact they are functioning as employees. If they only work for you, if you totally control what they do, if they do not have distinct task responsibilities, then the IRS or your state tax department may declare them as employees and you will become liable for collecting and paying payroll taxes, perhaps even retroactively. So tread carefully—you should discuss this issue with your accountant and check the IRS web site noted above to make sure you are within the tax law definition of contracted labor.

About Employees

If you are doing well enough to justify hiring employees, it is a good sign that you are doing it right. But remember that this is a critical and costly stage in the growth of your business. Be cautious. Recognize also that while hiring employees represents a major step forward to your business, you need to make sure that you have the right personality to be an employer. Can you make sure that your employees work for you and your business, and not the other way around? It is amazing how often the roles can be reversed. Can you be tough minded? Would you be able to fire someone who disregarded the rules of your business? Do you always avoid conflicts and disagreements? Are you able to stand up for what you believe in? Are you a leader? Can you inspire someone who is working for an hourly wage or salary? You really need to ask yourself these questions before taking on employees.

In the dog-breeding world, an employee hired to manage your kennels, or to run a kennel shift that includes feeding, administering medications, cleaning, grooming, managing your bitches through the whelping process, or doing puppy watches must have a special understanding and empathy for dogs. Employees need special skills and training if they are hired to deal with the public by handling any of the following: sales, boarding, grooming, stud services, training classes, registrations, warrantee contracts, and organizing special clinics and seminars. Remember that they are your face to your customers—they represent you and your business reputation. When you find a loyal and good employee, you have found gold. It is better to reward an exceptional employee with bonuses and perks than to drastically increase their base pay rate. This leaves them always striving to earn brownie points and receive more goodies.

If you make the decision to hire employees and you want your business to function properly, it is critical that you carefully supervise and train them during a probationary period until they have proven their skills and integrity.

Prepare an Employee Policy and Procedures Manual

Prepare an employee policy and procedures manual in which all of your rules and procedures are clearly described including (if applicable):

- the original employee application
- hiring data
- a complete job description
- wage and salary details including pay ranges, raises, bonus incentives and overtime
- holiday, sick leave, and vacation policy
- the employee statement of compliance agreement (make sure all employees sign it and receive a copy)
- relevant IRS forms
- proof of citizenship or eligibility to work in the United States
- time cards
- dress codes
- shifts
- equipment
- breaks
- telephone usage
- computer access
- fraternization rules relating to other employees and customers
- sexual harassment laws

- obscene language
- racial discrimination or religious harassment of fellow employees
- personal hygiene
- reporting requirements
- training and educational reimbursements
- reimbursement rates for mileage for driving one's own car for business purposes
- theft
- tardiness
- discounts on services or products offered by the business
- and anything else that's applicable to your particular business

If you can think of any other categories or you have an employee manual from another business that you can reference, do it. Make sure there is nothing illegal in the manual. Preface it with a disclaimer that basically says that if anything in the manual is subsequently found to be illegal, it was by no means intentional or malicious in content. Put a price on the manual that will be deducted from the employee's last paycheck if it is not returned in good condition and complete when they leave your employment.

The reason that employers require reimbursement or return of the P&P Manual is to lend it value and seriousness. It isn't just an obligatory notebook that someone is forced to provide to fulfill a legal requirement. It has value, is taken seriously, gets periodic updates put into it, and is a valuable training tool. This is the "bible" of your employee/employer relationship. In a small business it functions as your operational manual as well. If you design it properly, it leaves nothing to your employee's discretion and gives them a source for answers to almost all of their personnel questions or issues. It establishes a chain-of-command, procedures for filing complaints, and sets the tone of your professional approach to your business. In the event that a manager leaves, the P&P manual will provide continuity. Rules do not fluctuate every time an employee leaves your employment. Everyone is working under the same set of rules. It is simply a superior business practice. No matter how small your business may be—always act like it is a growing business and not a midget in its industry.

A Breeder Secret

A Non-Compete Clause
There should be a non-competition clause in your employee compliance agreement that says they cannot open a breeding (or boarding) kennel within a certain number of miles from your place of business and that they cannot contact your customers or solicit their business for a minimum of three years from the date they leave your employment. If they do, you have the right to sue for violating the employee agreement that they signed.

Additional Employee Policy Recommendations

Kennel workers should be instructed in safety procedures. They should be issued safety goggles. All hazardous chemicals should be described to them, and they should be taught how to handle them in a safe manner. You can obtain all necessary information for handling of hazardous chemicals from the manufacturer. Conduct a fire drill once a month. All employees should be shown all of the exits from the facility and where the fire extinguishers are located. Post a diagram of the facility with exits clearly marked. Require CPR and first aid certification on humans and on dogs.

All employees should be required to pass a drug test as a condition of employment. You can buy the home kits to do drug tests on employees or contact a company that does this service (that would probably be more expensive). This is a voluntary test, but if they don't do it, you don't have to hire them. Trust me, you don't want anyone using drugs on your premises. Check with your insurance company as to what other things you can require that would lower your risk and your insurance premiums.

If you can afford it, install video cams in your kennels so that your employees know that their interactions with the dogs are being monitored.

Employees should not be allowed to bring their friends or family onto your property without prior permission.

Employees should sign a confidentiality agreement that states they cannot disclose any personal information about you or your family to anyone.

If you run into a slow time in your business due to the economy or unexpected problems, you don't have to reduce their base pay or let them go. You can sit down with them, explain what is going on and why, and ask them to be patient and hang in there with you until things get back on track. Usually an employee who feels that you have been honest and given them the option to stay to help the business will take a temporary cut in pay, or take a temporary leave without pay. Since you may have rewarded them in the past with bonuses and vacation packages or other incentives, there is a good chance they will support your efforts to economize if they can until the crises passes. If you fall ill or have an accident that disables you for a period of time, these are the employees who will come to your rescue—because you were with fair them.

Hiring Outside Services

Periodically, you will need to hire outside services for your business. In some cases you can hire an independent contractor to perform some of these services as they can function much like an outside service. The following is a list of professional services that you may require:

- Plumbers
- Roofers
- Appliance repairmen
- Pet sitters
- Computer repairmen
- Lawyers

- Accountants
- Professional dog handlers
- Delivery services
- Glass repairmen
- Painters
- Landscapers
- Contractors
- Decorators
- Merchandisers
- Writers (ad copy)
- Photographers
- Advertising and marketing firms
- Graphic designers
- Veterinarians
- Vet technicians
- Canine midwife
- Dog trainers
- Groomers
- Business consultants
- Temp services
- Trash collection
- Security and alarm services

Small businesses and outside services usually work on written agreements. This requires signing basic, temporary service contracts. Be sure to read them carefully, and read the fine print, too. I do not accept the term boiler plate contract—there is always something that may come back to haunt you. Every contract is negotiable and make sure that you can live with it or ask for changes up front in writing. Some of these contracts call for early cancellation fees and penalties, add-on services, and miscellaneous related expenses to be paid for by the customer. Some require a minimum time period, such as a two-year contract. Some provide for periodic unilateral rate increases.

A Breeder Secret

Keep Your Social Security Number to Yourself
I advise you to not contract for services on credit, and if you don't then there is no reason for you to give any of these service providers your social security number or any other credit information (no matter what they say, I believe they sell this information). If they insist, go elsewhere, or offer to pay cash or pay by credit card (which you will pay off when you receive the monthly statement).

Never agree to an arrangement with an outside service provider without a satisfaction guarantee. If you do not want to be locked into a service contract, you might have the option of paying in advance. And if you do agree to pay for the first service in advance, there is no reason for them to care about your credit rating. If they provide good service for a reasonable price, it is understood that, barring a disaster, you will continue to use their services. If you fail to pay, they do not have to provide the service. They may try to hook you with a reduced monthly rate if you contract for two or more years. I would rather pay the full rate and be in charge of my own business than to be locked into doing business with someone I may not be satisfied with—or have to pass on a better offer that may come along. Ask for business references and check them out.

Believe it or not, there are some service contracts that require you to continue to pay for years into the future, even if you go out of business, or your facility burns down, or there is a natural disaster that prevents you from doing business. Many small businesses have been hit by such clauses. When you're considering services, shop around, and read the entire 20 or 30 page contract! They should all have a release clause, which is a 30 day notification cancellation clause that either party to the contract can activate by written notification. If you can't find it, ask for it.

Keeping Your Providers Happy

The best way to reward a good service provider is to send them referrals. Let them know when you are sending a referral. Veterinarians will sometimes give you a flat fee or a percentage discount on your bill for referrals.

Give your regular service providers a nice holiday gift. Two tins of cookies, a bottle of good wine, a fruit basket for the office—something that doesn't cost you an arm and a leg, but definitely promotes continued good service. An office gift is especially nice for the staff and workers who do not get much recognition or high pay all year. Write a nice personal message to the vet techs, the trash collectors, and the gardeners—even if you do not know them by name, you can send a note to their supervisor saying how pleased you are with their service, and asking them to please convey your thanks to those who actually do the work.

Tip the service guys and gals who come out regularly to provide monthly service— they will do a better job for you, and they will be more likely to respond to you in an emergency situation ahead of other customers who do not give them the recognition they deserve. I always ask the name of the person doing the job, offer them a bottle of cold water, and ask them how they like their job. Do I have an ulterior motive? Yes, to some degree, and that is that you never really know where your next puppy sale is coming from. Plumbers and drywall guys, contractors and landscapers actually make a good living—and they might spend $2,000 on a family pet for their kids. One of those other service providers may be working their way through college and in five years may be working for the city or the police department. Life is a game of connections. Make them, enjoy them, and share them. Personally, I have a fascination with people. I really do want to know if they like their job, if they have a family, or if they are going to school. You might be surprised at how many really unique and special people you can meet under the most unassuming circumstances.

Chapter 10

WHAT BREEDERS NEED TO KNOW ABOUT VETERINARY CARE

Today, dogs in the United States have access to better and more state-of-the-art medical care from better educated, better equipped, and more intelligent doctors and technicians than do many people. As a breeder, it is imperative that you take advantage of this by understanding what you need and may need in the future, and arming yourself with not just resources, but with at least one veterinarian (and maybe more) who you trust.

Veterinarians and Breeders

Having a good relationship with a good veterinarian is critically important for breeders. A good vet takes X-rays and reads them, he diagnoses problems accurately, performs complicated lab tests, and trains his own assistants and technicians. Your veterinarian should be an accomplished surgeon who performs surgeries by himself, with only the help of one or two veterinary assistants or veterinary technicians. While performing the surgery, he keeps a watchful eye on the anesthesia being administered by the technician. Most veterinarians today are proficient with sonogram and ultrasound technology—something hardly any human doctor can do accurately, in my opinion.

Not only can your veterinarian handle almost any treatment for your dog, but also most other small animals like cats, rats, guinea pigs, reptiles, and birds. In some cases, he is even equipped to treat exotic animals or farm animals. He does all of this without being able to fully communicate with his patients. Just think about the complexity and diversity of skills, as well as the vast base of knowledge he must have to do his job. All the while he must be vigilant because his patient can, and may, bite him, scratch him, or kick him! What is most amazing is that veterinarians are usually down-to-earth, regular gals and guys, real animal lovers who, even after 30 years of practice, still get teary eyed when they have to euthanize a patient.

To be honest, there are incompetent veterinarians, too. But as a professional dog breeder, you are going to learn how to choose a truly superior veterinarian who is what I refer to as a "breeder friendly" veterinarian, one who will work with you to provide the best care for your dogs and puppies. These vets understand that dog breeders need to perform common veterinary procedures themselves, and often understand veterinary medicine better than some vet techs and assistants. Dog breeders have the opportunity to experience, first hand, many procedures and techniques that are only occasionally observed in a veterinary practice. For example, breeders typically deliver many more litters than any veterinarian will in his lifetime. Breeders supervise many more breeding pairs than any veterinarian. And I can guarantee that as a professional dog breeder you will quickly become an expert in semen collections and artificial inseminations. In fact, my veterinarian used to ask me to do a semen collection on a dog from time to time in exchange for veterinary care. Fresh inseminations do not have to be documented on a special form or performed by a veterinarian (inseminations using frozen or chilled semen do need to be performed by licensed veterinarians).

A Breeder Secret

A Dog's Favorite Veterinarian

A professional breeder I know always had her champion dog bred by artificial insemination. She was afraid that he might pick up a disease from a natural breeding and that he would become obnoxious if he were allowed to actually breed a bitch. I disagree with this theory, but everyone has a right to his or her opinion. She would drive him over to her vet, a few miles from her kennels, have him collected, then return home with the semen to inseminate her females or any visiting females who were there for stud service. The result was that every time she would go anywhere with her dog, she had to take a route that did not go anywhere near her veterinarian's office, because her dog would become very excited if he thought he was going to see his favorite veterinarian!

When you are selecting a veterinarian for his or her competence and breeder-friendliness, take the time to interview everyone closest to your kennels—especially if you are able to get any recommendations about them from other breeders. Your veterinarian should be geographically close enough for you to get to the clinic within 20 or 30 minutes. If not, you will need to have some kind of rapport with a closer veterinarian—even if it is only for back-up. If you live where it may take an hour or more to get to a veterinarian, you may not be in an appropriate location to be raising puppies. Remember that when puppies are being born, everything is accelerated. They only have about eight minutes of oxygen before they must come out and breathe air. If the puppy is so stuck that you cannot get it out dead or alive, remember that there are probably other puppies stuck behind it, and you need a vet NOW! The farther you live from a veterinarian, the better equipped you must be. Later in this chapter I explain how to stock a kennel dispensary.

Recognize that a veterinarian's time is valuable, so make an appointment and pay for it as a scheduled exam. This should give you 15 or 20 minutes to sit down and discuss their philosophy about dog care as well as attitudes regarding professional dog breeders.

When you make your initial appointment over the telephone, ask the receptionist if the vet works with breeders at all or, better yet, if the veterinarian is also a breeder. If she hasn't got a clue as to what you are talking about, this vet is probably not who you are looking for, so move on. When you do arrive at a veterinarian's office for the first time, evaluate the staff. My experience is that bad attitudes on the part of the receptionist, vet tech, or vet assistant can translate into vet bills inflated to reflect the self-importance of the staff and a veterinarian who hasn't got a clue about what goes on in the front office. Obviously, you want to avoid such a situation.

All professional dog breeders should make it a point to know the receptionist, secretary, and all of the techs and assistants by name. This is how you get an appointment in the middle of a busy day at the clinic—because your dog is sick and you are a preferred customer! It could also have something to do with your personal interest in the staff and the huge fruit basket you send each year at Christmas time. Staff people who refuse to be friendly, down-to-earth, cheerful, and especially gentle with your dogs are not the people you want to have to work with in an emergency. They are more likely to turn you down when you really need their help.

Questions for Your Veterinarian

During the time you spend interviewing a prospective veterinarian, be sure to ask him or her these key questions (as well as any others you have that are particular to your needs).

1. How are prescription medications dispensed to dog breeders?

2. Does he or she support you having various prescription medications on hand at your kennel? This is very important because there are times you'll need certain medications before you can get them from the vet. Will the veterinarian support you in having the drugs you need to have on hand? See the list of medications you will need later in this chapter.

3. What is the vet's approach to emergency care—do they handle breeder emergencies, or do they send them to an emergency veterinary clinic? You want to know that if you have an emergency C-section in the middle of the night that your veterinarian will meet you at the clinic, call in the vet techs, and allow

you and some of your breeder friends to help resuscitate the puppies as they are born. In my experience, if you rely on an emergency veterinary 24-hour clinic for a C-section, the chances of you saving your bitch from an emergency spay or even death, and/or saving any of the puppies, is questionable.

4. Will they allow you to accompany your dogs into the back of the clinic for various medical procedures like holding the dog while they do X-rays or calming the dog while they attempt to extract a stuck puppy? The standard excuse for not allowing breeders in the back of the clinic is that insurance doesn't cover it, but I feel that if the veterinarian is that rigid he isn't going to help you or do anything for you as a professional breeder.

5. Will he or she take the time to educate you, to explain a diagnosis, and to include you in the decision-making process regarding your dogs?

6. Will they share relevant veterinary updates with you and keep you current on new medications and procedures that relate to your business?

7. Will the veterinarian consider supplying you with free samples or overstock items? A vet tech at one of the clinics I worked with would save overstock items, free samples, or things like silver nitrate sticks that were nearing their expiration date and give them to me when I would come in for puppy well checks or pre-breeding examinations because my veterinarian told her to take good care of me.

8. Will your veterinarian make house calls in special situations, such as for a recovering bitch with nursing puppies? My veterinarian once left for vacation in Hawaii the day after one of my bitches had a C-section. She wasn't doing so well when he left, and he was worried about leaving her. Can you believe that he called me twice from Hawaii, during his vacation, to check up on her! Now *that* is a remarkable veterinarian! The main reason I hated moving away from Colorado was that I had to leave my veterinarian.

The Care and Keeping of Your Veterinarian

The best way to avoid having your dog poorly treated is to cultivate a good working relationship with your veterinarian so that they feel an obligation to be there for you when you need them! So, all year long, when regular procedures are taking place and you are setting up an appointment, be accommodating, be flexible, never be insistent, be patient when you have to wait in the waiting room way past your appointment time—in other words, be the perfect customer. Always say thank you even though you are paying for their services. Pay your bill immediately and in full—do not quibble over five dollars this way or that way. Don't argue about a bill unless you believe there is a mistake on it. If a vet tech goes above and beyond their normal scope of caring and attention, give them a tip and verbally thank them for their special effort.

Above all, never misrepresent a situation as an emergency if it isn't one. If it's 4:00 a.m. and your bitch had her last puppy at 2:00 a.m. and she is resting comfortably even though you know there is at least one more puppy not yet born, do not call the vet and wake him if your bitch is not in hard labor for at least 20 or 30 minutes without producing a puppy (*that* would be an emergency). Do not wake him up until 6:00 a.m. at the earliest, because he may be in for a C-section delivery at 7:00 a.m. if you can't get your bitch restarted. Call the clinic and alert them of a possible C-section—even if you have to leave a message on the answering machine, try to find out what time the vet gets in and leave a message for him to call you as soon as he arrives.

If you find a breeder-friendly veterinarian, there are lots of nice things you can do for them. First, send them lots of referrals. They deserve at least that. I often recommended my veterinarian for a special award for veterinarians. Though he didn't get it, in my opinion he surely deserved a medal. I always sent him thank-you cards, flowers, fruit for the staff, even a book of dog names for his clinic. I even made up a stud dog notebook for his office. In it was a section for all the popular breeds, with plastic document covers and alphabetical dividers. I put my stud dog's information in it with a photograph. I told his office staff to ask other breeders to add to it until the practice had a good resource for healthy stud dogs.

So This Doesn't Happen to You

As a professional breeder, you will experience many great and wonderful things, and many frightening and ghastly things. I share these stories for your perspective and to make it real how important it is to find not just an "OK" veterinarian, but one whom you really trust.

In at least two cases, if I hadn't been a knowledgeable, experienced dog breeder, I would have lost my dog through the incompetence of a 24-hour emergency clinic. I refused their diagnosis and treatment, pointed out why they were wrong, and told them exactly what they needed to do to save my dog. In one case, I was able to keep a puppy alive by telling the young vet on duty what to do until the morning when my regular vet could perform the correct surgery. In the other case I ended up with a spayed showgirl because the veterinarian who performed the C-section had obviously never done one before, and he lacerated her uterus. To save her life, I told him to remove the uterine horns and sew her up as quickly as possible. She was so close to death that I doubted she would make it off the table.

I also had to force them to allow me to resuscitate the 10 puppies that would surely have died if left to the clinic's inexperienced staff. I stood in the middle of the clinic with the puppies laid out on a towel in front of me and showed the vet techs how to resuscitate a puppy correctly and quickly. Thank goodness, I had brought bulb syringes, Dopram, and dental floss with me. The stitching on my bitch was so poorly done that it was oozing blood when I loaded her into the back of my van. She ended up with a raging infection, barely alive, and on an I.V. drip in my home clinic for two weeks. My regular veterinarian made house calls and prescribed heavy-duty antibiotics and some painkillers that would not completely sedate the puppies that were nursing. I supervised the nursing puppies and supplemented them with yogurt and puppy formula. I just needed them to get the first days of mother's colostrum for immunity purposes. It was the worst mess I had ever seen in an E.R. in my entire life. Truthfully, except for the anesthesia, I could have done a better surgery myself at my kennels— and my kennel nursery was cleaner than the emergency clinic operating room!

Another time, I ended up taking another breeder's bitch to the veterinarian who normally cared for her horses. She had to go to work and her bitch was in hard labor, but only one dead puppy had been born. The bitch had been in labor for several days and was exhausted. I watched the veterinarian take his time prepping the bitch for surgery. He slowly ate his lunch, chatted with his wife on the telephone, and finally got the bitch on the operating table. He didn't even bother to wear a mask or wash his hands. While his vet techs ate burgers in the emergency room, wiping the ketchup and mustard on the surgical drapes, he very slowly and methodically removed eight dead puppies from the bitch. I'm not even sure they were all actually dead, but I watched him toss them into the trash can one after the other. I was sick to my stomach. The moral of this story is, take your dogs to a vet you know will do his or her best for your dog, and don't take them to a horse doctor.

Pharmaceutical Supplies and Resources

Setting up a well-stocked dispensary and an in-house clinic validates your claim to being a professional dog breeder. It imparts confidence that you can deal with many different medical situations and emergencies yourself instead of running to the veterinarian for every little scratch or tummy upset. Gradually, as your confidence increases, you will find yourself learning how to do more and more procedures yourself.

Don't be shy about asking your veterinarian and other professional breeders to teach you. When I first started breeding dogs, I learned tube feeding from a substitute veterinarian who was covering for the regular veterinarian while he was away at a seminar. I had been very upset about not being able to save puppies who were losing weight and crying, but were too weak to nurse. She put her arm around me and squeezed me. She looked into my eyes and said, "You are going to tube feed these puppies, and they are going to be fine. I promise. I am going to teach you how to feed them and how to hydrate them subcutaneously. You can do this; you are a smart lady who can do anything you put your mind to." I think she was one of the kindest and most wonderful people that I have crossed paths with in my 60-plus years! I went back to my kennel and brought the box of puppies to the clinic, where she spent two hours with me, tube feeding the litter, stimulating them all to go potty, checking them for dehydration and, one by one, having me hydrate them subcutaneously. At the end of two hours, all the puppies were sleeping peacefully in the warming box. They were clean, full of formula, and no one was crying. Not even me! I was grinning from ear to ear, and had gained the confidence that I needed to raise this litter of puppies.

I will never forget her patience and kindness. I have paid that good deed forward so many times that I have lost count of all the novice breeders I have taught to tube-feed puppies. I put that procedure into my DVD, *Whelping Healthy Puppies*, as another way to pay it forward. You, too, must always be ready to teach other breeders these types of procedures. Tube feeding saves lives. The more breeders who know how to do this, the more puppies will survive. Although I have it on my DVD and some other breeders have also demonstrated this procedure in their books and videos, it really should be taught hands-on. The first time I did it, my hands were shaking so badly that I had to struggle just to get the tube down the puppy's throat.

Getting Organized

Even in a relatively small space, you can actually do quite a lot. You need a small cupboard to secure your medications and supplies. An examination table or grooming table is a necessity. Good lighting is critical. A fluorescent lighting fixture would be the best—place it directly overhead. You can utilize pegboard on the wall to hang some of your equipment if you don't have the luxury of wall cabinets. I have used transparent shoe holders that hang on the back of a door and have about 30 pockets—they hold all types of items. I have used the top of my washer and dryer, with a big towel thrown over them, as an examination and grooming area for puppies. Your dispensary/clinic can also double as a grooming area. Make sure to disinfect the area before doing any medical procedures.

You need to be careful about how you store and secure your medical supplies—especially if you have children or cats around who could get into them. If there are other people working at your kennels or older children in the area, put your medications under lock and key. A small refrigerator is a definite plus, as it allows you to have chilled items close at hand instead of running to your regular refrigerator and trying to keep those items separated from your food items.

You have to have a way to secure a dog on a table. This can be done with a slip lead that attaches to a hook on the wall or to a grooming arm that is secured to the table. Be careful not to leave a dog attached to anything while on the table unless you are with the dog because it's possible that they might jump off of the table and hang themselves. If you are not using a traditional grooming table, make sure to put some type of rubber mat or other non-slip material like a throw rug with a rubber backing or a large thick towel onto the surface so the dog will not slip and slide on it. Have a shelf or counter top nearby where you can place the supplies you need for your procedure. Some grooming tables have a shelf on the bottom, but I find it inconvenient to reach while you are trying to apply medications or perform various procedures on the dog.

The best of all worlds is to have a bathroom set up just for the dogs where you can bathe and groom them. Not everyone has that luxury. If you do, have the tub elevated so the top edge of the side is at your waist level, and be sure to install a top-quality spray nozzle so that you can bathe dogs easily. A hinged or removable cover for the bathtub can double as a work surface. For small dogs, even a deep sink would be a wonderful asset. If you are showing dogs, a mirror in the grooming area is definitely helpful so you can observe all sides of the dog and see its general outline from the other side.

Ventilation is important. You should have some type of ceiling or wall fan that pulls the air to the outside, and some type of auxiliary heating that you can control easily. A high-volume hair dryer is a wonderful tool. It can be mounted on the wall or on the table. A professional hair dryer is not only for regular grooming, but also for quickly cleaning up a bitch before and after whelping. If you have an area available, you can wash her down with warm water and soap, then quickly blow her dry before she gives birth. Repeat the procedure again after all the puppies are born. It will go a long way in keeping your whelping box clean, avoiding teat infections, and maintaining a pleasant environment in your nursery. After a bitch is finished whelping, I usually clean off her rear the next morning and wash off her teats with soap and water, then rinse well, and dry.

A Breeder's Medical Supplies

Designate a place in your kennel where you will keep your first aid kit and supplies. In addition to the items listed below, you should have a few key phone numbers available. These are your veterinarian's regular telephone number as well as his emergency number or cell phone; the telephone number and directions to the local emergency veterinary clinic; and the hot line for the Animal Poison Control Center, which is (888) 426-4435 (a fee does apply). As I said earlier in this chapter, only the very best and dedicated vets will give you their cell phone number. You must promise not to use it for non-emergency calls, but do be a bit pushy about this—it could save your dog's life.

The medical supplies you must have on your premises should include tools and medications that will assist you in a variety of situations. This alphabetical list includes the standard items that should be in a first aid kit, as well as what a breeder should have on hand:

1. Activated charcoal
2. Antibacterial ointment
3. Antibacterial wipes
4. Assortment of scissors (blunt ended; small curved; suture removal scissors)
5. Baby formula bottles (either small animal feeders or premature baby bottles)
6. Bandages and gauze
7. Benadryl
8. Betadine solution
9. Bitch pants for bitches in season and sanitary pads to fit
10. Boric acid
11. Bulb syringe (baby nasal size with the soft rubber tip, not the hard plastic tip)
12. Centrifuge tubes to attach to baggies or plastic vaginas
13. Clipboard (washable) for charting temperatures and weights
14. Cotton balls—sterile
15. Cotton swabs—sterile
16. Dental floss, unwaxed (for tying off umbilical cords)
17. Digital thermometer with sterile plastic disposable covers
18. Ear cleaning solution (see recipe section later in this chapter)
19. Elastic bandages and butterfly clips
20. Elizabethan plastic collar (appropriate size)
21. Epinephrine injection for allergic reactions to stings and medications
22. First Aid Book for dogs
23. French tubes (for tube feeding newborns) in appropriate sizes for specific breeds
24. Gloves, Latex or Plastic—sterile (keep sealed until ready to use)
25. Glycerin—small bottle
26. Hair clippers
27. Hand disinfectant

28. Hand towels (two dozen, small white)

29. Health records (you can get these free when you order vaccines)

30. Hemostats for clamping the umbilical cords—at least two

31. Hydrogen peroxide

32. Ivomec injectable cattle wormer 1% (never give to Collies or Collie mixes)

33. KY Jelly (not Vaseline™ or udder balm, which are not sterile)

34. Lactated ringer solution or sterile saline solution (for puppy hydration)

35. Large and small heating pads with temperature controls

36. Liquid suture and a suturing kit

37. Muzzle (properly sized for your dog breed)

38. Mylanta™ (for external treatment of hot spots and rashes)

39. Nemex II (wormer for puppies and bitches)

40. No-rub contact lens cleaner (for cleaning eyes and removing tear stains)

41. Nutra Stat™ (a glucose treatment for bitches)

42. NutriCal™ paste (a high-calorie dietary supplement for mother and puppies)

43. Oxygen tank with regulator (do not use a non-medical tank)

44. Pain medications (per your veterinarian—do not give a dog Ibuprophen or Aleve)

45. Pediatric cough syrup *without alcohol* for severe kennel cough symptoms

46. Pill splitter

47. Plastic aquarium tubing that fits on 30cc syringes (for A.I.)

48. Plastic baggies or a roll of artificial plastic vaginas (veterinarian supply)

49. Pliers—needle-nose to remove thorns and porcupine quills

50. Propylene Glycol

51. Rubber bands (to secure plastic baggie to centrifuge tubes for artificial insemination)

52. Sanitary pads wrapped individually (for applying pressure to bleeding wounds)

53. Scale for weighing puppies

54. Self-adhesive bandages (Vet Wraps)

55. Silver nitrate sticks sealed in plastic (to chemically cauterize cuts and wounds)

56. Splints to fit the dog's legs—at least two padded and wrapped

57. Sterile pipettes to use in A.I. procedure

58. Stethoscope

59. Styptic powder

60. Syringes with screw-on needles (25- and 22–gauge sizes, one box of 100 each)

61. Syringes without needles, for use with tubing (30cc's and 20cc's)

62. Syrup of Ipecac

63. Vaccines

64. Water bottles for ice or hot water (soft type)

65. Wintergreen rubbing alcohol

Professional breeders give their own inoculations to their puppies. There are five reasons for this:

1. To avoid taking very young puppies to the veterinarian clinic where exposure to contagious diseases is a serious risk factor. Scales used to weigh the puppies are often not sterilized; examination tables may or may not be adequately wiped down. The vet may be using antibacterial disinfectants, but not anti-viral cleaning products that are more expensive and usually have to air-dry to be effective.

2. Because veterinarians charge high prices for an inexpensive vaccine/procedure which actually costs less than $2.00 per injection, .20¢ for the syringe w/needle, and takes 30 seconds to mix and administer.

3. Sometimes veterinarians use vaccines that have been compromised by incorrect storage procedures because the vaccines may sit on the floor of the clinic for hours or even days before the vet techs or office personnel open them, inventory them, and put them in the refrigerator. In a busy clinic these boxes may not be opened for quite some time. These "spoiled" vaccines are ineffective and puppies come down with diseases despite vaccinations. Breeders want to handle this important matter themselves and do not depend on technicians who may not take it as seriously as a breeder would. Breeders wait for vaccine delivery by FedEx or UPS and immediately move them from their ice packed chests to refrigeration. Vaccines delivered to breeders are delivered by next-day air on ice from the manufacturer or distributor. The vaccine has a lot number and date on each vial so if there is any problem with the vaccine, it is traceable back to the point of origin. The breeder has complete information that is not routinely provided by veterinarians on the health record. This information is entered on the puppy's individual record and is provided to the new owner. Breeders use a fresh needle for each puppy to avoid possible contamination. Some veterinarians dispense the vaccine from one large syringe to the entire litter of puppies.

4. Veterinarians may also purchase the least expensive vaccines that they can find. Some people believe that these cheaper vaccines have an inexpensive dilute used to mix them—which is a carcinogenic substance and this may be why we are seeing increased incidences of injection site sarcomas in relatively young dogs. Breeders also rub the injection site thoroughly to dissipate the vaccine under the skin—this may also defend again injection site sarcomas. It also keeps the area from swelling and causing pain. I have never seen a veterinarian massage the injection site.

5. Veterinarians may use large gauge needles to give inoculations or other injections to all the animals they treat. Except for what they use on horses and cows, they tend to use the same size needle for a St. Bernard full-grown dog as they

use on a six week old Terrier puppy. Breeders purchase small gauge needles that inflict much less pain on the young puppies. You can see them flinch when the vet gives them an injection—but when I give them one they don't even feel it. Using a smaller gauge needle increases the time it takes to fill a syringe with the mixed vaccine and to administer it—and veterinarians always seem to be in a hurry.

Giving subcutaneous injections is one of the easiest things that breeders do. I have never met a professional breeder who did not give their puppies their inoculations in-house. It is true that some breeders purchase modified-live vaccines while other use a more holistic approach and order only killed vaccines that, although safer, are less effective in creating immunity. In different parts of the country, and in different seasons of the year, there are different recommended protocols. Vaccine manufacturers and distributors make recommendations. It is the breeder's decision as to what vaccine to use, and when to administer it. Whatever their choice is—they would normally purchase the vaccines in packages of 25 individual doses, or bottles of 10 doses per bottle. These can be stored in the refrigerator up to a year (there is an expiration date on each bottle).

The only "breeders" I have met who take their puppies to the veterinarian for inoculations are inexperienced and are not being mentored by a responsible breeder. These people do not tube feed failing puppies, do not hydrate, do not remove dewclaws, do not administer wormers, and do not give inoculations. They don't know how to prepare a slide, or even how to take their dog's temperature or fill out a weight chart for the litter. They should not be breeding dogs. They usually have high mortality rates in their puppies. They continue to breed solely because they want the money. They have the vet give the *shots* (as they call them) so that they can tell buyers that the puppies "got all their shots" and sometimes they even have the vet remove the dewclaws and "stitch" the wound—a fairly barbaric procedure considering all the alternative methods of dewclaw removal available today.

Proper Use and Storage of Medications

Since you are going to have medications on hand, be careful about expiration dates, correct labeling, and correct storage. Keep an accurate inventory and dispensing log of all your medications to make sure they are appropriately controlled. I find that keeping good records clears my mind of extraneous details so that I can concentrate on the important issues at hand. Knowing that I have detailed records of all medications given to my dogs is reassuring, and also provides good information for the future about what works and what doesn't. Allergic reactions in individual dogs should be recorded also, so that they will not be given the same medications in the future. Check each dog's records prior to dispensing medications.

You should also know when to re-order medical supplies. Find out what the shelf life is of various prescription medications; that way, if you don't use all of the medication prescribed, you will know if you can keep it on hand for the future, or if you need to discard it. Never use old pill bottles with old labels on them to store different pills, and make sure to store all medication away from children and other animals. Do not flush medications down the toilet or pour them down the sink, as this could contaminate the ground water. Ask your veterinarian how to dispose of them safely—they may let you drop them off at the clinic where they dispose of toxic waste properly.

Prescription medications that you may need can be obtained through your veterinarian if you have developed a good working relationship with him. If your veterinarian refuses your request, you may obtain them from sources in Canada or Mexico where a prescription may not be required. There are also on-line sources. Be aware that not all on-line suppliers are legitimate and quality control is always a concern when you do not have personal knowledge of the source. If you network with other experienced breeders, they may assist you in identifying reliable sources of medications as well. You need to know that even a prescription from your veterinarian may be better than actually purchasing the medications from the veterinarian clinic. Prescriptions filled at some of the national chain pharmacies can be up to 50% less expensive than buying the same medication from your veterinarian.

By using the less expensive capsules and compounding them yourself with canned pet food, roasted liver, or cheese, you can save yourself a lot of money and make the medication more palatable for your dogs. Medications purchased from your veterinarian may not be compounded either—and you may have to do this yourself when dealing with a particularly bad tasting or smelly medication.

The following list features some of the prescription medications that you need to have on hand:

1. Amphoral (for puppy diarrhea).

2. Baytril (not for Collies or Collie mixes).

3. Calsorb or injection type calcium. Rapidly absorbing calcium supplement for bitches showing signs of eclampsia during whelping or lactation.

4. Dopram. A cardio stimulant for stressed newborn puppies who are not breathing and have no pulse.

5. Doxycycline.

6. Oxygen and Regulator.

7. Oxytocin. Obtain this from your veterinarian just prior to whelping date—for secondary inertia during labor, and for a clean-out shot after whelping is completed. Your vet will give you the correct dosage for the size of your bitch. You need at least three doses on hand, and these must be kept refrigerated.

8. Penicillin.

9. Terramycin (eye ointment).

Equipment to Assist with Medical Procedures

A well-equipped infirmary will save you hundreds of dollars and frantic trips to the veterinarian or emergency clinic in the middle of the night or on weekends and holidays. It not only gives you confidence to deal with the day-to-day health care needs of your dogs, but also helps you develop a solid preventative maintenance program. Having the right equipment and the knowledge to perform necessary procedures and tests is one of the major differences between a professional dog breeder and a hobbyist. You will have a much lower incidence of "misses" in your bitches and visiting bitches, a major reduction in parasitical and bacterial diseases, and the ability to properly manage your stud dogs. On-site identification and diagnosis of health issues that arise will allow you to address these issues before they escalate into serious threats. Having the right equipment will reduce the mortality rate of your puppies significantly.

The following list includes some recommended equipment:

1. **Centrifuge machine.** Most breeders don't have one, and it isn't absolutely necessary, but it can be helpful for spinning down various bodily liquids to prepare slides. Look for a used one from a medical office or clinic or just plan to get one when you find one or can afford one.

2. **Dehumidifier.** For humid and muggy climates.

3. **Dremel set nail grinder.** So much better than nail clippers.

4. **Fecal flotation system.**

5. **Hair dryer.** High volume with or without a heat setting.

6. **Humidifier.** Handy for dry climates or sick dogs.

7. **Incubator Box.** See building instructions below.

8. **Methylene blue stain.**

9. **Microscope (400X or stronger) with its own light source.** Offer to pay a vet tech to show you how to do vaginal smears, sperm counts, fecal tests, and so on. If you have a friend who is a registered nurse or a lab technician, he or she can demonstrate these procedures. Your other option is to take a basic lab class at a local community college; by doing this, you will be technically far ahead of almost all breeders. Some breeders even learn to perform basic blood tests.

10. **Microwave oven.** To warm towels, food, and medications.

11. **Nebulizer.** For dispensing medications via a fine mist. (Expensive but kits are available).

12. **Refrigerator.** Put your meds in a closed plastic container.

13. **Slides.**

14. **Whelping box.** With an attached floor heating unit, or a heated whelping nest. Build a solid large box that will be used for many years! For your personal comfort, it's nice to have a coffee pot, T.V. with a DVD player, cell phone or cordless phone, wall clock, thermostat on the wall of the whelping box, a small, very short stool to sit on in the whelping box, and a good friend to keep you company and assist.

Construction of the Incubator Box

Purchase a semi transparent 3'x 1.5'x 1' plastic bin with a detachable white lid. Drill 12 round holes 1" in diameter spread evenly into the lid. Drill a hole 2" in diameter in one side of the bin near a bottom corner. Disinfect the bin with a very mild bleach solution and allow it to air dry. Purchase a large heating pad with a regulator. Cover it with an old pillowcase and put it in the bottom of the bin. Pass the plug of the heating pad through the bottom hole of the bin. Place soft bedding on top of the heating pad (not too thick). Set the control to "low" and plug it into an outlet close to the whelping box. You now have the perfect place to put a chilled puppy, puppies you want to put aside while the mother is delivering their littermates, orphan puppies, or a place where puppies can stay warm and dry while you are cleaning the whelping box. This is also the box to use if you must transport puppies to the veterinary clinic. Just remember to plug it back in when you get to the vet. For large breeds you may need two of these boxes.

A to Z of Medical Procedures Handled by Breeders

You're reading this book because you are already a breeder or want to become one of the highest quality. So that you understand what it is you're getting into, I share this (partial) list of procedures that professional breeders routinely do themselves. Depending on the size and extent of your breeding program—and, of course, your dogs—you may be doing fewer or more of these.

Artificial Insemination. Perform artificial insemination, whether from semen collected from the stud dog or an actual insemination and elevation of the bitch. This is a detailed topic, and I suggest you study medical references and other available books on this subject to learn it properly. Essentially, you need to know how to collect semen and how to deposit it into a bitch. It isn't that difficult—but it isn't something you can really learn from a book. You should have an experienced breeder teach you how to do it—or at least allow you to observe the process at their kennels. Anyone with a champion stud dog will be collecting semen on a regular basis and doing A.I.s at their kennels.

If you are going to perform an A.I. on a bitch that you do not own, be sure to get written and signed permission ahead of time and make sure the owners initial a clause that says you are not responsible for any medical complications that may arise as a result of the A.I. procedure. Also, if you do not want a stud owner to perform an A.I. on a bitch you are having bred at their kennels, you need to state that in your stud service agreement. Just write a note on the bottom of the page saying that you wish to be notified before any A.I. procedure is initiated.

Take vaginal smears and prepare a slide to look at under the microscope. If you don't know how to stain and prepare a slide, ask the vet tech to show you. You'll need to learn this procedure for many other microscopic examinations as well. When you look at a slide from a bitch in heat, you are looking to pinpoint her fertile time so that you can facilitate a quick and easy breeding which will produce a litter of puppies. Most bitches are ready to breed between the tenth and twelfth day of their heat cycle. Some are ready earlier and some much later. I had a bitch named Lady who was never ready before the 19th day and was only fertile for two days. She produced huge litters of ten and twelve puppies and became pregnant every time she was bred.

To help you pinpoint the time, let's say that on the ninth day of her season, the bitch is "flagging," i.e. putting her tail to one side when you touch her above her tail. You would use a long, sterile swab to get a good vaginal smear and prepare a slide. Looking at it under the microscope, you can expect to see uniformly round cells with uniform nuclei (centers) that resemble the breakfast cereal Cheerios. This would signify that she is not quite ready to breed. On the eleventh day, she is still flagging and seems much more eager to play and posture (stiff legs and a bouncy attitude). You take another smear, and this time the cells look irregular and the nuclei are also not centered and are irregular in shape—some almost look square, resembling the cereal cornflakes. This means that the bitch is ready to breed. We refer to these cells as "cornified" (having corners) so in the world of dogs, we call that "Cornflakes." A helpful memory tip is that with Cheerios she is not ready to breed, but with Cornflakes she is ready to breed. There is nothing wrong with breeding her early if your stud dog will comply. Sperm live for five to seven days.

Birthing. Attend to the birth of the puppies, including turning and grasping stuck puppies, performing vaginal exams, and clamping and cutting umbilical cords.

Cleaning Ears. Clean infected ears and treat them with the following solution: mix one bottle of wintergreen rubbing alcohol with two tablespoons of boric acid powder. Mix well, shaking the bottle vigorously until all the powder is dissolved. Add two tablespoons of glycerin to the mixture, and shake well again. Fill a sterile cotton ball with this mixture and, holding the dog's head up, squeeze out the contents of the soaked cotton ball into the dog's ear. Massage the area directly under the dog's ear— you should hear a swishing sound as you massage the lower part of the ear canal. The dog may whine a bit, as it does burn if your dog has inflammation or sores in the ears. Do both ears. I take my dogs outdoors to do this, because they immediately want to shake their heads—and lots of debris will be spraying out. This is an old hunter's remedy used by most professional breeders (especially Sporting dog breeders). The wintergreen alcohol disinfects and dries out the ear, and smells good. The boric acid kills the fungus inside the ear, and the glycerin makes the mixture adhere to the inside of the ear canal. I promise you that in 90 percent of cases, if you do this procedure once a day for 10 days, your dog's long bout with ear pain and fungus will be ended. Also, repeat this remedy whenever you take your dog swimming. After swimming you need to dry out the ear and kill any fungus that entered the ear with the water. Once a week, you should always put a cotton ball around your index or little finger (depending on the size of your dog) and wipe out the ear as far as you can reach. The ball should come out almost completely clean with no brown or black debris or wax. If it isn't clean, repeat the treatment until it is clear. Do not put warm oil or any type of petroleum jelly in the ears of your dog as it just creates a warm, damp area for fungus and bacteria to multiply. You need to promote dryness inside the ears.

Dewclaws. Remove dewclaws and cauterize the wound.

Docking and Cropping. Dock tails (and, for some breeders, crop, or trim, the ears).

Euthanizing Newborn Puppies. Humanely euthanizing defective or malformed newborn puppies is painful, but necessary. Here is my advice—if the puppy has a cleft palate, badly deformed legs, or has intestines on the outside of its abdominal cavity (commonly referred to as a toothpaste puppy), the humane thing to do is to wrap this puppy in newspaper as soon as it is born (when you see the defect), and place it gently in the freezer. It will go to sleep and expire very quickly, without pain or suffering. If you stay up all night trying to save the pup, you will get attached to it during the time you are working on it. If you've kept a deformed or defective puppy overnight there is no way you can euthanize it yourself. You will be forced to take it to the veterinarian to have it put down and this is just too emotional.

Heartworm prevention. Almost all professional breeders mix their own heartworm preventative, as the commercially prepared type is very expensive. I am not telling you to do this. Check with your veterinarian first. I am only going to tell you what I do. I mix this 9:1 ratio, but you can double check the formula with your veterinarian or in a veterinary pharmaceutical text to be sure. It is 9 parts of propylene glycol to 1 part of 1% injectable Ivomec cattle/swine (available from Revival Animal) wormer (warning: do not give Collie or Collie Mixes Ivomec). I give this orally—0.50 cc (½ cc) for every 44 lbs of weight. I prepare either a cheese ball or a small liver treat to give immediately after squirting this into the back of the dog's mouth—as it is very bitter and they try to spit it out. The treat makes them swallow it. I give this once a month to prevent heartworms. I give it year around so that I don't have to have a blood test (teeter) done to confirm that the dogs do not have heartworms. You cannot give heartworm preventative medicine to a dog that is infected with heartworms—it will probably kill them, as the heartworms die, detach and clog up the heart and lungs even more. There is a treatment for heartworm—but it is extremely debilitating and personally, I wouldn't put my dog through it. They come out of the treatment after several months in a crate, nothing but skin and bones left, their spirit crushed, and I don't believe most of them ever regain their health. The heartworms do major damage to the lungs. Just because we have an option doesn't mean that we should always seize it as the appropriate choice.

Hydrating Puppies. A key procedure you must be able to perform is to hydrate puppies subcutaneously to treat dehydration. Checking for dehydration is easy. Pull up on the puppy's skin on its neck and let go. If it pops back quickly the puppy is not dehydrated. If it goes back slowly, the puppy needs to be hydrated. Depending on the size of the puppy, pull about ½ to 1 cc of lactated ringer into a small gauge syringe. Expel just enough to get all the air out of the syringe. Pull up on the puppy's skin at the back of its neck and insert the needle just under the skin and inject the liquid. Pull up the skin over each rear hip and repeat the process, using a new needle for each injection. The last thing you want to do is to cause any infection in your puppy. The needle should be sterile, and if you are careful to insert it only once, you should avoid contamination of the needle. You should then have three lumps under the skin of the puppy that will be quickly absorbed by its body. Repeat this procedure every four hours until the puppy is hydrated.

Inducing Labor. Administering Oxytocin intramuscularly to bitches in labor that are experiencing secondary inertia or as a clean out shot after whelping is completed. Be forewarned—your veterinarian is not going to dispense this powerful drug to you without carefully briefing you on its use and having enough trust in you to believe that you will not misuse it. Don't administer Oxytocin to a bitch that is in labor with contractions and don't administer it to a bitch that hasn't yet produced any puppies from this litter at all. When in doubt, call your veterinarian. As soon as you know she is in labor, call his office to give him a heads up and find out where he is going to be that evening. It is wonderful to have this drug on hand so that your veterinarian doesn't have to meet you at the clinic in the middle of the night, but instead can talk you through the process on the telephone. You need to be knowledgeable about the signs of complications so that you can seek out veterinary intervention when it is critical to do so. This drug is primarily used to restart contractions when a bitch stops in the middle of delivering a litter of puppies. This is referred to as secondary inertia. The uterine muscle is tired and the bitch's body is not producing sufficient petocin to keep the contractions going. By the way, putting some of her pups that were already born on her to nurse has been known to effectively restart contractions. Also letting her eat several of the placentas can also contribute to continued contractions. The clean-out shot is to make sure there are no retained dead or live fetuses, or placental material in the uterine horns after all the pups have been delivered. This helps to avoid infections. Sometimes you will be surprised at the birth of yet another live puppy when you thought she was done.

A Breeder Secret

Beware Raspberry Leaf Tea

Let me say something about raspberry leaf tea and raspberry leaf capsules. At one time, many dog breeders were recommending this natural product to help start, strengthen, or restart uterine contractions in bitches. However, too many breeders have reported a much higher incidence of stillborn puppies when they used this "natural" remedy. Many of us discussed this and the general consensus was that the raspberry tea may have caused such hard contractions that they crushed the puppies. In some cases the contractions were so hard that they caused the uterus to shred and hemorrhage. Not only did the puppies die, but the mothers who survived them had emergency spay operations. My advice is to steer clear of raspberry leaf tea.

I.V. Administration. Administering liquids and medications intravenously. Some breeders prefer to have the vet tech or vet assistant set up the I.V. needle, and then take the dog home where they can then monitor the drip and change bags as needed. This saves hundreds of dollars in hospital fees and greatly reduces the stress on the dog, who can come home and rest comfortably in familiar surroundings—especially a bitch that is on I.V. liquids after an emergency C-section and needs to be home with her puppies. Some experienced breeders will be able to set up the I.V. needle themselves and hook up the I.V. without a problem. Some of these things are very dependent upon what your veterinarian is willing to concede—and this is another good reason to carefully develop a professional relationship with your veterinarian before you find yourself in an emergency situation.

Life-Saving Techniques. Administering oxygen and performing CPR and other life-saving techniques on newborn puppies as necessary. Administer Dopram to resuscitate puppies.

Mastitis. Diagnosing and treating mastitis with hot compresses and appropriate antibiotics. Some bitches are prone to mastitis, which is a caking of the breasts. It may be caused by too much milk, or because puppies are not nursing enough, or because bacteria enters the teats from a dirty environment. Learn from my experience, and avoid having a horrible problem. Check your bitch at least three times a day for hard, hot breasts. At the first signs of a problem, immediately apply hot compresses to the affected area every two or three hours, check with your veterinarian as to which antibiotic you should use and how much to give. Make sure you give the bitch and her puppies plain cultured yogurt during treatment with an antibiotic. Just a small amount for each puppy every four hours or so. This will preserve the good intestinal bacteria, which helps them to digest their food. Left untreated, mastitis can result in massive septicemia and ultimately death.

Microchipping. You should microchip your own dogs and puppies. There is a special applicator needle with each chip. It is easier to do on larger breeds. Some small breeds may need an experienced person to do it. Ask another breeder who does it to show you. Some breed clubs hold microchip clinics where it is performed for a reduced rate. But, if you are a professional breeder, you should learn to do this yourself.

Minor Wounds. Attending to minor wounds and cuts that require wound cleaning, irrigation and sometimes suturing with liquid suture or conventional sutures. The key to success and to avoid infections is to make sure the wound is completely cleaned and irrigated properly. Keep cleaning and irrigating until you can't possibly imagine one germ surviving. When in doubt, have it done by a veterinarian.

Shots. Inoculating all of your dogs (any vet tech can teach you how to do this—it is extremely easy).

Skin Care. Bathing and treating skin irritations with various soothing home remedies. Many skin irritations are caused by food allergies. In most cases, preparing and cooking your dog's food for about three or four months should clear up the problem, after which time they can be weaned back onto a special food.

I owned a Pekingese who was 10 years old. A groomer nicked her by accident, and she contracted a terrible staph infection that almost killed her. Her poor little body was covered with bleeding sores from her scratching and digging at herself, I tried all sorts of remedies from the veterinarian. Steroids, medicated shampoos, antibiotics, bland prescription food, etc., but nothing helped. Toward the end she was on sedatives to stop her from constantly scratching and crying. As I held her in my arms, the veterinarian called me from his clinic and told me that it was time to think about her quality of life and maybe I should consider euthanizing her. I said, "Absolutely not. I am not ready to let her go this way." I put her in my car and drove to a holistic healer that I knew from dog training classes who was also a well-known breeder and exhibitor. The recipe she gave me to help my dog was one cup of brown rice cooked with fresh chicken broth, a cup of steamed carrots, ½ cup of steamed green peas, ½ cup of steamed green beans, a cup of boiled and de-boned chicken (if your dog is allergic to chicken you could use lamb or beef), ½ tsp of garlic powder, and ½ tsp iodized salt. Mix it all together. That was enough food for a week. Ling Ling ate that diet and nothing else for four months. She recovered completely. Her coat grew back to be thick and beautiful. I then slowly transitioned her to Avoderm™, which can be ordered over the internet from www.breeders-choice.com/avoderm.htm or purchased at select health food markets and independent pet stores.

As a topical solution for dry skin or skin irritations, you can use an oatmeal based shampoo and, after rinsing with warm water and white vinegar (a 50/50 mix) and again with plain water, make up a big batch of regular, but strong tea–10 bags to a quart of boiling water (which makes three or four quarts). Let the tea cool and use it to rinse off your dog. (I learned about this from a doctor in Israel who prescribed it for babies with eczema.) Of course, if your dog is white and you plan to show your dog, it may discolor its coat.

I also use Mylanta on hot spots. It has aluminum in it, and will dry up a hot spot in about 24 hours. Many breeders in Florida and other humid climates are familiar with this remedy.

Swimmer Pups. Attending to swimmer pups, doing appropriate physical therapy and correct skeletal support to correct the deformity. Swimmer puppies are usually too fat because they are either getting too much food, or their mother's milk is like high-calorie cream. These pups get so heavy that they cannot get up on their feet to support their weight, and without intervention, their chests get flatter and flatter and they appear to be swimming around the box like seals. This is a serious condition that needs immediate attention. Remove them from their mother and wean them as soon as possible so that they will continually be looking for her and moving around. Tape their front legs together with surgical tape leaving a small distance between the legs. Place rolled up towels or newspapers under the box liner to create valleys and hills that they have to climb over. Tape them on their sides to a stiff board for 20 or 30 minutes 4 or 5 times a day. Massage their rear legs and hold them on your lap with their front legs parallel and against your body—and encourage them to put weight on their rear legs and push off of your hand. This process takes time and patience, but without it—they will die. Veterinarians are not versed in how to deal with these puppies—so it is up to you to save them.

Tube Feeding. Tube-feed newborn puppies.

Weaning Procedures

One of the most important skills a breeder needs to have is to become competent with weaning procedures. When it comes to weaning puppies off mother's milk, a lot depends on the breed you are working with. Small dogs typically do not have a major problem nourishing the two or three small puppies that they produce. Although mastitis could become a problem for them, with adequate attention and supervision it can be easily managed. Some bitches will wean their puppies at four or five weeks just by making themselves less available, and cutting the nursing sessions to half or even a quarter of the time that they are willing to lie down and nurse their puppies. Some bitches will push their pups away and even growl at them if they attempt to nurse between meals. On their own, they will cut back on their food. But you cannot rely on that, so you must monitor how much the mother is eating. This is another excellent reason not to leave food around for dogs or puppies to nibble on at will.

At around three weeks of age, make water available to the puppies. Use water feeders that hang on the side of the whelping box, crate, or playpen the puppies are in. The puppies will quickly learn how to lick the ball and get a drink from the feeder, and most importantly, they will not track excrement into the water bowl, which would introduce bacteria into the water supply. Amazingly, this is one of the main reasons that so many breeders complain about their puppies getting diarrhea. This is such a common complaint that you would think most breeders would have figured this out by now.

You might hear breeders say that hanging water bottles just don't work right and create a wet pool in the puppy pen or whelping box. The secret to having a non-dripping water bottle is to pay a little more and buy a good one, and to fill it all the way to the top with no air bubbles trapped inside the bottle, screw the top on tightly and turn it over only once to hang it on the side of the pen. Tap the little steel ball once with your finger and let it reseal itself. If you have made sure there are no air bubbles, and you have filled it all the way to the top, it will not drip. Purchase new water bottles every year as they tend to dry up and the seals and plastic can become brittle. Never use a glass one as you don't want anything breakable in the nursery!

Puppies can get runny stools for a number of reasons, so it's helpful if you can eliminate their source of water as one of them. Runny stools may be caused by excessive bacteria in the intestines, or a lack of digestive flora in the intestinal track. This could be the result of antibiotics that are given directly to puppies, or antibiotics obtained through their mother's milk. Spoiled food can create excessive bacteria or too much food may not be digested properly.

In the whelping box, if it is made large enough, you can position a nice puppy bed a few inches higher than the rest of the box (depending on the size of your puppies). Do this by securing an upside-down wooden box to one side or a corner of the whelping box so it won't move. Make it just large enough for the puppies to sleep in it, and high enough off of the floor so that they have to climb in and out of it. Their instinct is not to eliminate where they sleep, so use this instinct to your advantage.

Smart, well-bred puppies will go all the way down to the other end of the box to pee and poop on the newspapers. I have even had litters of puppies that were smart enough to go through an opening in a barrier that I had made about two-thirds of the way down and use the last one-third of the box as a bathroom exclusively. They were so cute as they would crawl out of the sleeping area onto the floor of the whelping box and waddle down to the little door in the barrier, go through it, do their business, go back through the door, and waddle back down to the bed and climb up and into the box. Sometimes they would stop along the way to have a drink from one of the water bottles along the wall of their box. Fashioning something like this in the whelping box will make your life easier as all you have to do is pick up the newspapers in the designated area periodically.

As the puppies are gradually weaned, they should be nursing less often and for less time when they are nursing. At this point, you should start feeding the puppies. When you begin to feed the puppies, their mothers immediately stop cleaning up after them. It simply changes the smell of their poop, and the mothers refuse to eat it—which is a good thing, because it would make the mothers sick.

When you switch to feeding the puppies, put towels or old blanket sections inside the raised bed. All around the pen, and outside of the bedding, put newspapers. Newspapers are absorbent, and you simply roll them up a few times a day and throw them in the trash bin. Collect old newspapers year round and put them in neat stacks, using brown paper grocery bags (the exact perfect size for this) to package them in manageable bundles. (By the way, if you do this, you can get the daily newspaper delivered and write the expense off of your income taxes for the year because you are using it for puppy box liners.) Don't use puppy pads or anything that is made from cloth as you do not want any of your puppies to become accustomed to peeing or pooping on anything made of cloth or carpeting. You can use pads and quilts, blankets, and faux sheepskins for newborn puppies to age three weeks to line the whelping box, but then put them away for the next litter.

Under normal circumstances, I only use puppy formula for a few days to make the transition from mother's milk easier for the puppies. Warm up the mixed formula in a pan, and when it is very warm to your touch, slowly stir in some Gerber's Baby Rice Cereal™ (this also helps to keep the stools firm) until you have a thin gruel. To keep this warm, put the pan inside another pan of hot water or use a double boiler. Put a few tablespoons of the mixture in a small, shallow saucer, pick up each puppy individually, and put them on a table or surface that is a comfortable height for you (so as not to kill your back leaning over).

Use a clean towel on the surface to help the puppy keep from slipping and sliding, and also to absorb spilt cereal. Put the saucer down in front of the puppy. Dip your index finger into the cereal and bring it up to the puppy's mouth. Some puppies will immediately begin to lick and then go for the bowl of cereal as though they had been doing this all of their life. Others need some encouragement and you actually need to put some into their mouth before they get the connection. Teach each puppy to eat from the saucer. This process seems like a big effort and some breeders just put all the puppies on the floor, put a big bowl of cereal down, and let them go for it. But before you decide what you want to do, read the following true story.

With my very first litter of puppies I filled a flying saucer dish with cereal. This is a dish that is round and has a raised area in the middle supposedly designed so that the puppies can't actually get into the bowl (which they do anyway). They all seemed to be lapping the cereal—about 10 puppies in a circle around the edge of this big bowl. The telephone rang in the nursery and I went over to the wall and picked it up. It was a friend and she talked for about ten minutes, telling me something interesting and funny. I lost track of the time and didn't keep an eye on the puppies. When I hung up and turned around, there, in the middle of this flying saucer dish, was a big gray clump of puppies. They were all fast asleep, and their tummies were full—and they were all stuck together with rice cereal, which became an incredibly sticky glue that had dried like cement. It took me an hour to dissolve this gluey mess with buckets of warm water, dozens of wash clothes, a basket of towels, and a hair dryer set on low to dry them. It was a horrible experience. I was crying and very afraid that I would never get them free of this block of cemented rice glue. After that experience, I listened to another breeder's advice: "Teach puppies to eat properly before you allow them to eat at a trough like little pigs."

I believe that teaching puppies to eat one at a time ensures that they will not be sloppy eaters. Just like kids, they have to be taught how to eat neatly and efficiently. You will probably only have to go through this exercise once or twice before the puppies will know exactly what to do when you put the saucer down in front of them. I also wipe each little face when they are finished eating. On the third day of weaning, feed the puppies on the following schedule: 8:00 a.m., 12:00 noon, 4:00 p.m., 8:00 p.m., and 12:00 midnight. Their longest stretch will be from midnight until 8:00 a.m.

This is a difficult schedule for you, because it takes about an hour to feed a litter of eight to twelve puppies. You have to prepare the food and put it down on the floor of the feeding area of the nursery. Take all the puppies out of the puppy pens and place them onto the floor. Call out "Come Puppies, Come" because this is how you teach your puppies to always come when they are called, for the rest of their lives! You are programming them. Whenever they hear the word "come," they will salivate and run to the person who is saying it.

The puppies will race to the feeding dish, devour their puppy food, and then they will proceed to pee and poop all over the floor. Prepare a plastic bag and have a roll of paper towels in your hand. As each puppy eliminates, wipe it up immediately and throw the soiled paper towels in the plastic bag that is hooked to the side of a puppy pen. Make sure it is attached where the puppies cannot reach it.

When all of the puppies have finished eating and then eliminated, the floor will be fairly clean because you have been vigilant about picking up the mess as it occurred. Remove the dirty puppy-feeding dish or feeding dishes (for a large litter, use two of them). Return the puppies to the puppy pens or to the whelping box, depending on their age. If they are in puppy pens, pull out the trays under the pens and roll up all the dirty newspapers where excrement has fallen through the grid onto the trays below. Always line the trays with newspapers because it is so much easier to clean this up than to try to clean off the trays. Have some disinfectant ready in a spray bottle and use this to wipe off the trays before you reline them with newspaper and roll them back under the puppy pen floors.

While the puppies are busy eating, you can use the time to clean off the puppy pen grids with a brush and disinfectant, or wipe down the whelping box with disinfectant and paper towels. You have to work quickly and efficiently if you want to stay ahead of the potential mess. As you scoop up each puppy and put them back in their pens, wipe off their coats with a baby wipe, including feet and toes. There is always at least one puppy who poops twice—you will quickly identify who this is and let him run around for an extra five or ten minutes until he does his thing! When they are running around after eating and playing together in the nursery, get out some toys for them to play with.

Remember to gradually decrease the puppy formula and replace it with the puppy kibble. (See the Puppy Weaning schedule below.) Reduce the liquid so that eventually the puppies are eating regular puppy kibble. Sprinkle hot water over it to ensure that it remains slippery and will not stick in the throat of a puppy, but don't soak it. At this point, the puppies may be eating too fast, in which case you should spread their food out on a cookie sheet to slow them down so they do not choke.

Don't Forget Mom

During the entire weaning process, your most important task is to monitor the mother's situation. Reduce her food substantially, cutting it by 30 percent the first week, by half the second week, and by the third week she should be back to her normal pre-breeding portion. At the end of the first week, if the puppies are doing well on their transition to regular food, remove the mother's access to water. Give her one cup of water three times a day for three days. Her milk will begin to quickly dry up. She will be a little uncomfortable, but you are saving her from getting mastitis, which can lead to infection and even death. I know that I keep repeating this warning, but you *must* pay attention to these issues, as they are very serious.

You should be able to completely wean the puppies off of their mother's milk within a week or two at the most. By the end of that first week, you should be able to put her in the whelping box, pick two of the smallest puppies, and put them on her for no more than five minutes several times a day. This is to relieve any pressure, but not to stimulate more milk production. Move them around to different teats so that they are sucking on all of her functional teats at least for a few seconds.

Puppy Weaning/Feeding Schedule: Weeks 4 Through 24

Week 4	Puppy formula—mix according to directions	8:00 a.m.
	Gerber's Baby Rice Cereal—thin gruel	12:00 noon
	Serve warm	04:00 p.m.
		08:00 p.m.
		12:00 midnight
Week 5	Puppy formula	8:00 a.m.
	Gerber's Baby Rice Cereal—gradually decrease	12:00 noon
	Ground puppy kibble—gradually increase this	04:00 p.m.
	Gerber's Baby Beef or Chicken—2 Tbsp	10:00 p.m.
	Serve warm	
Week 6	Ground puppy kibble—coarsely ground, sprinkled with hot water—to make it slippery	8:00 a.m.
		3:00 p.m.
	Serve warm	10:00 p.m.
Week 7- 6 months	Regular puppy kibble, sprinkled with hot water—to make it slippery	8:00 a.m.
		3:00 p.m.
	Serve at room temperature	8:00 p.m.

Preventive Care

The most cost-effective thing you can do in your breeding program for the success of your kennel operation is to practice preventative care with your breeding stock. I will assume that you purchased the very best dogs that you could find—your breeding plan starts with choosing superior genetic combinations that will stack the deck in your favor. This applies to genetic diseases as well, not just conforming to the breed standard.

Feed the Best to the Best

Don't be cheap when it comes to what you feed your dogs. Some cheap foods end up costing you more in health care costs as you deal with ugly, dry coats and a lack of stamina and vigor. Poor nutrition will eventually deplete your bitches, and the size of their litters will diminish. Your stud dogs will produce less and less healthy sperm if their nutritional needs aren't met.

Feed high quality, naturally preserved food, with vitamin E used as a preservative. Try to avoid corn-based dog food—corn is for chickens. Barley and rice are better sources of vegetable protein, but the really important part of the food formula is animal protein. Your dog should be getting most of its protein from animal sources. It should also be getting vegetables and fruits because in reality dogs lean more toward being omnivores (eating both meat and plant materials) than most people would assume. My dogs love fresh apples, green beans, and carrots.

In the wild, dogs are omnivores because they tear open their prey's stomachs and eat the grassy contents as well as the flesh. It is almost impossible to find a commercial dog food that has 90 percent of its protein from animal sources. Get as close as you can, though, because the alternative—feeding the BARF (bones as raw food) diet—is not only risky, depending on the raw meat source, but also expensive and problematic to store. It could still be justified except for the fact that when the puppies leave you, they will probably not go to a home that will accommodate this special raw meat diet.

Find a practical alternative—feed a high-quality commercial dog food and mix in fresh vegetables, fruits, and regular portions of boiled chicken or beef. Supplement your dog food with Omega 3 fatty acids (fish oil) to promote beautiful coats and prevent cancer. Give glucosamine and chondroitin to build and maintain joint cartilage. There are some excellent reference books on canine nutrition, so educate yourself, but don't spend three or four hours a week preparing complex diets.

Physically Fit

Breeding dogs need to be in top physical condition—in proper weight and physically fit. Some breeders use a modified treadmill with removable rails on either side to keep the dogs from jumping off. If you want to put your dogs on such a treadmill, be sure to supervise them even if the rails are in place, and attach a disconnect tab to their collar just in case they slide off for any reason. When I lived in Colorado, I used to stand on a steep hill overlooking a meadow and throw tennis balls for at least an hour. I had ten Labradors retrieving them back to my hand. Up and down the hill, up and down the hill they ran—needless to say that they were all about muscle and strength and deep breathing. We were living at 8,000 feet above sea level at the time, so they learned to breathe deeply. What a difference in health and energy. My arm got tired, and I even thought about teaching them to use a pitching machine so that they could continue to play this game until they became tired. But I don't think it would have worked because half of their fun was jostling each other to see who got the balls back into my hands the quickest. They probably would have knocked a pitching machine over. Labs never tire of retrieving—I think they could do it around the clock if you let them. I have seen Labradors in the field who were literally gasping for breath, having run all day on doubles and triples (multiple bird retrievers at distances in excess of 150 yards, on land and in the water), but still tapping their toes on the ground in anticipation of just one more run for the birds! At that point one, can see why Labradors are so popular with hunters.

Limiting Outside Exposure

One of the hardest things for many new breeders to understand is that if you have breeding stock you cannot do in-house rescue work like fostering or in-house training. No matter how much extra room you have, or hours in the day, or a burning desire to rescue poor neglected pooches, you cannot bring any rescue dogs into your kennel without endangering the health of your dogs and their puppies. There are simply too many parasites, communicable diseases, venereal diseases, and airborne diseases to be able to protect all of your puppies and dogs from contracting them. So, if you have the resources, and you want to help in a rescue project, send money or supplies, or volunteer some of your time at the shelter as a trainer, a dog walker, a groomer, or whatever you are best at. Make sure that you change your clothes and shower *before* you interact with your own dogs at home. Use those disposable shoe booties, too.

Kennel Cleanliness

Keep your kennel runs clean. Keep your whelping boxes clean. Do your kennel laundry with disinfectant, making sure to wash all regular bedding at least once a week, and changing out whelping box blankets two or three times a day. If you are using newspapers in the whelping box, make sure you change them out and wipe the surface underneath with a disinfectant before you replace the bedding and return the puppies to the box. Use bleach or a laundry disinfectant on all your bedding.

Make sure you have hair screens on your drains if your kennel has a central drain or individual drains in each kennel run, as the dog hair that will build up is substantial. It tends to trap fecal matter and smells terrible, too. Use bleach and change out the water in the mop bucket often. Use a squeegee to clean off your kennel floors, and if you have compressed air, blow the kennels dry. Use rubber boots and rubber gloves, and possibly safety glasses, when cleaning the kennels. If you don't have compressed air, you can use an industrial-type mop that's been well rung out, and the floor will dry within minutes. In the winter, you can use a heater with a blower motor for the kennel floors. I do not like those plastic sub-flooring tiles or slats as they tend to trap dog hair and various debris from food, dog poop, and muddy dog paws. If you have Dogloos™ or plastic doghouses, they are elevated off of the cement floor and are easy to mop out. Dry debris like dried mud, dust, or dog hair can be vacuumed with a shop vacuum from the floors and also from inside of the Dogloos. Make sure to empty the shop vacuum after each use so that it won't develop bacteria and begin to smell bad.

Once a week you can rinse it out and sit it in the sun to dry. If you have chain-link dog runs, you will need to scrub them periodically with disinfectant and brushes. This is not an easy task and requires some elbow grease. Another option is to clean them with your steam cleaner, but you need to either be very tall or use a ladder so that you can angle the steam cleaner wand toward the ground and still get the top portion of the chain link. Use a degreaser and a deodorant product.

If you are operating a medium-sized kennel with eight to ten dogs or more, you should sit down and draw up a very detailed maintenance schedule for the kennel facility. Here is an example of a typical schedule that is posted daily:

Scheduled Kennel Maintenance—Today's Date: _____

Frequency	Due	Description of task	Completed	Initials
Daily	1/1	Wash dog bowls/dog toys w/soap & water, dry (dishwasher is great)		
Daily	1/1	Pick up and dispose of dog poops, mop urine & disinfect floor as needed		
Daily	1/1	Vacuum dog runs and doghouses		
Daily	1/1	Empty shop vacuum		
Daily	1/1	Pick up outside dog poops		
Weekly	1/7	Pressure wash and dry kennel runs		
Weekly	1/7	Clean windows and doors		
Weekly	1/7	Clean/vacuum ventilation filters, wipe vents, wipe/dust or vacuum ceiling fans		
Weekly	1/7	Wash out shop vacuum and dry		
Weekly	1/7	Empty trashcans and poop buckets, dispose of poop properly		
Weekly	1/7	Disinfect grooming/dispensary area		
Weekly	1/7	Check supplies—make shopping list		
Weekly	1/7	Launder bedding, replenish paper towel dispensers and plastic bag dispensers		
Monthly	1/31	Clean light fixtures, kennel walls, light switches		
Monthly	1/31	Clean/disinfect outdoor potty areas (pea gravel) with bleach solution. Remove debris, dog hair, weeds, etc. Sweep walks, trim plants or trees as needed. Discard old bones/chews.		
Monthly	1/31	Apply pest control chemicals around the building, and around food storage area.		
Monthly	1/31	Replace ventilation and heating filters.		
Semi-Annually	4/1 & 9/1	Do complete deep cleaning of entire facility using steam cleaner (rented?), including chain link, walls, flooring. Replace food receptacles and storage bins as needed, etc. Paint as necessary.		

A Breeder Secret

Schedule Security

If you keep to a maintenance schedule, your kennels will always sparkle with professionalism. You will never be uncomfortable with any visits by buyers or official inspectors. Your kennels will always be in superior condition and your dogs will be healthy and clean! You will never be overwhelmed by a gigantic task of cleaning up a huge mess. Bacteria and fungus will never gain a foothold in your kennels.

Grooming

To make sure your dogs are always in top cosmetic and physical condition, post a grooming schedule in your grooming/dispensary area. On it, include all grooming requirements for your breed, dates to give heartworm preventative, appointments for teeth scaling, and especially a monthly schedule for applying flea and tick preventative if these are problems in your area. If you get into the habit of taking care of your business as a highly paid kennel manager, you will feel good about your accomplishments, you will always know exactly what is going on with each dog that you own, and at the end of the day, you will never feel guilty about neglecting your dogs or your business.

Another health maintenance tip: When traveling with your dogs to a show or elsewhere, do not use the rest areas along the highway to let your dogs out to eliminate. Stop somewhere else along the road for this. The public rest areas along major highways are breeding grounds for all types of dog diseases deposited there by hundreds of dogs traveling along that route. You don't know what your dogs might contract there. The same rule applies at dog shows; if you can possibly avoid the general areas set up for doggie bathrooms, do so. If you can't, wipe off the dog's feet, underside, and rear end with a baby wipe treated with some mild disinfectant or antibacterial cleaner after you've let the dog use the area. Just be careful with what you use as dogs are sensitive to various chemicals.

Snake Proofing Dogs

There is a snake proofing method that should be performed on dogs who are going to be hunting or exercising in areas where rattlesnakes are present. Check with your local Gun Dog club to obtain more information on this process and find out if and when the club will be doing this for members' dogs. There is also a rattlesnake vaccine that is available from your veterinarian.

Avoiding Accidents

Accidents do happen—sometimes they are simply unavoidable. However, just as with children, there are some things that we can do to avoid having them happen to our dogs. Here are some suggestions:

1. Depending on your breed, teach all puppies to swim, and teach your own dogs where the exits are from the swimming pool. Mark the exits with a white cone, rock, or pot.

2. Always crate or belt your dogs in a vehicle. Make sure that the crate is secured to the vehicle. Purchase special canine safety belts that attach to your regular seat belts of the car.

3. Do not have poisonous houseplants or poisonous shrubs or flowers in your garden.

4. Keep medicine out of the reach of dogs and children.

5. Keep cupboards closed and install child-proof devices on the cabinet doors.

6. Do not leave any food out on counter tops.

7. Store all chocolate in upper kitchen or pantry cupboards, secured in closed plastic containers. Never leave any chocolate candy on tables or counter tops.

8. Teach your dogs to exit from your vehicle only on your command. Never allow a dog to leap from the car without your giving the command to do so—too many dogs have died this way leaping out into traffic. Put a leash on a puppy in training while it is still in the vehicle and walk it out of the car on the driver's side only, using the command you choose for this.

9. Teach your dog to exit your house only after he sits on command—and the minute he is outside the door, teach him to sit again and wait for your instructions. Many puppies have been hit by cars in front of their own homes.

10. Teach your puppy never to go into the street without his leash and without you.

11. Teach your dog the "leave it" command. If he tries to pick up anything while on a walk, or in the field or anywhere else, command him to "leave it," at which time your dog should immediately drop it or stop going toward it.

12. Make sure your dogs are trained to come when they are called. This should be a solid, reliable recall. If you have a field dog that will be working in the field, the most important command is the recall whistle—three blasts from the whistle and the dog should immediately turn around and run as quickly as possible to you. This is taught for the dog's safety. Should he be running toward a busy highway; an oncoming truck; an approaching vicious dog, bear, moose, mountain lion; or other dangerous situation, he needs to respond immediately to your whistled command to turn around and run back to you quickly.

13. Microchip your dogs, and if they are not show dogs (because show dogs cannot wear collars as it ruins their coat), put a simple leather buckle collar on them with a tag that has your telephone number and their microchip number engraved on it. The yellow plastic tags that come with the chips eventually break and fall off, so put the number on a metal tag with the dog's rabies and licensing tags. If they make too much noise clinking together, put some surgical tape on the back of each tag. Remember, better safe than sorry!

Chapter 11

PREPARING PUPPIES FOR THEIR FUTURE

Preparing puppies for the transition to a new home or for a working position requires a methodical plan. An ethical and professional breeder's goal is to create the genetics, health, and mental attitude that are crucial to allow a puppy to grow into a wonderful family member. It is a breeder's responsibility to prep each puppy so that the transition to a new home is as smooth as possible. The puppy must be mentally and physically ready for its new life.

Conditioning the Brood Bitch for Motherhood

Insuring that your puppies get the best possible start on life begins with the brood bitch. You have either purchased a very well bred puppy bitch with a sterling pedigree, or you have bred a superior bitch puppy with excellent credentials. In either case, she is a blank canvas. These are the steps you will take to develop her properly for her future role as a mother:

1. **Teach Her Clean Habits.** Housetrain her before she is ever allowed to live in a kennel run. This consists of taking her out to a pre-designated area away from

your house where she is encouraged to eliminate. When she performs properly, praise her and bring her back in the house immediately. Going out to pee and poop is not to be confused with going out to play. Even if you only bring her back into the house for a few minutes and then take her out to play, the message is different. The commands you choose for potty must be consistent, and focused on the behavior you desire. I use "potty, potty" and when the desired behavior occurs I reinforce it with "good potty, good potty." Crate train her so that she will never have an accident inside of the house, which includes attached or covered areas like the laundry room, garage, porch, etc.

2. **Teach her to eat properly.** During her weaning period, you will feed her by herself in a small dish that is too small to stand in. She should not be allowed to slop her food. You will consistently wipe off her face and her paws after eating. She will eat on a small carpet or towel so that anything that drips will be absorbed and she will never become accustomed to walking around on a slimy or smelly surface.

3. **Train her key behaviors.** There are a number of key behaviors the brood bitch should learn. I recommend you begin training her at the age of seven weeks. These behaviors include:

   - **Stand.** The stand behavior is critical for a brood bitch who needs to be able to stand up when you need her to no matter what is going on. The "stand" command is also very helpful during breeding and when her temperature needs to be taken.

   - **Give.** When she is a puppy, train her to give you toys and the like and to wait patiently to get them back. In the future, you will have to take puppies away from her to resuscitate them, cut and tie their cords, to weigh them, etc. You cannot have a brood bitch who will not allow you to take anything you want from her without her protesting or threatening you.

   - **Leave It and Off.** Train her to get off of furniture or beds and stay away from certain items. This is important because if she is never allowed on sofas, chairs, or beds, she will not decide to whelp her puppies there.

   - **Wait.** Similar to "leave it," you want her to be able to stop if she is moving away from you, especially if she is heading somewhere you do not want her to go.

4. **Handle her all over,** including her anus and vulva. She should not have any problem with you touching her there. Periodically, take her temperature with a digital thermometer that beeps. She will quickly learn that she must stand still until she hears the beep.

5. **Let her watch the breeding sessions at your kennel.** Crate her in a corner of the room so that she can watch the process, experience the smells, and learn. Dogs learn from observation. When Camille was a puppy, every afternoon she sat behind the chain link fence of the exercise yard and watched me train one of my hunting dogs. The sessions were 30-minute obedience drills—repeated basic verbal commands and whistle sits and recalls. Two weeks later I took Camille out to the same area to begin her basic obedience training. There was no need to

train her, because to my delight she had memorized all of the exercises and even executed them almost perfectly! That was an eye opener for me, and it saved me hours of unnecessary training of puppies over the years. I would just let them watch from afar. The very smart ones, like Camille, would learn everything quickly and easily. Some slower puppies needed extra work, but even they had a basic understanding of what was expected of them and were much easier to train than a puppy that begins basic obedience without any observation time.

The first time she comes into season, put her in with one of your experienced brood bitches, if you have one. An experienced brood bitch will teach your puppy that it is okay to be mounted, and she will learn that despite all of her in-house training, she is not a human and it is okay to copulate with a dog. This will be very helpful when it is time to breed her.

Physical Care of New Puppies

Stage 1. Birth to Four Weeks
A new life slips into this world, wet and blind, deaf and helpless. Most of the time I will turn the puppy over to tie and cut the umbilical cord, and then suction the liquid from the puppy's mouth and throat. I vigorously rub that puppy with a warm, dry hand towel until I hear it crying. Once I hear that first cry, I can slow down a bit—the frenzy to ascertain and preserve life now shifts to a lower gear. I talk to the mother, telling her how nice her new puppy is. She is frantic now, wanting instinctively to lick her baby. Just another moment, please!

I check with a penlight to make sure the roof of the puppy's mouth is one solid piece with no split (cleft palate), and I carefully look at the legs and paws. I hold the puppy up next to my ear to listen to its breathing. Warm, sweet puppy breath fills my nostrils, and I smile. No gurgling noises from liquid in the lungs, no bubbles coming out of the nose. This puppy is perfect. I gently blow my breath into its nose so that some of my scent is left there (they do that on newborn colts to imprint them with human scent after the first moments of their birth). I hold that puppy against my neck for a moment and hum loudly, as though doing a meditative "Ohhhhhhmmmmm." The puppy can't hear anything, but it can feel the vibration of my hum. Then I kiss this puppy on top of its head and I give it back to its mother.

The mother is relieved to have her pup and begins to tend to it herself. As time goes on, she learns to accept my interventions and she learns to wait to receive her puppies from me. I am a believer in that ancient philosophy between dog and human. For dogs, all good things should come from the hand of a human. I never free-feed my dogs or puppies, so food doesn't come miraculously from the ground, it comes from my hand. Puppies do not appear on the floor of the whelping box, they come from my hand to their mothers. If there is something drastically wrong with them, their mothers never receive them.

A Breeder Secret

What to Do for Mom
Refer to your whelping DVD and whelping reference books for instructions on how to physically care for the mother so that she will maintain her health and take good care of her puppies.

Everyday, I change the bedding and newspapers in the nursery at least two or three times. When I perform this housekeeping, I develop a ritual for the puppies and for the mother. She gets taken out to relieve herself, stretch her legs, and take some breaths of fresh air. She might get a few minutes of grooming or a special treat of beef bullion and a hard-boiled egg. She might get her breakfast or lunch or dinner, depending on the time of day. While she is eating or moving around in the outside pen, I am handling her puppies. I try to handle them the same way everyday. I move them one by one into a preheated plastic incubator box while I wipe out the whelping box, disinfect it, dry it, and install clean bedding. Then I take each puppy and hold it up to my ear so that it is touching my neck and I hum loudly. I blow softly on the puppy's face and stroke its head and back gently. Kisses all around and back to the box. I bring their mother back in. This ritual goes on until the puppies are walking.

By interacting with them this way, the puppies learn my scent and they learn that nothing bad happens when they are in the hands of a human. I believe the humming is soothing and they learn to associate it with calmness, petting, ear and chin scratching, etc. Keep the puppies very clean. Wipe off their mom's teats when she comes back in from outside. Wipe off her feet with a mild disinfectant, too. Always wash your hands before you handle a puppy at this early stage.

Stage 2. Four Weeks to Six Weeks

At this age it can be ascertained if a particular puppy was brain damaged during the stress of birth. If it was deprived of adequate oxygen or had some other brain defect, it will show up at this age. Such a puppy may be difficult to connect with and will not play well with its siblings. I refer to this as puppy autism. The pup will poop and pee anywhere without regard to where it sleeps or eats. Later it will be almost impossible to housetrain this puppy. If it is deaf, it will not learn the bite reflex and will grab onto its siblings or your fingers and bite down hard. I learned about deaf puppies from a Dalmatian breeder. Even squealing loudly will not stop the painful biting, and it will have to be taught bite inhibition by squeezing hard on its toe when it bites too hard. It is a slow and difficult lesson to learn. Brain-damaged puppies need to be medically evaluated to make decisions about their future before they grow into large, untrained, unruly, or even dangerous dogs. The options are limited to extremely kind-hearted adopters who do not have any other dogs and have the time to train a "special needs" puppy, or in severe cases, euthanasia.

A Breeder Secret

Deaf Puppies Can Thrive

Deaf pups can be beautifully trained if that is their only issue. They do better in a home without other pets and without small children. One can use vibrations on the floor (wood floors are best), hand signals, and mental imaging to convey commands and expectations, praise, and joyfulness. The main issue with these dogs is not to surprise them or scare them with sudden unexpected physical contact that may cause them to bite in fear. It could be a scary world for a little puppy that cannot hear.

Stage 3. Six Weeks to Twelve Weeks

At this stage, puppies can now start to be separated into puppy crates at night. They are completely weaned by this age. At first they will cry, but after a few nights they will curl up next to their stuffed toy and go to sleep. In the morning, each one should be picked up and taken outside to the puppy potty area. They will immediately use it—and get lots of praise—then be returned to the puppy yard where breakfast awaits. After breakfast, it is back to the puppy potty area. If the weather is nice, it is a good time to put the pups outdoors with their mother or father. Make sure the area is secure and they cannot wander away or get hurt. Mom and especially dad will protect them from birds of prey or coyotes if this is a large breed. Smaller puppies and parents must be supervised at all times as it is not safe to leave them outdoors by themselves. If the weather is not suitable for outdoors, they can be put in a kennel run for a few hours as long as there is a raised bed for them to nap on and lots of toys to play with. Outdoors, I provide sand for the pups to walk on, rocks to climb over, and bridges to cross and go under. There should be mounds of dirt and little hills to climb, as well as areas with grass to walk on.

If it's warm enough, you can teach certain breeds to swim by seven weeks of age. It takes a little patience and effort. The best way is to get into the water with them. Smaller puppies can be taught to swim in a bathtub with warm water. Once they learn, they enjoy this wonderful exercise. Remember to dry their ears out after swimming. It is wonderful to teach puppies to swim now because if their owners have a pool, they will be so pleased to not have to worry about them every second. You must educate the owners with pools to take their puppies into the pool and show them over and over where the exits are located. One way to teach this is to place a small white traffic cone where the stairs are to get out and play a game with the puppy so that whenever it exits the water and touches the white cone it gets a treat.

If you can do it safely, you can further expand the puppies' world by taking them outdoors and letting them walk on grass, dirt, cement, rocks, and through water. It's a terrific experience for them. I used to take mine for walks in the woods (two at a time). They will follow you closely at this age.

A Breeder Secret

Flies

A word of caution here about putting puppies outdoors—flies are a breeder's worst enemy. They spread Parvovirus as they land on infected feces or contaminated water sources in the area, and then they land on your puppies or their food. Setting up a big fan aimed at the puppy exercise pen keeps the flies off of the puppies.

Socialization

There are plenty of books and videos on the socialization of puppies, and most forward-thinking dog folks understand how crucial this process is to insure a behaviorally healthy puppy. New research is coming in all the time that shows there is a clear link between good socialization techniques and good behavior later on in life. As a breeder, doing a good job socializing your puppies is very important. Recognize that success in socializing your puppies is one of the key factors that will determine whether or not puppy buyers will come back to you, and, at least as importantly, send you referrals. Along with that motivation is the even more important factor of ensuring those puppies a forever home because the truth is that a socialized puppy has the greatest chance of being integrated into his human family *for life*.

Socialization can begin almost from birth. As noted above, handling, humming, and speaking to puppies are all beneficial things to do in this early stage. This is such an adorable and fun stage of development. They begin to wrestle and play with each other. They should learn to love the feel of your hands on them, and when you lift them to your ear, they should actually snuggle and lick your neck. I recommend humming to them, but you should also talk to them in a clear voice. When I have an especially wiggly puppy, I have it sit on my lap until it relaxes its body. As soon as it relaxes and sits still, I release it. Soon pups like these begin crawling up onto my lap, getting a tummy rub, and then leaving. They realize that it is not a trap and not something to resist or hide from.

There will be special puppies in the litter that will always run to you and want to be held. That is great, but it is the one who hangs back, who waits in a corner or only follows the others, that needs the most physical contact and reassurance. Likewise, a puppy that is too busy to be held or cuddled needs to learn to accept contact. Hold that puppy on your lap and talk to him quietly. To avoid distractions, take him out of the room where the other puppies are playing.

Teaching puppies to follow you at an early age is the way to begin to install a solid recall, an important behavior for any dog to learn. At an early age, I will say, "Come Puppy, Come" as I drag a towel around the floor. Most of them will chase it, toddling and sometimes falling down. They quickly begin to react to the word "Come."

Adding toys to the nursery floor will enrich a puppy's experience. At first, they will investigate them, but are mostly interested in each other and my hands. But over time puppies will begin to react to the toys more intently. After a few weeks, when I empty the toy box onto the nursery floor, the puppies are delighted. Some of them will already have a favorite toy. Anything with a rope on it is a big hit in the nursery. Other fun toys are big empty plastic milk jugs. They grab the handles with their teeth and drag the jugs around on the floor. Many pups, especially Labs, like big toys. They will tackle almost anything, trying to drag it or pounce on it. Tug of war is also popular, and several puppies will join in. They also play "train," grabbing each other's tails, creating a train of three or four puppies, though someone always lets go and falls into the puppy behind him. There are a few yelpers. No matter who jumps on them, they yelp loudly. If a brother bites another brother or sister, the victim will cry pitifully. If that doesn't cause an immediate release, a puppy growl is the next reaction. These are all good things because the puppies are learning the proper way to interact with each other.

You can make toys for the nursery that will teach your puppies to be fearless explorers and increase their mental abilities. A plastic trashcan with the bottom cut off, just about twice as big around as a puppy, makes a terrific tunnel when taped sideways to the floor with duct tape so it doesn't roll. Pups love going through it, or barking at a littermate who stays inside the tunnel and doesn't come out the other end. Cement blocks make great places to climb and teach the puppies about going up and down steps. Don't pile them high—just two at the most. I like to tape a four foot, one half inch thick and one foot wide plank to the floor to get the puppies used to walking on it. After a few days, when all the puppies are used to walking on it, I tape one end to the cement blocks and the other end to the floor—now you have two toys: a ramp to go up and a tunnel to go under. Later you can tape each end to the top of a cement block. The pups like to walk across this bridge.

A closet mirror on a plastic backing (not glass) is a great toy. Tape it to the bottom of the wall in a horizontal position so that puppies can see all of their littermates' images. It's fun to watch them running back and forth from one end to the other, pawing at the reflection. Eventually, a very smart little guy will try to look behind the mirror. Put down pieces of carpeting, plastic grass, and a sandbox if there is enough room. Make it small enough so that you can throw out the sand if one of the puppies mistakes it for a bathroom. I don't advise using kitty litter because puppies might try to eat it. Hard clumping cat litter (the type that forms solid chunks when any liquid comes into contact with it) can kill kittens and puppies as it can cause a blockage in their intestines if they ingest it.

As they get older, I begin to desensitize my pups to sounds. Since my dogs are bred to hunt, they need to get used to sharp and sudden sounds. I will sometimes drop heavy telephone books on the floor far from their box. Every day I drop them closer and closer. I slam the door when I leave. While these steps are not necessary with many breeds of dogs, getting any puppy used to the kinds of sounds they will encounter in their new homes should be part of your socialization program. For example, I run a vacuum cleaner around all of my puppies until they leave for their new homes, and this could be applied to any breed. Your goal should be for the puppies to ignore and not react negatively to these loud sounds because they become accustomed to them—they should continue playing without fear. If we pre-condition puppies to accept sudden loud noises, using treats and praise, we can teach them to love not only the sound of a gun, but other potentially scary things like thunderstorms and vacuum cleaners. It is easy to run the vacuum cleaner around the puppies from the age of four weeks until they leave for their new homes.

If some of the puppies in the litter are intended to be shown or participate in indoor competitions of any type, they need to be conditioned to the sounds of a dog show arena. The way to do that is to attend a large indoor show and to record the sounds. Some breed clubs have tapes of show sounds in their library expressly for the purpose of puppy conformation training. Bring home the tape or CD and play it while the puppies are eating or playing. Soon they will learn to relax around those unique noises such as the loud speaker, dogs barking, or many people talking or applauding at the same time.

A Breeder Secret

It Works!

Puppies who are intended for a life as working gun dogs need to be fearless around the loud bang of a shotgun. I once sold a puppy to a woman in the Midwest. She already had a Golden Retriever puppy that she had purchased elsewhere. She called me about three weeks after she received her puppy from me. She was excited on the telephone as she told me that upon hearing thunder and lightening, her 12-week-old Lab pup had jumped up on the window seat to watch "the light show," wagging his tail and looking expectantly at her for a treat, while her Golden pup, of the same age, had run scurrying under the bed, shaking in fear. She was delighted with her Lab puppy's reaction, but she wanted to know how she could address the terror of her Golden Retriever pup.

During all of your exercise and play times with the puppies, invite other people to participate. Have them spray the soles of their shoes with a parvocide like bleach and water and ask them to wash their hands before touching the puppies. I have paid teenagers to come and play with my puppies for an hour in the afternoons. Make sure the people understand that the puppies need to be picked up securely (with one hand under their chest and one hand under their rump), held on laps, rolled over on their backs for tummy rubs, and talked to all the time. If you have young children playing with puppies, make sure that they are told to squeal loudly if a puppy gets mouthy with them—but never to hit or kick the puppy. I always ask younger kids to sit on the floor on a blanket when playing with puppies. Make sure they are spending some time with both men and women. There are some puppies that dislike men, because they have never been around them. Make sure none of your puppies suffer from that phobia.

Properly socialized puppies will not hide behind furniture or crouch down close to the floor. They will not be afraid of loud noises, strangers, or different floor surfaces. They won't bark at umbrellas, or cower under the bed when there is lightening or a thunderstorm. They won't become terrified from fireworks on the Fourth of July or New Years. When they see people, they will come running with wagging tails because as far as they know, only good things come from people! If you never scold or yell at any puppy, and you always reinforce "Come!" with food, you will have wonderful, friendly little puppies. If you squeal loudly every time they get mouthy with those sharp little milk teeth, by the time they go to their new homes they will not be biting anyone. As you squeal, also push your hand farther into their mouths. Do not pull it away from them as that becomes a great game of tug of war for them.

Continue to handle their feet a lot, cutting their nails, and spreading their toes apart in your hands. There are far too many dogs out there that will not allow their owners to cut their nails or handle their feet. That is the fault of the breeders, and there is no excuse for it. The same applies to their teeth. Open their mouths and lift up their lips to see their teeth. At first they will resist, but if you give them a piece of puppy kibble every time you do this and say the words "teeth, teeth," they will quickly adapt to it. For show dogs this is very important. For other dogs it is also a very good practice to be able to inspect and even scale their teeth as needed.

All puppies should be accustomed to being groomed before they leave their breeder. Bathing, nail trimming, and brushing should all be routine by the time they go to their new homes. You should never get a call from the new owner saying that they are unable to cut their puppy's nails or give it a bath. In your original instructions to the new owners you should supply a grooming instruction sheet. Nail trimming diagrams and instructions can be found in many supply catalogs. If you call the catalog companies, they will send you as many catalogs as you need for your puppy packets.

Teach the puppies to focus on your face. Do this on a table or counter top, or while sitting on the floor. Show the puppy a treat and let him sniff it, then slowly move the treat up to your face. As soon as the pup makes eye contact with you, move the treat from your face directly to his mouth and say his name. Soon the pup will be looking straight up at you trying to make eye contact with you. Have a treat held between your lips. As soon as the contact is made and held for even a second or two, drop the treat from your lips. By the time he is ready to go to his new home, he will be seeking out human eye contact and human connection.

For Show or Hunt Pups

You will be so far ahead of any other breeder when you properly prepare your puppies that are destined for show homes and/or field work. Many of these procedures would also be appropriate for any working dog. Use common sense and figure out what you can do for a special purpose puppy to make it the best candidate that you can.

Show Pups

If the puppy is going to be a show dog, you will want to start stacking this pup at around five to six weeks of age. Stack the puppy and have someone photograph them from the side and from the front. A trick to getting a young puppy to maintain his stack long enough to get a good photo is to hold him cradled with his head pointed toward your right hand and his tail pointed to your left hand, rest his body on both of your hands and rock him forward and backward about 10 times rather quickly. This gets him just dizzy enough to make him stand still for a few seconds when his feet are placed on a table. Always place his rear feet on the very edge of the table so that if he moves them backwards, he begins to fall until you catch him. This teaches him not to move his rear feet once you plant them. Lower his front feet carefully so that they line up perfectly under his shoulders.

Looking at the photos taken this way gives you much better information than any other way you can look at the puppy's conformation and structure. At five to six weeks (though this varies somewhat by breed) he will have the same proportions that he will have as an adult dog. After the age of six weeks he will go through various awkward stages of development where one part of his body will grow before another. At eight or nine weeks, you will not be able to give him a solid evaluation for balance and show quality.

Following Exercises. Following is a great skill for a future show dog (any dog, in fact) to learn. From the ages of six to twelve weeks, puppies will naturally follow you, without a leash. If you walk briskly along a path, they will follow you when you make clucking noises. If a puppy is going to be a working dog, you will want to reinforce his following instincts before he leaves your kennels. Take him out for a walk by himself—just the two of you. Make sure this is not after a meal. The best time to work with a puppy or young dog is about an hour before a meal is due because at that time they are hungry enough to pay attention to you (the source of their food) and not so famished that they can't focus on the training.

If the puppy wanders off and doesn't focus on you, hide behind a tree or a wall. When he discovers that he is alone, most pups will panic, start to cry, and run around looking for you. Let him fret for a minute, then step out from behind the tree or the wall, and call him to you the same way you always do, by saying, "Come puppy, come." He will be delighted to see and hear you. Give him lots of praise when he runs to you—and if you have a treat in your pocket (which you should always have), reinforce that "come" with a treat (just a piece of puppy kibble). A healthy puppy will pay more attention to your whereabouts after this exercise. They won't forget the feeling of losing you, and will follow you closely after that. Train all of your puppies off lead before you ever put a collar on them. It is the easiest thing to do because it is very natural for them. Even after putting a collar and lead on a puppy, don't drag them around; instead, entice them to follow you by using a treat and praise.

For Gun Dogs

Even if you are not a hunter yourself, if you breed any of the hunting breeds, you must have an excellent understanding of what is required of them in the field. That is how you create the best possible puppy that can fulfill the expectations of their new hunting owners. This will also help you dispel misinformation and to educate the puppy buyers in the proper training methods for their puppy. You certainly do not want to stand by while some ignorant trainer talks your buyers into putting an electronic collar on a five- or six-month-old puppy for quick results. If nothing else, give your buyers the information they need to make good choices for their puppies.

For puppies you know will be going to hunting homes, begin their specialized training between six and twelve weeks. Randomly hide duck wings and small canvas puppy bumpers with pigeon feathers attached to them under bushes or behind trees. Put them in places where the puppy can find them relatively easily. Walk along with the puppy until they scent the bumper, and either lock-up[4] or pick it up. Remember to praise them. If they lock up, fire your starter pistol and throw a rock or something where the hidden bumper is located. Tell the puppy to fetch. Throw a white canvas bumper scented with pheasant scent and watch the pups mark the short throws and retrieve the bumper, delivering it to hand. When you throw a bumper scented with duck scent, also have someone blow on a duck call in the vicinity of the fall. It will only take a short time before these little guys are locking up on point and learning the fetch it up command.

Remember that locking up is a hereditary trait and cannot be taught. Pups will either lock up, or they will simply go directly to the bird. Locking up is only a positive trait if the breeding line also includes superior scenting ability. As a hunter, the last thing you want is a retriever who locks up too close to a covey of wild birds and ends up flushing them before you can get into gun range to shoot them. The fact is that none

---

[4]Locking up refers to a gun dog who scents a bird, freezes with his nose pointed straight toward the bird, his tail straight out in back, and one front leg tucked up bent at the elbow. The dog will hold this stance until given the command to flush the bird so the gunner may shoot it as it flies up.

of the retriever breeds can compete with the scenting ability of pointing and flushing breeds like the German Shorthaired Pointer, English Spaniel, Springer Spaniel, Brittany, Pointer, and others. Hunters who prefer upland game will often hunt with a pointing breed and use a retriever to mark and fetch the fallen birds. When hunting ducks, nothing can surpass the natural ability and perseverance of Labrador Retrievers and Chesapeake Bay Retrievers, who will hunt under the harshest conditions without complaint or refusal.

A Breeder Secret

Marking the Middle
A training tip about puppy bumpers is to wrap both ends of the bumpers with duct tape. Puppies do not like the feel of the tape in their mouth, so they learn to pick up the bumpers in the middle where there is only canvas or plastic. This is how you teach them to eventually pick up birds in the middle of the bird's body and not drag them by the head or tail feathers.

I taught my puppies to play in and love the water by taking them to a pond that had a gradual slanted incline from the banks. The shallow water extended at least six feet out from the banks. I took puppy toys with me and threw them in the water just a few feet from the shoreline. The puppies learned to play in the water. I would throw bumpers for their mother, who would retrieve them across the pond, swimming out and back. Soon all the puppies were swimming as well, following their mom.

Some pups will naturally dive to retrieve something that sinks. I had a female who absolutely loved to dive under the water. She would pursue any duck under the water. When ducks are wounded, they will dive to get away from a dog. I usually trained my hunting dogs with dead ducks because I couldn't bring myself to shoot them. I would get them from trainers doing advanced training. They would work their dogs on freshly shot birds and at the end of the day give the dead birds to me. I put the birds in my freezer in the kennel and the night before a training day I would take it out and let it defrost. When dead ducks are launched over a pond, they tend to hit the water and sink. Suzy would scent them off the top of the water and dive down even five or six feet to retrieve them! I just had to be fanatical about treating her ears after every outing; in fact, if you take your puppies swimming, don't forget to treat their ears afterwards. Remember, moisture in a dog's ear is a bad thing.

A Breeder Secret

Mark Training
Dogs are drawn or sucked to white in the field, so that's the color bumper that's used to help train puppies to easily see a bumper as it is launched and falls. At 10 to 12 weeks, a well-bred retriever will be able to accurately mark the fall of a white bumper within a reasonable distance. Orange bumpers and cones are always used for blind retrieves, where the dog has not been able to mark the fall and gets direction for the retrieve exclusively from the handler.

Guns

Puppies who will be future gun dogs need to attend a gun conditioning day at the local gun club or training area to ensure that they won't be gun shy. If the puppy is sold out of your geographic area, refer the buyers to hunting dog clubs in their area where they can participate in this. Puppies are conditioned to the gun by walking them through a field while a gunner shoots a shotgun about 200 yards away from them. Every time he fires the shotgun, the owner gives the puppy a treat. Usually an experienced gun dog is brought along to set the tone. When a gun dog hears a gun he gets turned on and starts looking for the birds to fall. He has no fear—only joy in the hunt. Puppies pick up on that, and start wagging their tails, too.

I once participated in a gun conditioning exercise at Fort Carson, Colorado where at least ten pups were being conditioned to the gun at the same time. Ten guys and gals were crossing the field with their pups on lead, feeding treats as the gunner fired from the hillside. By the end of the day, three sessions were completed (don't work puppies too long on any exercise). The pups were within 20 yards of the gunner, and they were still wagging their tails. This is actually a good exercise for any puppy, even if it is not a hunting dog, because it builds confidence and for the rest of their lives they will not fear loud noises like firecrackers, lightening, or thunder. Remember when I talked about dropping heavy books on the floor and slamming doors in the nursery? Now you understand what that was all about.

Chapter 12
MANAGING A STUD DOG

Managing a stud dog begins at seven weeks of age. Do not be overbearingly dominant with a future stud dog. Although he must learn to curb his assertiveness, he should not be made to comply with the typical rules relating to dominance-like behavior that one might enforce on a puppy dog that is not going to be used for stud service.

If you are of the old school that believes dogs are functioning primarily on an instinctive basis with some repetitive conditioning by their human owners, you may want to re-examine that premise. A recent feature article in *National Geographic* (March 2008) titled *Minds of their Own (Animals are Smarter than you Think)* by Virginia Morell, quotes current research data from around the globe that demonstrates a much higher level of cognitive ability in the animal kingdom than is generally accepted. The article goes on to quote: "Animals need to find mates, food, and a path through the woods, sea, or sky—tasks that Darwin argued require problem solving." Another quote by

Alex Kacelnik, a behavioral ecologist at Oxford University is: "This is the larger lesson of animal cognitive research—it humbles us. We are not alone in our ability to invent or plan."

In my years as a successful stud dog manager, I learned some valuable lessons that I wish to share with those who have an open mind. Dogs are far more intelligent than most people are willing to concede. They learn in many of the same ways that we do. Just as our society has accepted the fact that self-esteem plays a pivotal role in the mental development of humans—the same applies to dogs. When they are intimidated and regimented and are forced to continually work in a repetitive and mentally non-stimulating manner, they can lose their confidence and their ability to function at peak performance levels.

A stud dog who is not allowed to experience a more than average degree of male assertiveness within his pack will not become that experienced, wise, take-charge type of stud dog that will "anchor" your breeding program. He will "miss" (not get the job done). Females only cycle twice a year on average. When he misses—you lose. If you are using him on outside bitches—you not only miss the stud fee—you also destroy your reputation for reliability.

Here are the rules for raising a future stud dog that I have learned from my personal experience. They are different or even the opposite from what most conventional dog trainers recommend. It is up to you to accept them or to reject them:

1. Give the puppy lots of praise and reinforce his self esteem whenever possible. Set him up for success. Don't necessarily require him to do something to get "a pat on the back." Don't insist that he earn praise as you would in a pet puppy.

2. Do not make him wait long in a "sit" position to get his food.

3. Allow him to go through a gate or doorway ahead of you when it is safe to do so.

4. When returning home from a walk or excursion, open the door and allow the puppy to enter first.

5. Prepare his food first and let him eat before the other dogs, who are watching—particularly before the bitches eat.

6. Let him watch all breeding done at your kennels. Put him in a crate in the corner where he can observe, smell, and learn.

7. When he starts to become sexually mature, do not run him with your working stud dogs. Put him in with your bitches. Later when he is an established stud dog, you can run them all together if you have firmly established yourself as the leader and you don't tolerate any dominant behavior between the males.

8. When you play tug-of-war with this puppy, end these sessions with him winning.

9. Do not train this dog to go into the "down" position when other male dogs are present. You can put him in a "sit" or "wait" position—but not "down". For the purposes of earning Obedience titles or the CGC designation (Canine Good Citizen) these short "down" exercises will not damage his attitude. Just don't do them excessively.

10. Allow him to mount all the pillows or toys he wants to. Even his littermates should not be off-limits. Later, when he is experienced—you can teach him to perform when you provide the bitch and tell him it is OK.

11. Examine him all over—including his testicles and penis. He should be conditioned to being touched anywhere without reacting negatively.

Maintaining a Working Stud Dog in Good Physical Condition

1. Feed high quality food.

2. Supplement with Glucosamine and Chondroiten to support adequate seminal fluid and with zinc and Vitamin E to support high sperm count and motility.

3. Provide physical activity to maintain good muscular development.

4. Check his temperature weekly during a grooming session when you go over his entire body checking for any irregularities. Check his testicles for sores, tenderness, or swelling; and check his penis for discharge.

5. Periodically check his sperm count using a "teaser bitch." Look at the specimen under the microscope and check quantity, motility, and deformities i.e., two-headed, without tails, etc. There will be a few of those—but drastic increases should be addressed by a fertility specialist.

6. Always breed him in the same room or area and never loan him out to anyone or take him anywhere else to be bred. He will be the master of his domain and will perform like a champ in his own "kingdom."

7. When he is "tied" with a bitch, lay them down on a blanket and hold the bitch's head securely. This will be much safer for him than having a bitch dragging him around and possibly injuring him.

8. Always clean and disinfect the breeding area before and after breeding sessions.

Frozen Semen
If you have a quality stud dog who is producing superior offspring, you might want to consider the collection and freezing of his semen for the future. This would be prudent in case he gets injured, dies from some unexpected illness, or becomes sterile. There are semen storage banks for dogs. You can research this through your breed club or on the Internet. I certainly regret not having done this on two of my best stud dogs. One became sterile and the other one experienced kidney failure and died within a few days at the age of 12. I lost the breeding lines because I had not anticipated these occurrences. The bitch line is still running in the East from one of my top males on a limited basis. Don't assume that your stud dogs are indestructible. It is best to have a back-up plan i.e., frozen semen or at least a string on several intact males out of your stud dog that you can go back to if you need to do that.

Its Not For Everyone
Stud dog ownership is not for all breeders. You cannot manage a stud dog if you are squeamish about getting some semen on your arm or you can't bear the thought of holding his penis to collect him or to guide him into a bitch. These are things that

Professional Dog Breeders do without batting an eye. It is just biology. You can wear latex gloves when you are managing a breeding. If you can understand that this is not "sensual," but it is all about pro-creation—then you will have it in perspective.

There are professional breeders who always go outside to other breeders for stud services. They are either limited in the size of their facility, or they are not physically able to supervise breeding sessions. There are also professional breeders who do not breed and raise their own stud dogs from their own bitches—they only purchase proven stud dogs from other breeders around the country. I believe that a truly professional breeding kennel will develop its own "signature look." When their dogs are seen in the show ring or at an event—it will be obvious to experienced fellow enthusiasts that the dog is from a specific breeding line. He will have certain attributes that will make him stand out from the crowd. Once you have achieved that special "look" and it is a positive statement—you are successful. You have reached your goal.

Very often your stud dog will end up being your personal companion dog. Most breeders will keep this dog for his entire life. A well-managed, healthy dog will produce quality puppies until he is 10 to 12 years of age. It would be difficult to part with this senior and difficult to locate a quality home for such an old dog. There would be no need to keep his sons for stud service unless you were introducing a completely different bitch line into your kennels. You might keep the sons who are top show prospects to promote your kennel reputation and then sell them to other breeders who will exhibit them. It is also fun to take the old guy to an occasional Specialty show and exhibit him in the Veteran's Class. These old show boys love the attention and the well-deserved applause they get from the crowd. Even an old retired hunter may enjoy the occasional day in the field when he is encouraged to show the young dogs how it is done.

Like many experienced dog breeders, I found the males to be the sweetest of the personal companion dogs. They are loving, protective, and intelligent. Having a superior stud dog is one of the "perks" of becoming a professional dog breeder. I was always proud to be seen with my stunning Champion dog. He was so well behaved and friendly that I could take him anywhere and not worry about his behavior. That is more than I can say for many children.

Chapter 13
TO SHOW OR NOT TO SHOW

Some people have asked me if it is absolutely necessary to be involved in dog shows in order to become a superior dog breeder. The answer is "No," you don't have to get involved in dog shows—but being involved makes it a whole lot easier to purchase high-quality breeding stock, to learn the breed standard, and to showcase your dogs. Other purebred dog venues can be pursued, including hunt tests, agility trials, obedience trials, tracking, and so on. Though it's not technically a necessity, I feel that if you do not plan to do anything with your dogs, you should not pursue this profession. Through this chapter you'll discover why.

One reason you want to be involved in shows and related activities is that you cannot own enough dogs to provide the genetic diversity you need to maintain vitality in your breeding lines. Therefore, it is necessary for you to be ever on the lookout for what's happening with your breed so you can consider what might benefit or improve your lines. Another reason is that having your dogs compete against others provides potential buyers the opportunity to confirm that your puppies are good quality—regardless of what you claim and believe. Showing that your dogs have performed exceptionally well in competitions maybe the only way to prove to the buyer that you have the best puppies available. If you were a buyer considering a $2,500 purchase you would likely want to see how the potential breeder's dogs stack up against others.

To do this, you don't have to become a rabid exhibitor and spend every weekend at dog shows, or at obedience trials or agility competitions, or at a hunt test. Most of the activities that you will be engaged in are weekly classes for conformation to teach your puppy how to behave in the show ring or weekly agility/obedience training sessions.

Getting your puppies into a show ring is good for them. It socializes them to strange new sounds, other people, and other dogs. If your dog has been properly trained for showing so that it performs no matter who is on the other end of the show lead, you shouldn't have a problem later on turning it over to a handler at ringside if you decide that is the best way for you to finish the dog's championship. In fact, some dogs will show better if they are excited about all the new faces and new smells around them. A dog that has been crated for three or four days is not going to show as well as a fresh dog who came straight from home or from the airport, is with its owner, and isn't stressed out from all the other strange dogs barking and whining around it in a cramped van or RV.

A professional dog breeder's secret is that even though it is competitive and hard to win in the show ring, with a good dog you can place in the ribbons—2nd to 4th place in the Open class or in the Puppy class. If you have a very popular breed, getting that first-place blue ribbon and photo with the judge may be difficult, but when the competition is fierce a placement is valuable.

A Breeder Secret

Hold for the Cameras
When you've earned a ribbon, you will be photographed with your dog and the judge. Show photos are always an asset to your website—make sure you get one.

Here is another professional dog breeder's secret. If you enter in the American Bred Class, which often has no competition, you could more easily receive a first-place blue ribbon and would go back in the ring for the Winners' circle. American Bred class is leftover from the days when many of the dogs being shown were from outside the U.S. The designation was to showcase the dogs being bred in the United States at that time. Today, the American Bred class is sometimes used by handlers or breeders who have multiple dogs to show and cannot fit them all into the Open classes. You can use it to get that blue ribbon that would not be forthcoming in the Open classes, either because your dog just doesn't have the pizzazz needed to win or because you are not an accomplished handler. If your dog is awarded first place in American Bred, you will be seen in the company of the best dogs, in the Winners' Circle, after all the other classes have competed. I don't think I have ever seen a winner from the American Bred Class awarded Winners Dog or Winners Bitch, and subsequently never BOB (Best of Breed), but it is a legitimate class that allows you the opportunity to showcase your dog. The judge will see your dog a second time, putting yourself and your dog in the ring with the best dogs.

I am not advocating that you avoid the Open class—and if you have a good dog, you might actually win. But, if you have shown your dog several times without placing in the ribbons, you might want to give the American Bred class a shot. A dog can be perfectly bred to the breed standard, have a beautiful coat and a smooth, flawless gait, but lack the spark of a truly exceptional show dog.

In conclusion, try it. As you have probably figured out by now, I believe in the motto *carpe diem* (seize the day). It would be good for your kennel reputation if you could learn to enjoy it and succeed in the show ring. If you just can't get into it, then encourage one of your kids to become a Junior Handler, or make a good friend out of someone who is a breeder/handler and trade them pet sitting or obedience training or something in exchange for showing your dogs. If you only have bitches and you always breed them to champion stud dogs, all of your puppies will be champion-sired—that's the justification for big stud fees. Even if you don't show your bitches, do make a point to help out at these events as a club member. The more you help out, the more cooperation you will receive from other breeders and exhibitors.

A Breeder Secret

Show Off Your Stud Dog
Everyone with a high-quality stud dog will either end up showing him or competing with him in some type of event. That is a good invest-ment because it will attract bitch owners to use him on their bitches. The reason AKC doesn't allow neutered or spayed dogs to compete in conformation classes is because the whole point of them is to ferret out the best dogs for breeding purposes.

Dog Show Etiquette Tips

Earning ribbons and championships on your dogs at shows is extremely rewarding and valuable for your business, but it's certainly not something to be done at all costs. Here are my personal standards that I feel should be upheld by everyone who shows a dog.

1. Never ask anyone not to bring a competitive dog to a show so that your dog will have a better chance of winning.

2. Never agree to not enter your dog in a show in order to allow someone else a better chance of winning.

3. Do not volunteer or accept a nomination on the judge's selection committee of your breed club or an all-breed club if you are planning on exhibiting any dogs that you own or co-own under any judge that you helped select—ever!

4. Do not converse with any AKC judges anywhere on the premises of the dog show whether your dog is entered in the show or not. This gives the appear-ance of impropriety. Watching professional handlers and breeders bending over the barriers at a dog show and whispering in the ears of the judges or huddled together in the parking lot with a judge, is one of the reasons that so many people drop out of the sport. I may be paranoid, but you have to admit that this practice reeks of favoritism and unfair advantages given to those who indulge in

it. When they come back and win with a mediocre entry, you have to wonder. Again, it is the appearance of impropriety that stings.

5. Do not mail winning show photos of your dog and its handler or of you and your dog, to the judge under whom you won at the show. If the judge wants a photograph, he or she can purchase one from the photographer at the show. Sending a photo conveys the request to put your dog up again the next time this judge sees your dog in the ring. The photos are meant to identify you or the handler so that the judge will remember it the next time he or she sees your dog. This is why many handlers always wear the same outfit or the same unusual or bright color at all the shows. They can't put their name on their jacket, but if they wear the same unique jacket at every show, people learn who they are and instantly recognize them.

A Breeder Secret

Another Ethical Dilemma
You may be told that all handlers send photos to judges and you should, too. Not only is this not true, but even if it was a common practice, it is still an unethical practice. Show photos are expensive, and the gift of a photo is a gratuity whether you intend it to be one or not. I hope that this practice is discontinued as more breeders appreciate the inappropriateness of it. Remember, do the right thing!

---

6. Do not advertise your dog in any publications with a photo of a judge awarding your dog a prize with a big "Thank You" under the photo, naming the judge. The name of the judge who put your dog up should not be mentioned at all. Judges should not receive recognition for putting up any individual dog. Published recognition is a form of gratuity. It promotes this judge for future assignments. Say "Thank You" in the show ring when you receive the ribbon; that is being courteous. Never mention it again to the judge.

7. When you are gaiting your dog around the ring, do not drop bait behind you on the floor to cause the other dogs to lower their noses to the floor. Do not run up behind another exhibitor in the ring while gaiting your dog thereby crowding their dog and causing it to lose its pace and focus and to look around at your dog.

8. While presenting your dog in the show ring for the judge's evaluation, do not push your dog out further toward the center of the ring so as to obscure the dog behind you. If the judge asks you to bring the dog to a particular location for individual judging, you must comply and that is acceptable. However, when the dogs are all lined up in a row so that the judge can take a comparative look at all of them, it is blatantly unfair to stack your dog one or two feet towards the center of the ring and out of line with the other entries.

9. Do not face your dog in the opposite direction to make it stand out in the ring at the end of the line after all dogs have gone around. This practically screams of a pre-established method of identification so that the judge will presumably identify which dog they are supposed to put up. It is just too suspicious. A good

judge who is judging fairly will penalize these types of behaviors in their ring and will not award any ribbons to a dog that is handled in this fashion. It is the judges who police the show ring and it is their job to remove the incentives for this type of handling. Anything a Junior Showmanship exhibitor is not allowed to do should also be barred from the regular rings.

10. Do not activate squeaky toys behind a dog that is being stacked for the judge's examination, causing the dog to be distracted and lose its stack.

11. Do not stand outside the ring with a bitch in season to distract a competitor's male dog from showing well while the judge is judging him. Also, do not stand outside the ring with a bitch in season if you have a dog in the ring who will turn on and strut his stuff if he gets a whiff of her. Do not agree to do this for another exhibitor.

A Breeder Secret

What a Bitch Can Do to a Dog
If you have ever watched a Malamute dog in the ring when a bitch in season is walked past the ring, you will understand the effect she can have. It is like a metamorphosis. The male dog will begin to puff up before your eyes, stacking himself in a perfect kinetic stack with his tail and ears up. I swear the males grow two inches in height, and their expression is one of eager anticipation. When they move, they are incredibly impressive. An "outside-the-ring" assistant handler knows exactly when to walk a bitch by the ring and when to walk her away from the ring so that the effect is on one dog and not on the others. This is entirely unethical.

---

12. Do not agree to pick up a judge or judges from the airport and take them to their hotel. If they are ethical, they will rent a car, hail a taxi, or take the hotel shuttle. The time you spend with them in the car creates a window of opportunity for unethical conversations. If necessary, the club can offer to pay for a taxi and an ethical judge will understand the reasons behind that decision.

13. Do not attend the judge's dinner the night before a show in which your dog is entered. All kinds of improper introductions and situations can arise. This practice of hob-knobbing with the judges the night before a dog show is highly suspect. The AKC judges' guidelines suggest that judges are asked not to engage in any behavior that would give the appearance of impropriety. It would seem much better if the judges would just dine with each other, with the AKC officials, and perhaps with the show superintendent's staff and avoid socializing with club members.

14. Do not have cosmetic surgery performed on your dog to make it more competitive in the show ring. This includes practices such as ear surgery to correct poor ear set or shape (a common practice in some breeds), dental work to correct a flawed bite or missing teeth, and much more. The show is about identifying the best breeding stock; when you cover up genetic flaws yet offer your dog as a stud dog, you are misleading other breeders, failing to disclose pertinent facts, and misleading puppy buyers as to the quality of your dogs.

15. Never substitute one dog for another in the show ring or at a performance test. For example, don't take your Champion dog into a ring or your Master Hunting dog up to the line as a replacement for one of your dogs who isn't competitive, then apply the points or passes to your other dog. This is cheating.

A Breeder Secret

No-Fail Identification

One of these days, microchips will become mandatory and a dog's chip number will have to be put on the entry form of any event in which he competes. Each dog will be scanned as it enters the show ring or other competitive events to verify its identity. I would support such a change wholeheartedly to stop the practice of substitutions. We need to utilize modern technology to police our own sport.

---

16. Do not make nasty comments or curse or swear when your dog doesn't place in the ribbons. No matter what your opinion of the judging, keep it to yourself in the show ring. Your options are to document the poor choice, describe why it is a poor choice, and make an official complaint to the show superintendent; or forget it and choose not to show under that judge again. Just make sure you are being objective—which is not often an easy task. If you haven't had your hands on the winning dog to compare it to your dog, there is no way you can be sure that your dog is really better. From my experience, putting your hands on a dog to go over it can be very revealing. When I watch judging, I look for the judges who make a thorough physical evaluation of each dog by carefully and methodically going over it with their hands. Chances are their evaluation will be much more meaningful than the judge who spends most of their time staring at the dog's face or at a row of hand-stacked dogs, paying little attention to substance and movement. You can tell the judges who are considered "movement" judges because they will turn and watch the dogs gaiting all the way to the end of the line. Judges who don't understand movement or structure will merely watch the down-and-back looking for the obvious flaws that anyone can learn to recognize. Movement judges will want to see the side movement on every dog and they will put up a dog that is structurally superior regardless of the cosmetics.

In summary, let me say that in order to bring these practices to an end—and to clean up the dog show sport so that it is fair, honest, and uniformly judged—it is necessary for ethical breeders to actively recruit and assist honest and intelligent new breeders, and to instill in them a strong ethical and moral sense of responsibility to maintain scrupulous and impeccable integrity. If you know firsthand, beyond a doubt, that someone is breaking the rules, blow the whistle. If you remain silent, the corruption will spread.

Chapter 14

SELLING OR PLACING AN ADULT DOG OR BITCH

The hardest task of a professional dog breeder is to cull their kennel breeding stock. Do not assume that culling is synonymous with euthanizing dogs; rather, it is a term generally used among dog breeders in reference to reducing the number of dogs one owns, or to replacing existing dogs with better or younger dogs to enhance your breeding program. While it is difficult, it is also necessary to the health and longevity of your breeding program, as your goal is to produce the best quality puppies from the best quality dogs available. In this chapter, I'll explore some of the reasons you may need to cull your kennel and some of the ways to go about it.

Reasons to Cull

There are many reasons that you may want or need to remove a dog or bitch from your breeding program. The following are just some examples, based on my personal experience.

- You have a dog whose puppies do not meet your breeding standards of quality, temperament, or health.

- If a dog or bitch that you are breeding has been bred to two different quality breeding lines and has produced mediocre or poor quality puppies that do not meet the breed standard both times, you cannot in good conscience continue to use that dog or bitch for breeding. No matter how good the dog or bitch appears to be, or is on paper, it is genetically an inconsistent dog. This should be a reminder that when you purchase your breeding stock, you should try to see the entire litter if possible. If you looked at the entire litter of puppies that it came from, you might find that it was the only puppy that was high quality, in which case it was a fluke. If it cannot reproduce that same quality, then it is not worthy of your kennel name. Make sure you spay or neuter this dog yourself, because when others see it, they will think it is breeding quality.

- You have a bitch that has contributed significantly to your kennel, you have kept a daughter back from her, and it is time to spay her and retire her from breeding.

- You have a dog who is terminally ill and surgery is not a feasible option. The dog is suffering from either a disease it contracted, an accidental injury, or a vicious attack by another dog. Euthanizing the dog is your only option.

- You have a stud dog who has become permanently and irreversibly sterile.

- You have a dog who is dog-aggressive and fights with your other dogs. He or she cannot be left alone with your other dogs or children. I can say without a doubt that there is no room for a vicious animal in any breeding kennel—or in a home. A dog must be evaluated before it can be placed or euthanized, and any dog that is aggressive with people without provocation should always be euthanized.

- You have a dog who produces incorrect color (assuming color type is relevant to your breed). He or she carries a mutated or recessive color gene that keeps popping up in its litters. If this is the case, the dog is worthless to any professional breeding program and must be removed from it.

- You have a bitch who produces too many puppies in each litter. By the time you raise her litters you are exhausted and physically depleted. She suffers through pregnancies that are unbelievably difficult for her. She is tired and even with a once-a-year breeding program she looks worn out for months after weaning her litters. This trait tends to run from mother to daughter, so don't hold back a bitch puppy from this girl—you will have the same problem. Avoid this problem in the future by not purchasing bitch puppies from an extremely large litter.

- You have a bitch who is a bad mother. She has to be made to nurse her puppies. She is terrible at keeping them clean or stimulating them to pee or poop. When they are born she refuses to take the sac off or cut the umbilical cords. You have to keep a constant vigil when she is with her puppies, as she has no qualms about lying on them and suffocating them. If one crawls away she has no instinct to go get it and put it back with the litter. She leaves all the work to you. Three weeks after whelping she steps out of the nursery and refuses to return. She nips her pups if they want to nurse. She doesn't want to play with her puppies or keep them warm at night. We refer to these bitches as "non brood bitches." If you have a bitch who kills and eats her newborn puppies, she certainly can't be part of your breeding program unless you are prepared to muzzle her during whelping and perhaps for the first 24 to 48 hours until her hormones level out.

- You have a stud dog who is not good at his job. He just hasn't learned to adapt himself to different bitches, or he can't figure out how to copulate properly even after getting lessons from your resident experienced matriarch bitch. He suffers from continued premature ejaculation. He can't tell the difference between a bitch in season and a bitch that isn't in season. He wants to breed everything in sight, including you! He is difficult to collect and will not allow you to assist him in achieving a natural tie. Every time you attempt to guide his penis, he immediately jumps off and quits. Maturity isn't improving his skills.

- You have a stud dog who is rough and too aggressive with the bitches. He knocks them onto the ground, grabs them by the neck skin, drawing blood, and comes up tied. If they resist, he bites and snarls at them. He constantly marks his territory, peeing on everything in his domain. He attempts to rape bitches that are not in season. He mounts all the male dogs and growls at them, instigating fights if he can. He questions your authority and ignores basic commands.

Making Appropriate Placements

From the examples above, you can see that there are many reasons why a dog might not work out in your breeding program. Often these issues won't affect the dog's placement as a non-breeding companion animal at all. That doesn't mean you should be too hasty in getting rid of the dog.

When placing a retiring brood bitch, you should be careful to fully consider what is in her best interests. Ethically, you need to create a situation for her that ensures she will be properly loved and cared for the rest of her life. To make this happen, it is better for her to be under seven years of age. Optimally, she should be around five or six years old. By that age she should be a fully trained, possibly titled, CGC certified, healthy bitch. Anyone with a busy lifestyle who appreciates a lovely girl who is housetrained and obedience trained should be more than happy to get her.

Whether to sell her or give her away is a serious question. If you know the person very well—and you know that they are responsible and will love the dog and give her a forever home—then consider just asking for the cost of the spay and final health check. If you are considering someone you do not know well, I would ask for at least $400 to $500 dollars, plus shipping costs. People tend to take better care of something they paid for. If she is a fully trained and titled gun dog at five years old she is in her prime and is worth several thousand dollars to a serious hunter. She could work for at least another four or five years. Don't cheat yourself out of getting what she's worth, but consider the home first.

Aggressive dogs are the hardest to place and if you had raised your puppy properly you most likely would not be faced with this problem. However, sometimes we are given adult dogs because a breeder passed away and left you a dog in their will or for some other reason. Rehabilitating an aggressive dog is extremely difficult and they can never be completely trusted. You have to follow your conscience, but I would always elect to euthanize a dog that had bitten or attacked a human being without any possible provocation. If this dog was a sweet puppy and adolescent and suddenly became aggressive, the first thing to do is to have a physical examination performed. The dog may be in pain, have a brain tumor or some other debilitating disorder that has drastically affected his temperament. If the malady is addressed, perhaps your sweet dog will reappear. By the way, bitches do have PMS symptoms, so don't make evaluations about dog aggressiveness by her behavior just before her heat cycle.

I was once offered $3,000 for a brood bitch I was retiring. Suzy was five years old and had a Senior Retriever hunting title as well as WC and Canine Good Citizen certificates. She was a beautiful girl, extremely sweet-natured, and obedience-trained. The man who wanted to buy her was an avid hunter. He had seen her working in the field the year before and watched her ace a hunt test in Kansas. But when I sat down to interview him, I found out that his wife did not allow dogs in her house. He would have to house her in an outdoor kennel run with a doghouse. She would be his only dog, and he worked full time. This meant that she would only be allowed out of the dog run when he was at home and she would not be allowed in the house at all—even though she was a perfect house dog. She had slept on my bed for three years. I simply could not bear to think of her being locked in a cell 22 hours a day and only allowed out when he had the opportunity to go hunting. I told him it was not a good choice for her. I found a wonderful forever home for her as a therapy dog, living inside a house and going to hospitals two or three times a week. I gave the dog away, passed on the $3,000, and felt no regrets about it. Money and material things enhance our physical lives, but our souls are nourished through doing the right thing.

While writing this book I received a letter from the elderly couple who adopted, Suzy, telling me that after years of wonderful hospital work, she had passed away. They were so kind to write to me and thank me for giving them such a wonderful dog. I have an oil painting of Suzy on the wall of my bedroom. An AKC hunt test judge painted it. She produced beautiful artwork for greeting cards. As Suzy came out of the water after a test, the judge snapped a photograph of her. When she had published the greeting cards made from this painting, she sent the painting to me. I see it every single day as I open my eyes in the morning. I remember Suzy and all that she contributed to the world in her life—certainly more than some people can claim.

A Breeder Secret

Harder on the Breeder?

When a dog or bitch is kept as a pet, it is a major commitment. Unless you have unlimited resources and space, every dog that you keep is taking up the space of a dog that could be a productive asset. It is hard to give up a dog that we have raised from a puppy, loved, trained, and socialized. Some breeds are easier than others to transition to a new home. Sometimes I think it is harder on the breeder to part with their retired dogs than it is for the dogs to make the change.

Friends, Relatives, and Seniors

Sometimes a relative or friend who knows the dog will be happy to take him or her as a pet. They can see past their age and appreciate their many superior qualities. This is much easier for the dog, as well. They are not so traumatized by moving to another home when they are already familiar with their new owner.

An older, healthy dog who is trained is a good alternative for senior citizens who wish to remain in their home and be independent for a few more years. The dog gives them a reason to get up in the morning, get dressed, and go outside. It keeps the senior from feeling so alone, and gives them opportunities to talk to other people when they do go for a walk or to the park. Dogs attract children and other dog lovers, and this is especially true when there is a fine example of the breed on the end of the lead. Veteran dogs are still very impressive.

If the dog is a medium or large breed, it will tend to protect an elderly owner quite well. Even a small dog can be a serious deterrent to an intruder. My 10-year-old Pekingese actually chased a strange man right out the door of my kitchen one night, while tearing a piece of his pant leg off! I slammed the door behind him and called the police. She did not hesitate to attack him. Fortunately, he was unprepared for that and turned and ran. Of course, Pekingese owners know that all Pekes believe they weigh 200 pounds and rule China. This just demonstrates the power of self-confidence.

A Breeder Secret

Retired Stud Dogs

Placing retired stud dogs is an unusual practice. A stud dog is viable until around the age of 10 or 11 years if he is properly maintained. At that age, he should be retired to your front porch or next to your fireplace. It would be an extreme situation to have to place a dog at that age. He has earned his keep—and a gentle, easy retirement.

Facilitating the Transition to a New Home

Transitions are best done with scent conditioning. Once you know who the new owner is going to be, get a T-shirt or some article of clothing from him or her. Request that it not be laundered so that it still smells like the person. Bring it home to your dog that you are planning on transitioning. Keep it in a plastic bag and for four or five consecutive days, take it out and let the dog smell it before being fed their meals. In addition, take the article of clothing out two or three times a day and let the dog smell it, then give the dog a treat. What you are doing is positive reinforcement—associating that scent with something good.

By doing this, when the dog actually makes the transition and smells that scent which he or she has come to associate with food and treats, the dog will relax and his instincts will tell him that there is nothing to be afraid of. He will be pre-conditioned to accept this scent as something good. If possible, have the new owners visit and take the dog for a walk, or meet them in the park and let them interact with the dog for a few hours. When you feel that the dog is ready to make the transition, complete it. Don't call to talk to the dog on the telephone and don't drop by to visit the dog. Don't undermine the building of this new relationship. Make it as easy on the dog as possible. Unless the new owner is a long-time friend or a family member, it is best to make a clean break with the dog. You will grieve the loss of this dog in your home, but take comfort in knowing that you've placed him or her in the best home possible, where the dog will be treated like royalty.

Chapter 15
HELPING OWNERS COPE WITH LOSS

I don't know what your personal beliefs are about life and death, but one thing is a universal fact, human beings grieve, and they experience utter sadness and despair. When their loss is one of a dog who has provided unconditional love and daily companionship, often for over a decade, the grief they experience can be shattering. As professional dog breeders, it is often we who are called upon to console and help guide individuals and families following such a loss. Being a dog breeder means learning to function in many roles.

Listening and Consoling

I have played marriage counselor, disciplinarian, mother figure, consultant, child psychiatrist, dog behavioral specialist, Rabbi, and personal dog trainer. Was I qualified to play those roles? Yes, because I am human and I can empathize with a fellow human being (or a dog). But my biggest and best qualification is that I can listen. If you can listen to someone who is in pain, making them feel that it is OK to talk about their grief, you will guide them down the road to recovery. It never fails. The key is to let them feel safe in expressing their sadness. Crying together is good. Talking about the dog they lost is good. Don't worry about making them feel worse by talking about their pet and companion; this is what they need to do before they can get better. Don't ever belittle their feelings or say something like, "It was just a dog. I can get you another one." If that's the way you honestly feel, you might want to consider a profession other than dog breeding.

Experiencing a Loss

I'll start this section with a story. Jeff was a family man, about 40 years old. He bought a handsome black male pup from me so that he and his father-in-law could go duck hunting and have a great dog to retrieve for them. He had always wanted a really good hunting dog. He came to visit my kennels several times with his father-in-law. They brought pheasant wings and duck wings, duck calls, and even a live pigeon one time. When they were happy with what they were seeing, Jeff gave me a deposit on a black puppy—but took his time picking out the exact one he wanted. He named him Beau, and came to get him when he turned seven weeks old. Beau was a born hunting dog from the day he could climb out of the whelping box. I doubt I ever saw him without something in his mouth. He loved to carry everything around, but would bring it to you whenever you asked him. He was a big boy, with lots of substance and bone—a blocky, solid, classic Lab, with a bit of leg. I personally love that combination—that few inches over the breed standard is such a benefit in the field.

Jeff spent over 1,000 hours training Beau to be the best gun dog any man could own. His father-in-law spent almost every weekend helping Jeff train his puppy. They lived near a big pond, so Beau got to work in the water almost every afternoon, all summer long. By September, they were completely in sync. Beau was ready to work. He turned in a superior performance and by the end of hunting season Beau was an accomplished gun dog. His great breeding line of National Field Champions and Field Champions culminated in one awesome bird dog. Jeff called a few times during hunting season to tell me how impressed he was with Beau and how much he appreciated this wonderful dog that I had sold to him. It made my heart glad to hear of Beau's successes.

I got a call from Jeff's wife about a year and a half later. She was crying softly on the telephone. Then she told me what had happened. Beau had been poisoned one night by some psycho who threw poisoned meat over their fence, where Beau found it and ate it. Jeff had found him in the back yard, dead. This had happened over a month before she called me. She asked for my help because she was afraid that Jeff was going to grieve himself to death. He wasn't sleeping, wasn't able to go to work, wasn't able to eat, or to interact with his family. No one could get through to him. He was suffering from profound sadness and depression. He was ashamed to go to a therapist or tell his family doctor that he couldn't handle losing his dog.

Not only had Jeff lost his dog, he had lost his best friend. Jeff had never faced death before. He still had all of his grandparents, aunts, uncles, and friends. He had never experienced the loss of a loved one before. He had grown up without pets, so had never lost one. Some of his friends were critical of his reaction to the loss of his dog. He couldn't concentrate on his job or even look at his children without bursting into tears. He felt that he wasn't a "man" anymore, because this weakness in his emotional makeup had never surfaced before, and he didn't know how to cope with it. Jeff couldn't remember a single time that he had cried because of a personal tragedy. This 40-year-old man had escaped mortality. He had never attended a funeral in his life.

A Breeder Secret

Getting Help Through the APLB

The Association for Pet Loss and Bereavement (APLB) is a place where people who are grieving the loss of a pet can go for support. It was founded by Dr. Wallace Sife in the late 1990s, and is now recognized world-wide as an excellent resource for those in such need. Dr. Sife is the author of the book *The Loss of a Pet*—the first such book of its kind, which went on to win numerous awards. The Association can be reached through its website, www.aplb.org.

The next day, after thinking about how I could help Jeff, I called his home and talked to him for over two hours. I listened and understood his severe pain. In my life I had lost many friends in the wars in Israel. I lost my father when he was only 52. Having always had dogs since I was a young child, I had lost a number of them over the years. Being a breeder, I had fought death toe to toe and sometimes I had lost the battles. Being a woman, I had lost several friends to breast cancer and I had lost a full-term infant at birth. But the reason I could help Jeff was because I know that dogs have souls and I believe that Jeff and Beau will be reunited at some point. Because I have faith that this is the way of life—and that dying is not even close to being the end of our existence—I was able to convey a surety and a peace that had eluded him.

Jeff's wife called me later to say that he was doing so much better after our conversations and that he had gone to a grief counselor as I had suggested. A year later, I sold another puppy to Jeff with the understanding that he would try hard never to compare this puppy to Beau. I asked him to let the new puppy (a yellow pup this time so that he would not be expected to act like Beau) make his own unique impression on Jeff and his family. I purposely sold him a puppy that had a different breeding line than Beau—I wanted their personalities to be different, so that Jeff and his new puppy, Cody, could bond without reminders of Beau getting in the way.

Practical Ways to Ease the Pain of Loss

Here are some things you can say and do that will help people who have lost their dogs get through this extremely sad time:

- If you have a good photo of the dog as a puppy, have it framed in a tasteful frame and give it to them to put up in their house. Write the dog's name and birth date on the back of the photo. I have edited my own digital photos on a photo software program so that they look like oil paintings. If you can get a more recent digital photo from a family member and do the same thing, that is even better. Memorializing a dog this way is a good thing; it helps people maintain their connection to their dog.

- Write them a letter from their dog. You may feel silly doing this, but it works! Say thank you in the letter for all the simple joys they shared—being my friend, for taking me on long walks, for teaching me to hunt, for taking me to shows, for letting me play with your children, for making me a part of your family, for being my best friend—whatever you know that they have done with their dog. If a family member can share with you some specific experiences they had together like vacations or camping or anything memorable that you can talk about in the letter, get the details and include those times. What you are trying to show them is that their dog had a good life with them no matter how brief it might have been.

- Ask them questions about the best things they remember about their dog. For example, "What is the funniest thing your dog ever did? What surprised you about your dog? How smart do you think your dog was? Did you have a special term of endearment you used with your dog? Did your dog run in his sleep? Did he sleep on his back or lay in some weird pose? Did you ever think your dog was laughing at you?"

- Call them at least once a week for several weeks after their loss and check on them, asking how they are doing. This shows you are taking their loss seriously, letting them know that you understand how badly they feel, and that you accept their grief as a normal reaction.

A Breeder Secret

When to Get a Puppy After a Loss

If the people you're counseling want to buy a puppy right away, tell them you think it is really much better to wait a few months at least. They deserve to have that time to grieve and the puppy doesn't deserve to be constantly compared to the dog that passed away—it just can't measure up to that. It takes at least three or four months before one can freely enjoy a new puppy. Children seem to recover much faster and a new puppy is a distraction for them, but is it advisable to keep children from grieving? Would you want them to grow up like Jeff—never learning how to work through grief and pain? Kids need to learn these lessons. By bringing a new puppy into their home as quickly as possible, you are depriving them of this very important lesson in life.

You need to be prepared to take as much time as is necessary to empathize and sympathize with a grieving dog owner. Some of the people to whom you sell puppies will become more closely bonded with their dog than with any other being on Earth. When they experience the loss of that dog, it is very hard for them to share the pain they are suffering. Some people make fun of the loving connections between dogs and their owners; I feel sad for them because they don't understand, and have never experienced, the incredible bond between a human being and their dog. Many pets are surrogate children to people who, for whatever reason, were never able to experience parenthood. Or they are second children or grandchildren for those whose children have grown. Or they are simply members of the family like other "children" in the home. Imagine how you might feel if your child passed away. This is the level of emotional pain that they are experiencing.

Reaching Your Destination

You now have the moral foundation that supports the practical applications of this book. As you learn them, you'll be reminded that the ethical aspects of dog breeding are inextricably connected to almost every part of the process, from keeping your kennels clean to providing an invigorating and interesting environment for your dogs and puppies. Morality is not just a frame of mind or about being legally or financially honest. It is also about your daily life and how you create order from chaos while providing safety and security for your dogs, your family, and your customers.

Resources

Recommended Reading

Canine Reproduction and Whelping. A Dog Breeder's Guide. Myra Savant-Harris R.N., Dogwise Publishing.

The Complete Dog Book. Official Publication of the American Kennel Club. Ballantine Books.

Cytology of the Dog and Cat. Victor Permann, DVM, Ph.D.; Richard D. Alsaker, DVM, MS; and Ronald C. Riis, DVM, MS. American Animal Hospital Association.

Deafness in Dogs and Cats. www.Isu.edu/deafness/incidenc.htm

Diagnostic Veterinary Parasitology. Joann Colville, DVM. American Veterinary Publications.

Dog Owner's Home Veterinary Handbook. Delbert Carlson DVM, and James Giffin, MD., Howell Book House.

Kennels and Kenneling. Joel M. McMains, Howell Book House.

The Merck Veterinary Manual. Merck and Co. Inc., John Wiley and Sons.

Plumb's Veterinary Drug Handbook. Donald Plumb, Blackwell Publishing

Puppy Intensive Care. A Breeder's Guide to Care of Newborn Puppies. Book and DVD. Myra Savant-Harris R.N., Dogwise Publishing.

Skin Diseases of Dogs and Cats: A Guide for Pet Owners and Professionals. Dr. Steve A. Melman, Dermapet.

Successful Dog Breeding. The Complete Handbook of Canine Midwifery. Chris Walkowicz and Bonnie Wilcox, Howell Book House.

Veterinary Clinical Parasitology. Margaret Sloss, Russel Kemp, and Anne Zajac, Iowa State University Press.

Whelping Healthy Puppies. (Video 63 minutes/DVD Format). Sylvia Smart, Keepsake Productions.

Web Sites (information and products)

www.akc.org. American Kennel Club.

www.bigdogbeds.com. Big dog beds.

www.breeders-choice.com/avoderm. Breeder's Choice, Avoderm Natural™

www.buzzle.com. Buzzle, dog related articles.

www.carealotpets.com. Care-A-Lot Pet Supply.

www.deltasociety.org. Delta Society, therapy and assistance dogs.

www.dogwise.com. Leading source for books and DVDs on dogs.

www.DrsFosterSmith.com. Doctors Foster and Smith, veterinary products and information.

www.homestead.com Homestead web hosting and site design.

www.irs.gov/businesses/small/article/0,,id=99921,00.html. IRS site relating to independent contractors.

www.landcoproducts.com/products/milkreplacers.htm. Landco, superior puppy formula.

www.PennHIP.com. Hip evaluation information.

www.petedge.com. Pet Edge, excellent source for grooming supplies.

www.revivalanimal.com Revival Animal Health, best source for medicines and infirmary supplies, vaccines, etc.

www.unicahome.com. Unica Home, source for unique doghouses.

www.valleyvet.com. Valley Pet Supply, good source for toys.

www.vetamerica.com. Vet America, Puppylac milk replacer source.

Advertising and Marketing

AKC (*AKC Gazette*). (212) 696-8295. Breeder and classified advertising.

BowTie Inc, Fancy Publications (*Dog Fancy, Dog World*). BowTie Classified, 800-546-7730, (213) 385-2222. Leading magazines for breeder advertising.

Jeff Sengstack, Digital Video and DVD Authoring. Complete guide from software recommendations to professional tips.

AUTHOR BIOGRAPHY

Sylvia Smart owned a breeding kennel, Black Forest Flying Labs, for more than 15 years. She bred Labrador Retrievers, specializing in top quality hunting dogs; and healthy, robust, and sweet tempered companion dogs. She owned the number three AKC ranked Labrador Retriever in 2002. The kennel operation was always relatively small, with no more than five or six brood bitches and one or two stud dogs at any given time. Since retiring from breeding, she is focusing on her writing career and produced a DVD, *Whelping Healthy Puppies*. Along with her career as a breeder, Sylvia was active in many dog clubs and associations and was part of the management team for the Los Angeles Olympics in 1984. Sylvia's focus now is mentoring and advising other professional breeders. She currently shares her life in Arizona with two adult Chocolate Labrador Retrievers and a Silver Standard Poodle. Sylvia may be contacted through her website, www.sylviasmart.com.

INDEX

A

accidental breeding, 56, 73
accidents, avoiding, 146-47
accounting software, 77
accountants, and IRS, 84-85
activity clubs, 34
Advantix, 67
aggressive dogs, 172
all-breed clubs, 34
American Bred class, 165
American Kennel Club (AKC), 6
Amphoral, 131
ancillary products and services, 103-04
Animal Poison Control Center, 127
appliances, 71
arbitrator, 24
artificial insemination, 133-34
Association for Pet Loss and Bereavement, 178

B

backup generator, 66
banking, 76-78
balance sheet, 78
Baytril, 131
Benadryl, 68
birth collar, 99
birthday cards, 101
birthing, 134
bitches
    conditioning for motherhood, 148-50
    during weaning, 141-42
    foundation, 54-58
    reasons to cull, 171
    in season, 74
Black Forest Flying Labs, 61
blocky/show type Labs, 53
B-matches, attending, 48
boarding, 103
books, 47
breed
    how often to, 55
    large, 39
    by popularity (AKC), 41-43
    small, 39
breed clubs, 14, 47
    code of ethics of, 56
breeders, networking with, 31-32
Breeders' Club discount program, 80
breed encyclopedias, 41

breed evaluation worksheet, 51
breeding, accidental, 56
breeding rights, 54
breeding stock, obtaining foundation, 46-49
breed-specific publication, 47
breed standard, 47, 52-53
brochure, 87
brood bitch
    co-ownership on, 22-23
    retiring, 172
budget, 78-79
business, setting up, 76
business checking account, 76
business plan, 108
business transactions, 14
buyers, rewarding, 101-02
buying in bulk, 80

C

calcium, 131
Candlewood Kennels, 57
capital investments, 81-82
CDs, for puppy packet, 98
cell phone reception, 65
centrifuge machine, 132
checking account, business, 76
cherry eye, 10, 12
chewing, destructive, 69
children, involving young, 109
classified ads, 92
cleaning, ease of, 69
clubs, participating in, 34-36
code of ethics, breed club, 56
cold weather, 66-67
college scholarships, 111
come when called, 140, 147, 153
commitment to excellence, v, 93
concrete slab, for kennel, 69
Continental Kennel Club, 45
contracts, that work for you, 14-15
co-ownership, 22-25, 54
cornified cells, 134
corporations, 76
costs, cutting, 79-80
cougar, 74
covenants, conditions, and restrictions (CC&R's), 65-66
crate training, 149, 152

cropping, 134
cull, reasons to, 170-72
customer considerations, 40

D
dangerous dogs, 39
deductions, income tax, 82-84
dehumidifier, 132
dehydration, 67, 135
demographics, dog world, 48
desktop publishing software, 87
dewclaws, removing, 134
diarrhea, 138
digital camera, 48, 89
disclaimers, 15
disinfect, 71
DNA profile, 51
DNA testing, 52
docking, 134
dog breeder associations, 14
dog food, buying, 80
doggie septic systems, 66
doghouse, 71
Dogloo, 71
dog-related activities, 36
dog-related associations, 34
dog shows
  etiquette for, 166-69
  going to, 45
  research at, 49-50
dog sports, learning about, 31
Dopram, 70, 131
Doxycycline, 131
Dremel set, 132
dress well, 49
drug test, 117
dual champions, 53

E
ears, cleaning, 134
eat, teaching puppies to, 140
emergency care, 122
emergency clinic, 124
employees, 114-17
energy, 71-72
energy conservation, 71
energy-efficient appliances, 71
Epinephrine, 68
Estradiol cypionate, 56
ethics, 7-8, 36-37
Eukanuba Invitational, 31
euthanizing, 134
exhibitors, talking to, 49

expenses, with professional handlers, 26
exposure, limiting outside, 143-44
express agreement, 14
exterior cosmetics, 73
eye contact, 156

F
facility evaluation, 68-74
family involvement, 107-12
fecal flotation system, 132
Federation Cynologique International
  (FCI), 45
Feeding puppies, 139
Feet, handling, 155
Fencing, 73-74
Field Trial News, 57
field type Labs, 52
fire alert stickers, 70
flagging, 133
fleas, 67
flies, 152
fluff factor, 50
food, 142-43
food allergies, 137
following exercise, 156-57
foundation bitches, 54-58
foundation stock, co-ownership of, 25
Foundation Stock Service (FSS), 44-45
free-bait
frozen semen, 162

G
gait, dog's, 49
genes, recessive, 58
genetic defects, 21
genetic diversity, 164
genetic issues, 10
get, 11
gift certificate, 101
give, 149
grooming, 103, 146, 156
grooming areas, 70-71
guarantee, 90
  for stud dog breeding, 27
guilt, inference of, 16
Guerilla Marketing, 87
gun conditioning, 159

H
hair dryer, 126, 132
hair screens, on drains, 144
handling, teach dog to accept, 149
hazardous chemicals, handling of, 117

health checks, required for breeding, 27
health clearances, 56
health insurance, 79
healthy stock, choosing, 51-52
heartworm, prevention, 134-35
heat, 67-68
heating system, 66
highest and best use, 114
home owner's association, 65-66
house, exiting from, 147
housetraining, 148-49
Howley, Mary, 57
humidifier, 132
humidity, 68
hunt dog training, 35
hunt puppies, 157-59
hydrating puppies, 135

I
income tax, 82-84
incubator box, 132-33
independent contractors, 103, 114
inducing labor, 135
infirmary, 70-71
inoculations, 129-30, 137
insurance companies, 40
insurance coverage, 103
integrity, 7-8
internet access, 65
internet product sales, 106
I.V. administration, 136

K
kennel area, 69-70
   cleanliness of, 144-45
kennel blindness, 53
kennel dog, 74
Kennel Club (U.K.), 45
kennel name, iv, 102
   choosing, 60-62
kennel runs, 71, 74
kinetic stance, 50
kitchen, 70-71
knowledgeable, becoming, 47-49

L
labor, inducing, 135
land use regulations, 62-65
lawyer, 15
lease agreement, 54
leave it, 147, 149
liability issues, 39, 76
life-saving techniques, 136

line-bred, 11
line breeding, 58-59
litters, overly large, 39
locking up, 157
loss
   experiencing, 177-78
   ways to ease the pain of, 179-80
   when to get a puppy after, 179

M
magazine ads, 91, 92
maintenance schedule, for kennel, 144-45
mark training, 158
mastitis, 110, 136, 138
medical procedures
   equipment for, 131-33
handled by breeders, 133-38
medical supplies, 126-30
   proper use and storage of, 130-31
mentor, 32-33, 49
methylene blue stain, 132
microchipping, 137, 147, 169
microscope, 132
microwave oven, 132
mileage/trip book, 77
mirror, 154
Miscellaneous Class Breeds (AKC), 43
money, 50
mouths, handling, 155
movement, dog's, 49-50
Mylanta, 137

N
national breed club, 34
nebulizer, 132
networking, with other breeders, 31-32, 36
newsletters, 105-06
newspapers, 139
non-compete clause, 116
North American Hunting Retriever Association (NAHRA), 34

O
OFA, 56
off, 149
Open classes, 165
Operation Referral, 32
outcross, 11
outside services, 117-19
ownership, 76
oxygen, 131

Oxytocin, 70, 131, 135

P

partner, 107
  unsupportive, 108
partnerships, 74
paying yourself, 80-81
PayPal, 91
pea gravel, 72
penicillin, 131
personal liability, 76
pet-sitting business, 103
pharmaceutical supplies, 125-30
photos, 89
physical condition, 143
pick of the litter, 27
placements, making appropriate, 172-74
plastic items, 69
policy and procedures manual, 115-16
politics, of dog world, 8
predators, 74
premium, 46
preventive care, 142
price, of puppies, 95
print advertising, 91-92
professional handler, 25
  contracts with, 26
psychology of sales, 93
public rest areas, 146
puppies
  brain-damaged, 151
  deaf, 151
  physical care of new, 150-52
  purebred, 6
  switching, 9-10
puppy adoption months, 91
puppy autism, 151
puppy bed, 139
puppy contracts, 15, 17-20
puppy formula, 139
puppy kibble, 141
puppy packet, 98-101
puppy pads, 139
puppy starter kits, 104-05
pyometra, 55

R

rare breed program, 45
rear structure, poor, 49
record keeping, 76-78
referrals, 96-98
refrigerator/freezer, 70, 132

regional breed clubs, 34
registration papers, sale of, 46
reimbursement policies, 15
release clause, 119
repeat sales, 96-98
reputation, international, 45
restrictive registrations (AKC), 46
retail product sales, 104
return policies, 15
ribbons, 35
rosettes, 35
runny stools, 139

S

sales
  over the telephone, 94-96
  psychology, 93
satisfaction, guarantee, 119
scent conditioning, 174
secondary inertia, 135
self-education, 88
semen collection, 121
seminars, 32
senior citizens, older dogs for, 174
service provider, rewarding, 119
shoulder, loaded, 49
show catalogs, 46
show puppies, 156-57
Simerdown Kennels, 61
skin care, 137
Small Business Administration, 104
small business organizations, 65
small dogs, 68
  potty area for, 72
Snake Away, 67, 68
snake proofing dogs, 146
social functions, 108
socialization, of puppies, 152-56
sole proprietorship, 76
sounds, desensitization to, 154
special events, 32
stacking, 50, 156
stand, 149
structure for dog breeding, 68
stud dog
  contracts, 27-28
  co-ownership of, 23
finding, 59
  line-bred, 58
  managing, 160-62
  reasons to cull, 172
  retired, 174
  sterile, 8

substitution of, 9
summer camp, 104
swim, teaching puppies to, 146, 152
swimmer pups, 138

T
teenagers, involving, 110-12
telephone etiquette, 94-96, 109
Terramycin, 131
thank you for adopting me letter, 100
therapeutic benefit of dogs, 112
ticks, 67
toys, for puppies, 153
transition to new home, facilitating,
    174-75
trash bins, 73
tub, elevated, 126
tube feeding, 125, 138
typey, 9

U
United Kennel Club (UKC), 6, 45
USDA Health Certificate, 21

V
vaginal smears, 133
vehicle
    crate or belt dog in, 146
    exiting from, 147
ventilation, 126
veterinarians, 120-25
veterinary expenses, 20-22

W
wait, 149
warranty, 15
warranty contract, 17-20
warranty replacement expense, 90
wasps, 68
waste disposal, 72-73
water
    disposal of, 72-73
    supplying to kennels, 67
water feeders, 138
weaning prodecures, 138-42
weaning schedule, 142
weather, 66-68
Web cam, 90
websites, 47, 87-91
Westminster dog show, 31
whelping box, 132
whelping factors, 39
whelping/nursery area, 70

wiring, exposed, 72
women, as breeders, 108
wounds, minor, 137

Z
zoning issues, 62-65

From Dogwise Publishing
www.dogwise.com
1-800-776-2665

BEHAVIOR & TRAINING

ABC's of Behavior Shaping; Fundamentals of Training; Proactive Behavior Mgmt, DVD. Ted Turner

Aggression In Dogs: Practical Mgmt, Prevention & Behaviour Modification. Brenda Aloff

Am I Safe? DVD. Sarah Kalnajs

Behavior Problems in Dogs, 3rd ed. William Campbell

Brenda Aloff's Fundamentals: Foundation Training for Every Dog, DVD. Brenda Aloff

Bringing Light to Shadow. A Dog Trainer's Diary. Pam Dennison

Canine Behavior. A Photo Illustrated Handbook. Barbara Handleman

Canine Body Language. A Photographic Guide to the Native Language of Dogs. Brenda Aloff

Clicked Retriever. Lana Mitchell

Dog Behavior Problems: The Counselor's Handbook. William Campbell

Dog Friendly Gardens, Garden Friendly Dogs. Cheryl Smith

Dog Language, An Encyclopedia of Canine Behavior. Roger Abrantes

The Ethical Dog Trainer. Jim Barry

Evolution of Canine Social Behavior, 2nd ed. Roger Abrantes

Give Them a Scalpel and They Will Dissect a Kiss, DVD. Ian Dunbar

Guide To Professional Dog Walking And Home Boarding. Dianne Eibner

Language of Dogs, DVD. Sarah Kalnajs

Mastering Variable Surface Tracking, Component Tracking (2 bk set). Ed Presnall

My Dog Pulls. What Do I Do? Turid Rugaas

New Knowledge of Dog Behavior (reprint). Clarence Pfaffenberger

Oh Behave! Dogs from Pavlov to Premack to Pinker. Jean Donaldson

On Talking Terms with Dogs: Calming Signals, 2nd edition. Turid Rugaas

On Talking Terms with Dogs: What Your Dog Tells You, DVD. Turid Rugaas

Play With Your Dog. Pat Miller

Positive Perspectives: Love Your Dog, Train Your Dog. Pat Miller

Predation and Family Dogs, DVD. Jean Donaldson

Really Reliable Recall. Train Your Dog to Come When Called, DVD. Leslie Nelson

Right on Target. Taking Dog Training to a New Level. Mandy Book & Cheryl Smith

Stress in Dogs. Martina Scholz & Clarissa von Reinhardt

The Dog Trainer's Resource. The APDT Chronicle of the Dog Collection. Mychelle Blake (*ed*)

The Dog Trainer's Resource 2. The APDT Chronicle of the Dog Collection. Mychelle Blake (*ed*)

Therapy Dogs: Training Your Dog To Reach Others. Kathy Diamond Davis

Training Dogs, A Manual (reprint). Konrad Most
Training the Disaster Search Dog. Shirley Hammond
Try Tracking: The Puppy Tracking Primer. Carolyn Krause
Visiting the Dog Park, Having Fun, and Staying Safe. Cheryl S. Smith
When Pigs Fly. Train Your Impossible Dog. Jane Killion
Winning Team. A Guidebook for Junior Showmanship. Gail Haynes
Working Dogs (reprint). Elliot Humphrey & Lucien Warner

HEALTH & ANATOMY, SHOWING
An Eye for a Dog. Illustrated Guide to Judging Purebred Dogs. Robert Cole
Annie On Dogs! Ann Rogers Clark
Canine Cineradiography DVD. Rachel Page Elliott
Canine Massage: A Complete Reference Manual. Jean-Pierre Hourdebaigt
Canine Terminology (reprint). Harold Spira
Dog In Action (reprint). Macdowell Lyon
Dogsteps DVD. Rachel Page Elliott
From Hoofbeats to Dogsteps. Rachel Page Elliott
In Search of the Truth About Dogs DVD. Catherine O'Driscoll
Performance Dog Nutrition: Optimize Performance With Nutrition. Jocelynn
  Jacobs
Positive Training for Show Dogs: Building a Relationship for Success. Vicki
  Ronchette
Puppy Intensive Care: A Breeder's Guide To Care Of Newborn Puppies. Myra
  Savant Harris
Raw Dog Food: Make It Easy for You and Your Dog. Carina MacDonald
Raw Meaty Bones. Tom Lonsdale
Shock to the System. The Facts About Animal Vaccination... Catherine
  O'Driscoll
The History and Management of the Mastiff. Elizabeth Baxter & Pat Hoffman
Work Wonders. Feed Your Dog Raw Meaty Bones. Tom Lonsdale
Whelping Healthy Puppies, DVD. Sylvia Smart